LAW, CRIME AND SEXUALITY

LAW, CRIME AND SEXUALITY

Essays in Feminism

Carol Smart

SAGE Publications
London · Thousand Oaks · New Delhi

Editorial selection, introductory material and Chapters 1
and 13 © Carol Smart 1995

First published 1995

 SAGE Publications Ltd
6 Bonhill Street
London EC2A 4PU

SAGE Publications Inc
2455 Teller Road
Thousand Oaks, California 91320

SAGE Publications India Pvt Ltd
32, M-Block Market
Greater Kailash – I
New Delhi 110 048

British Library Cataloguing in Publication data

A catalogue record for this book is available from the British
Library.

ISBN 0 8039 8959 8
ISBN 0 8039 8960 1 (pbk)

Library of Congress catalog card number 94-069678

Typeset by Type Study, Scarborough
Printed in Great Britain by Biddles Ltd, Guildford, Surrey

Contents

Acknowledgements

The editor and publishers wish to thank the following for permission to use copyright material.

Academic Press Ltd for 'Feminism and Law: Some Problems of Analysis and Strategy' from *International Journal of the Sociology of Law*, 1986, 14(2), pp. 109–23; Blackwell Publishers for 'Law's Power, the Sexed Body and Feminist Discourse', *Journal of Law and Society*, 1990, 17(2), pp. 194–210; JAI Press Inc for 'Proscription, Prescription and the Desire for Certainty?: Feminist Theory in the Field of Law', *Law, Politics and Society*, 1993, 13, pp. 37–54; Open University Press for 'Feminist Approaches to Criminology, or Postmodern Woman meets Atavistic Man' in *Feminist Perspectives in Criminology*, eds L. Gelsthorpe and A. Morris (1990) pp. 70–84; Pluto Press for 'Feminist Jurisprudence' in *Dangerous Supplements: Resistance and Renewal in Jurisprudence*, ed. P. Fitzpatrick (1991) pp. 133–58; Routledge for 'Criminological Theory: its Ideology and Implications Concerning Women', *The British Journal of Sociology*, 1977, 28(1), pp. 89–100, 'Legal Subjects and Sexual Objects: Ideology, Law and Female Sexuality' in *Women in Law*, eds J. Brophy and C. Smart (1985) pp. 50–70 and 'Legal Regulation and Male Control' in *The Ties That Bind*, C. Smart (1984) pp. 3–23; Sage Publications Ltd for 'The Woman of Legal Discourse', *Social & Legal Issues: An International Journal*, 1992, 1(1), pp. 29–44; The University of Calgary Press for 'Law, Feminism and Sexuality: From Essence to Ethics?', *Canadian Journal of Law and Society*, 1994, 9(1), pp. 1–23; Virago Press for 'Unquestionably a Moral Issue: Rhetorical Devices and Regulatory Imperatives' in *Sex Exposed: Sexuality and the Pornography Debate*, eds L. Segal and M. McIntosh © 1992.

1

Introduction

This collection of essays has two main objectives. The first is quite simply to draw together an organized and focused collection of papers which have been published in a wide range of different journals and books. Bringing these papers together will not only make some work more readily accessible for students, but will also demonstrate that there exists a corpus of intellectual work which varied sites of publication can often disguise.

The second objective is of a different order. The papers are written by a feminist within the sociological tradition who focuses on substantive and theoretical issues in criminology and socio-legal studies. Although all these perspectives and foci come together in one person, both institutional and intellectual boundaries often mean that work defined as criminology is not read by socio-legal communities (and vice versa), what may be written for a feminist audience may not be read by sociologists, and many sociologists and feminists ignore anything which looks as if it is about law. This kind of fragmentation occurs elsewhere of course and is not necessarily problematic in as much as it represents the growth and diversification of sociology and of feminist scholarship. However, it does mean that there can be a considerable ignorance about certain kinds of intellectual developments which do not fit into standard categorizations. So this book tries to defy this fragmentation to some extent by, at the very least, bringing some elements together in a coherent whole and, at best, by revealing the relevance of specific substantive and theoretical debates to wider knowledge projects. This book will hopefully establish the extent to which this kind of feminist project is constantly informed by, and informs, wider debates in sociology, criminology, socio-legal studies and feminist theory and philosophy.

There are of course important sub-goals as well. This is a book for students and so it intends to provide new generations of students some understanding of an intellectual history with some of its shifts and developments. I cannot, of course, claim that this collection is representative of a range of intellectual traditions but the work that is presented here demonstrates a clear development of ideas which in turn links into wider intellectual movements. We can speak of this as a knowledge project – albeit that this may give it a false sense of purposive direction which really overestimates the author's control over her own intellectual development. But it has, with the benefit of hindsight, become a project. The kernel of this project has been to demystify law and to render its workings more transparent. This, in turn, has always been linked to a gendered emancipatory project – although the very idea of emancipation from constraints and oppressions has been transformed of late.

There are a number of things I would like students to take from this collection. The first is that theory need not be too hard or too inaccessible. I write this in the full knowledge that some of the pieces in this collection are not necessarily the most straightforward essays I have ever written. But the arrangement of the essays does allow the reader to follow the progress of ideas and to see the groundwork from which subsequent thoughts have emerged. This should provide some foundation for understanding why some ideas become particularly important and why they are taken up and developed later. For this reason it is probably better not to dip into the book as such, but at least to read an entire section and to read the introductions to each section which provide important guiding ideas.

I would also like students who do not have a great deal of knowledge of law and legal processes (including the criminal process) to take from this collection a deeply textured concept of law and how it works. Although one of my aims is to make the workings of law transparent, this does not mean that I want to make the workings of law appear simple or one-dimensional. As is the case with our understandings of economic or political systems, the more we study legal systems the more we can appreciate how difficult it may be to change them or to 'use' them for 'emancipatory' purposes. We begin to understand that the odd reform here or there (no matter how hard won) may have little impact or may even be counterproductive. And so I want students who may be committed to change (as most sociology, social policy and feminist students are) to become more sophisticated in their understanding of law. I would like many more students to hesitate before they call for legal reforms as solutions to problems they have identified.

Finally, I would want students to become more fully aware of the extent to which law is implicated in our everyday lives. There is still, I fear, a tendency to assume that law becomes relevant (sociologically as well as personally) when something has gone wrong, for example in the case of divorce, or a physical assault, or an accident. However, law does not sit on a shelf, so to speak, waiting to be lifted off when the occasion demands. It can be said to frame our lives in terms of the possibilities available to us, or we could go further (as I do in later papers) to say that it operates as a discourse which constructs legal subjects such as rape victims or lone mothers. I hope, therefore, that readers will gain some understanding of this form of deployment of power which is too often simply treated as an epiphenomenon of something else more important (such as, the economic base) or as a minor influence in a society where institutions such as the media, the labour market or the family are seen to be automatically more significant (see Kingdom, 1991).

Knowledge, politics and action

The papers which have been selected here have been chosen to portray the development of certain themes as clearly as possible. This means that this is a book about knowledge and ideas more than a book about actual laws, actual criminal processes, the actual effects of reforms and so on. Work on such topics is important but would not have served the purposes of this collection because such work is often bound by the historical moment in which it is produced, it is not always transferable out of its immediate context and does not necessarily provide intellectual tools for readers to 'think' about law in other contexts. There is therefore much talk here of ideologies, discourses and narratives (the terms change as ideas change) and little of the terms and nuances of legislation, the impact of the rape trial on abused women, or the form that a law against pornography might take. There is little point in reading this book to find the current state of domestic violence legislation, for example, or to discover the newly developed practices of the police in this field.

This is a book about ideas with the aim of generating more ideas and debate. But these are not intended to be ideas for ideas' sake. A major concern throughout the collection is the question of the relationship between knowledge and politics. In the papers that were originally published in the late 1970s and early 1980s, it will be discovered that I found this relationship relatively straightforward. Later it becomes more difficult. But before plunging into this vexed question it might be useful to provide a guide to the epistemological developments represented in these papers. To do this I shall borrow shamelessly from Sandra Harding's typology of feminist knowledges (Harding, 1986). Harding refers to feminist empiricism, standpoint feminism and postmodern feminism. This organization of feminist thought can be seen as replacing the dominant categorizations of the 1970s and 1980s, namely socialist feminism, radical feminism, liberal feminism and so on. It is, therefore, in some ways a newer method of slicing the same cake but it necessarily gives greater weight to the construction of knowledge than the avowal of a particular politics.

This does not mean that there are no politics in Harding's categories but the political implications of these different feminist positions are less easy to construe. For this reason I shall map the question of politics onto her typology and I shall explain later why I think it is important to do this.

Harding's typology does not represent a simple chronology although there is a sense in which feminist empiricism can be said to come first, with standpointism building on its insights. Then postmodernist feminism seems to emerge out of some of the dissatisfactions of standpointism and realism.[1] Notwithstanding this progression, it is clear that all three types of feminist knowledge exist at once even if this is a conflictual co-existence. Yet it is also the case that individual writers may slide between these divergent epistemological stances. Perhaps it is most common for standpoint feminism and postmodern feminism to rely, every now and then, on the products of feminist empiricism, even while being particularly disdainful of this epistemological mode. These categories are therefore rarely absolutely 'pure' and it is important to acknowledge this. They operate more like ideal types than strictly discrete entities. Thus certain papers in this collection 'tend' more towards one particular mode than another and I doubt whether the reader will find pure examples of any.

Feminist empiricism

I associate feminist empiricism most closely with the work produced during the late 1970s and early 1980s. Obviously theoretical work was being produced then, but this was the era when, in sociology and criminology at least, one of the main concerns and demands of feminism was for more studies *on* women. Women were absent; there was a clear sense in which we had no sociological knowledge about the lives of women. Feminist scholars rushed to fill these gaps, even while appreciating that the sociological methods available might not be ideal. Women were, in a sense, a new and uncharted territory and there was an eagerness for knowledge of them (us).

This knowledge was never regarded as neutral knowledge, however. Feminist empiricism has been criticized for presuming the possibility of objective knowledge or, at least, the existence of empirically verifiable facts. These criticisms have weight but, to some extent, miss the point. While feminist empiricism did subscribe to the notion of an objective, directly knowable social world, it was none the less committed to a political agenda and to the production of change. It may have been epistemologically conservative (from our vantage point now) but it was not necessarily conservative in other ways. Denise Riley (1992) for example argues that feminist research in the 1970s was directly geared to making demands on the state. This empirical research developed within a particular framework of understanding in which it was presumed that empirical knowledge could be presented to the state and that 'emancipatory' policies might eventually emerge. Although success was never naïvely presumed to follow automatically, none the less the research was seen as part of a political project for change. Riley argues:

> the British women's liberation movement formulated demands to a (solidly unresponsive) State, so that there was nothing academic about this interest [in research]; it was understood to be sharply political. Those of us who could somehow manage to research these questions saw our investigations as 'at the service of' feminist politics and campaigns. (1992: 124)

Thus feminist empirical work *on* women, was always intended to be *for* women, even though the relationship between this *on* and *for* was never fully explored and did not become a focus of attention until a clearly formulated standpoint feminism emerged. (The best example of this early approach in this collection is Chapter 2.)

Standpoint feminism
In Harding's typology the shift to standpointism asserts even more clearly the need for knowledge to be *for* women. But standpointism is differentiated from empiricism more in terms of its focus on the status of knowledge and the importance of methodology. For standpointism, feminist politics does not reside in the ultimate impact of knowledge upon the world (although this is important) but in the way that politics produces knowledge which will 'inevitably' forward the interests of women because it is generated from the perspective of women. From this epistemological position it is argued that if knowledge is generated correctly it will do good or, at the very least, will unassailably be in the service of the feminist project.[2] This is what Jane Flax has referred to as 'innocent' knowledge:

> By innocent knowledge I mean the discovery of some sort of truth which can tell us how to act in the world in ways that benefit or are for the (at least ultimate) good of all. Those whose actions are grounded in or informed by such truth will also have *their* innocence guaranteed. (1992: 447)

Unlike feminist empiricism, standpointism articulates quite carefully the way that knowledge and politics are related. But this relationship is identified at the *point of production* of knowledge (that is, knowledge from the perspective of women) rather than being explored at the *point of dissemination*. That is to say, an effect is presumed. The taken-for-grantedness of this effect rests on the assumption that there is a 'body' upon whom the knowledge will impact. Typically this 'body' is the state or an arm of the state or, at the very least, some bloc of interests which can be influenced instrumentally.

Standpoint feminism has therefore been especially powerful as a mode of 'knowing' in the field of feminist legal theory and feminist criminology. This is in part because the law (whether civil or criminal) has tended to be viewed as just such a bloc (of male interests) or as an arm of the (patriarchal) state. Pringle and Watson (1992) have cautioned against precisely this formulation of the state:

> Marxists and many feminists [have] assumed that the state has an objective existence as a set of institutions or structures; that it plays a key role in organizing relations of power in any given society; that it operates as a unity, albeit a contradictory and complex one; and that there is a set of coherent interest, based on underlying economic or, in the case of some feminisms, sexual relations, which exist outside the state and are directly represented by or embodied in it. (1992: 55)

The problem with standpointism, therefore, is not that it misconstrues the deeply political nature of the construction of knowledge, but that it assumes that this (good/innocent) knowledge goes out to work on or influences an organized, objective, purposeful institution or set of institutions.

From the vantage point of the 1990s this sort of feminist scholarship can be seen to be problematic in another crucial way. Put simply, it tends to speak in a 'falsely universalising voice' (Barrett, 1992: 207). This means that early standpointism, like the Women's Movement from which it was derived, spoke unproblematically of 'we' and of the category of women. This issue is discussed in greater depth in later chapters and so will not be fully developed here. It has also, since Riley (1988) wrote *'Am I That Name?'*, become a major focus of concern for both standpointism and postmodern feminism alike. The discovery of difference has meant that many of us who were writing in the 1980s look back with some anguish on the unselfconscious references to 'us' or 'we', and to bold policy statements which it was presumed would meet the needs of women-in-general. (The best examples of this standpoint orientation can be found in Chapters 4, 8 and 9.[3])

Postmodern feminism
This is the title Harding gives to her third 'type' of feminist epistemology. However as authors such as Barrett (1992), Butler (1992) and others have argued,[4] this title can be problematic. It often confuses poststructuralism with postmodernism, and then proceeds to treat an incredibly diverse range of writers as if they were the same and were dedicated to the same project. This project is often then

depicted as the desire to undermine feminism, or at least to rob feminism of its political relevance and purpose by denying the existence of women. Rather than reproduce arguments that are available elsewhere or which appear later in this volume, however, it may be more useful to provide a very straightforward guide to what I regard as the key issues of both poststructuralism and postmodernism since many of the chapters that follow fall predominantly into this framework. Necessarily this means that I am presenting the elements of both which I have drawn upon and found insightful, rather than attempting an overview.

The poststructuralism which influences the papers that follow derives in many ways from the work of Michel Foucault because it was in his accumulated work that there was the earliest and clearest articulation of a poststructuralist project. The influence is incremental but starts with the questioning of Marxist concepts of power and the idea of a unified state from which all power derives. These ideas are reflected in my early rejection of the idea of law as a unity which in turn reflects the interests of a patriarchal state or a bloc of male interests (see Chapter 8). Linked to this rejection of a Marxist approach is the refusal to posit a general theory of law and patriarchy. Instead there is a clear preference for more specific, local or historical analyses of connections between laws, events and persons. As Pringle and Watson argue:

> Foucault shifts the emphasis away from the intentionality of the state to pose questions about its techniques and apparatuses of regulation. . . . He aims to show how these mechanisms and technologies get annexed and appropriated to more global forms of domination. But these interconnections are not to be read off from a general theory; in each case they have to be established through analysis. (1992: 56)

This means that poststructuralism does not have to lose sight of the global, but it is never taken-for-granted nor is it presumed that everything inevitably operates to reproduce it or can be understood in terms of some derived purpose indelibly etched into the global scenario.

The Foucaultian concept of power has sometimes been seen as the complete antithesis of feminist notions of power (Alcoff, 1988; Di Stefano, 1988). However, not all feminists agree and many point to the way in which feminism has always identified diverse types of power and the power that women themselves can deploy. Poststructuralism, therefore, does not seek always to depict women as the powerless ones, while none the less recognizing that there are specific modes of deploying power in ways which are expressly gendered. The assertion that women can and do deploy power does not therefore mean that poststructuralists are asserting that women 'have' as much power as men or that because both 'have' power we can take power out of the equation and treat men and women as if they were the same. The deployment of power is not random and what feminists have added to Foucault's work is the recognition of the gendered nature of the patterns that are formed (see Bell, 1993).

The next key element of poststructuralism of course is its focus on discourse and the idea of the discursive construction of the subject. This emphasis shifts attention away from the idea of pre-given entities (for example, the criminal, the prostitute or the homosexual) towards an understanding of how such subjects come into being at certain moments. This entails a significant shift in perception away from the idea that people exist in an a priori state, waiting for institutions to act upon them, towards thinking about subjects who are being continually constituted and who also constitute themselves through language/discourse. Poststructuralism thereby destabilizes the 'individual', allowing him/her to become more fluid and diverse. This notion of diversity has, of course, been given even greater attention by writers more usually described as postmodern.

Finally, the other most important element of poststructuralism is its focus on knowledge and its disinterest in Truth but fascination with the processes and methods of distinguishing Truth from Falsehood. Foucault's insights into what we might call ways of knowing and his insistence that these are modes of deployment of power has provided a new focus for political action. Thus we can shift our understanding of law(s) away from the concept of it being an institution, towards the idea of law as discourse which is, in turn, a significantly powerful discourse because of its situation in the hierarchy of knowledges and its power to subjugate other discourses (namely, law's version of rape versus women's versions of rape).

At this stage we have moved quite close to what I regard as the key elements of postmodernism, and indeed there is a great potential for overlap. However, although we can construct poststructuralism and postmodernism on a philosophical continuum, so to speak, there remains for me one very important distinction. Postmodernism is a critique of epistemology. It makes us rethink and reconsider the foundations of what we think we know. But poststructuralism is more intimately involved with the construction of local knowledge. I am invoking an old distinction here which may not be entirely appropriate but, when I think about feminist work which is postmodern, I conjure up intellectual work which theorizes about theories and subjectivities. When I think of poststructuralism, I conjure up intellectual work which theorizes about discourses, relationships, subjects, documents, representations, bodies and so on. I think the former is vital because it is challenging how we can think and how we can do. But it is equally important to be doing the latter, namely reading the documents, talking to the subjects, analysing discourses, viewing representations, denaturalizing concrete bodies and so on. As Hekman argues, 'Foucault's analysis does not abandon the subject, but reconsiders subjectivity; his analysis is neither abstract nor subjectless, but, rather, an exploration of concrete bodies and their situations' (1990: 69).

The distinction I am making is not meant to be an old fashioned 'slur' on postmodernism or a new way of saying that postmodernism is concerned with the ephemeral while poststructuralism is concerned with the real. Both deny such simplistic dualisms and depictions. But ultimately I would argue that for the feminist sociologist, if not the feminist philosopher, there is a need to keep returning to social relationships. This does not mean a return to empiricism (meaning a naïve belief in a direct access to an unmediated reality) but a continual process of 'establishing through analysis' the status/locus of one's knowledge.

So what are the key elements of postmodernism? The first element that comes to mind is the place where postmodernism and poststructuralism most overlap and this is in the rejection of the Cartesian human subject from whom action and thought are assumed to flow, and who exists in an a priori sense, in essence, outside culture.[5] The postmodern critique of this subject is probably best expressed in the work of Susan Hekman (1990) but has been taken forward by Judith Butler (1990) in her critique of feminism's retention of essential sexual difference. It is Butler, although not she alone, who has done most to challenge the universalizing concept of Woman. Criticisms of this universal woman pre-date Butler's formulation of course. The argument that feminism hailed Woman when really it only spoke to a small group of white, middle-class western women has long been a grassroots political complaint. But Butler's formulation of the problem has gone beyond the idea of building a rainbow coalition of women as a political response to the criticism. Instead, she explores the presumed natural differentiation between men and women, ultimately to argue that we are not sexed by nature and then gendered by culture, but that in the process of being gendered we are also sexed. In challenging this fundamental binary divide (as fundamental to much feminism as well as conservatism) Butler invokes a very fluid subject who was sexed as well as gendered, but who had no essential being, and certainly no opposite pole (man) from which to derive meaning and identity.

It is this kind of argument which has caused alarm to a feminist scholarship which has always presumed that it was ultimately producing knowledge for women and that women constitute a fairly clearly defined and uncontroversially given interest group. As Butler argues, for many 'politics is unthinkable without a foundation' (1992: 3). She goes on to argue that this form of politics, based as it is upon the humanist idea of the a priori, rights-carrying subject, is only *one* conceivable form and not the only form that politics can take. She also, with others, argues that anti-foundationalism (that is, the rejection of this human subject) does not mean that real women do not exist. As she argues, being constituted as opposed to given in nature, even if this constituting is never fully complete or finalized, does not make the subject a chimera.

It is this debate about the supposedly vanishing Woman that I find generates so much antagonism against postmodern feminism and so much irritation among students. This is discomforting for feminists who are part of this intellectual movement because, as Flax (1992) has argued, the adoption of this position is often equated with a kind of treachery and abandonment of all that is held dear to feminism. It is seen as a form of 'guilty' knowledge; a kind of Trojan horse in the heart of feminist endeavour. In a way this is surprising because it seems clear to me that postmodernist/poststructuralist emphases on diversity and fluidity, have their roots in feminist thinking and feminist critiques of orthodoxies about women as a homogeneous, biologically given category. The fear of postmodernism/poststructuralism derives in large part from the misconception that it is an 'alien' form of philosophizing, imposed from outside by a few trendy (probably French) male theorists and taken up by some fifth columnists who were always shaky in their commitment to the cause anyway. This 'image' of postmodernism/poststructuralism is ironic in some ways because it perpetuates the disavowal of women's scholarship. These ideas are attributed to a few high status men, and the fact that many women were working with these ideas already and formulating ideas around difference and tackling epistemology, is ignored. The intellectual graft is credited to the famous men, and the women theorists are disdainfully regarded as mere acolytes or intellectual groupies.

This is not to say that postmodern/poststructuralist thought is not disruptive; it clearly is. What it most disrupts is the assumption that scientifically produced knowledge fuels politically correct actions and strategies. It disrupts the idea that women's experience can be read as an oracular utterance which can be harvested to produce a Truth which alone carries political force. As Jane Flax has argued, this proposition is based on two problematic assumptions. The first is the assumption that there is a supremely satisfying methodology which will not only produce Truth, but which will persuade all doubters of its veracity. This ignores the way that the production of knowledge is always contested and rests on a hope that there will be a final contest in which diversity will coalesce. Second, it is based on the presumption that in politics it is Truth which prevails. This is, arguably, a naïve view of politics and underestimates completely the influence of values and conviction[6] and the way in which Truth (evidence) can be disregarded.

Standpointism has perhaps taken feminism up a difficult alley where politics is concerned. Standpointism gives priority to knowledge produced in the academic context. It requires that this production follows quite precise rules and it also requires a feminist academic to act as interpreter and disseminator of this knowledge (namely, Maureen Cain's work discussed in Chapter 12). It participates in creating hierarchies of knowledge and legitimizes this by reference to the promise of a good political outcome. In contrast postmodern/poststructuralist feminism offers no such guarantees and I suppose that it is this which most frustrates its critics. There is no clear emancipatory project here in the sense of programmes of action and Utopian visions, and this feels like a betrayal for many. But perhaps we should consider why the promise of something manifestly improbable (since we cannot transcend power) holds such sway. We should also ask how long we must wait for the good political outcome, and how we will know it when it comes, for surely such a promise must have a time limit and some criteria for judging success?

My doubts about standpoint feminism and about realism in general are most clearly articulated in Chapters 12 and 3 respectively. But they also inform most of the papers originally published after 1989. I leave it to the reader to judge whether these later papers abandon the link between knowledge and politics or whether they are struggling towards a new articulation of this complex relationship. Certainly this relationship is a major preoccupation of mine and the papers that follow are therefore a kind of series of case studies, each written from within a historical moment and each engaging an aspect of the key concerns of feminist thought current at the time. What should become clear is that feminist scholarship has developed from a form of grappling with the mainstream, in which there were no or few women's voices, to transforming (to some extent) this mainstream and starting to grapple with itself as it becomes more aware of its (our) own role in the production of knowledge. There are now many feminisms and engagement between these forms is inevitable and productive, even if painful. This collection is intended to be a contribution towards this painful engagement.

Notes

1   I do not discuss these concepts in depth here because they are dealt with more fully in Chapters 3 and 12.
2   These issues are discussed in greater length in Chapter 12.
3   I was never a fully fledged standpoint feminist any more than I was ever a naïve empiricist. The reader may therefore find that my papers reflect 'tendencies towards' rather than precise examples of each epistemological genre. Remember the point I made earlier about Harding's categories being 'ideal types' anyway. It is probable that few writers/thinkers fit the categories exactly.
4   See for example the essays collected in Butler and Scott (1992) and Barrett and Phillips (1992).
5   Hekman summarizes this approach as one in which 'Man is the source of all truth; he sets himself up as one who constitutes himself' (1990: 65).
6   It might be useful to consider an anecdote here. Some years ago I was involved in a campaign to prevent certain changes to the UK law on divorce. Many groups were called to give evidence to a House of Commons Select Committee. Among them was a group from a prestigious university who had been carrying out meticulous research on the economic consequences of divorce for women. Their methodology was savagely attacked. Not because it was poor quality, but simply because it is always possible to attack methodology from some opposing methodological stance. Their research was therefore treated as discredited and their findings disregarded. However, while giving evidence, the group I was with was confronted by an inquisitor who produced a letter from a constituency member. This letter was treated as more real and influential than the research, but also as a statement of commitment to a set of values which were in the ascendancy. We failed to prevent the changes to the law. But was this because the research was not quite good enough? Were we not able to win the argument because the methodology was flawed? Had there been a larger sample would the political outcome have been different? I doubt it. The conviction that men were hard done by on divorce prevailed in spite of the weight of the evidence. Although this is a mere anecdote, this is perhaps a good example of the problem of presuming that Truth (even if we can acquire it) will be at all influential in the political sphere. We may not want a political system that disregards research completely, but we need to be conscious that it will not be research findings which bring a desired transformation of the political system into existence.

PART I
CRIMINOLOGY

Introduction

In the first section of this book I concentrate explicitly on criminology. These two chapters are more or less like bookends in that they frame my intellectual concerns from 1977 to 1990. They have certain themes in common but the first paper is demonstrably written within the 'feminist empiricism' approach while in the latter I am much more influenced by what can be loosely called postmodern feminism. They are bookends also in that my early intellectual work started in criminology but I abandoned this field (in the sense of rejecting the discipline and not its focus of study) and only returned explicitly to address criminology in 1990. When I wrote the first paper I was probably a criminologist, by 1990 I was probably not. This does not mean that there is nothing of interest here to students of criminology, however. Although the criminological paradigm does not dominate, readers will find that the substantive concerns of much feminist criminology are here. Later chapters address issues of rape, pornography, prostitution and criminal law's regulation of sexuality. It is simply that I discuss these important issues within a slightly different framework.

Both chapters in this section address fundamental problems within criminology. The problems have changed slightly with the passage of time but the very idea of the criminological project has remained the core issue that I address. The main difference between the two pieces is that in the first I appear to argue that criminology (until 1977) was immensely problematic until the dawning of feminist work which brought with it the promise of transformation. In the second, I acknowledge the changes feminism has introduced but I still think that criminology remains a doubtful project. Put more accurately, I reject the specific criminological project which remains wedded to a belief in the empirical discovery of causes of crime which are deemed sufficiently predictive and precise to be able to alter specific cultural patterns of behaviour. I have moved away completely from the search for causes and cures which still seems to preoccupy the self-confessed criminologist.

In the first paper I compare common sense with science and critique dominant theories of female crime on the basis that these accounts merely present everyday sexism as science. By 1990 I no longer presume that there is a science which is transcultural or transhistorical in this way. I use a different conceptualization of knowledge. This does not mean that the kind of criticisms made of the traditional criminologists are untenable, but it does suggest that I was then working (unwittingly) in the mould of feminist empiricism. This term is touched on in Chapter 1 and is explained more fully in Chapter 3, but for brevity here it means that I then thought that the accumulation of more empirical knowledge would lead to 'better' and probably more effective interventions. This approach also implies an ability to establish facts which are unassailable. It is this faith in the discovery of useful facts (and, related to this, their causes) which is abandoned in Chapter 3. In particular I am critical of a form of positivism which suggests that not only can causes of crime be identified, but that research can provide solutions. Thus, ironically, the first paper ends with a call for more feminist research and the second starts with an appreciative acknowledgement of all the feminist research that has been carried out, but suggests that some of this work, my own included, may have been problematic in that it has kept afloat a criminological project which cannot recognize its own limitations.

In both chapters I treat criminology as a form of knowledge or a discipline, and it should be recognized that it is this self-referencing knowledge project that I critique. I do not suggest we abandon enquiries into issues such as rape, domestic violence, child abuse or even theft and drug abuse. Rather I suggest that these issues are artificially conflated by the claims of criminology to be the study of criminal acts when arguably we should be deconstructing the meaning of crime, not concretizing it. Thus, I suggest that rape and child sexual abuse should be located in the study of sexuality, domestic violence in the study of marriage/family life, theft in the sphere of economic activity, and drug use in the study of health and so on.

My concerns, then, are with modes of theorization and articulation. In the first instance I concentrate on how dominant sexist ideologies perpetuated by mainstream criminology can feed into policies and practices. In the second instance I focus specifically on realist criminology and its tendency to sustain a faith in the discovery of causes and the promise of policy to ameliorate and improve social circumstances. In the first I suggest the ideologies are misleading and thus give rise to problematic policies for women. In the second I suggest that causes can no longer be presented in such a simplistic fashion and that our knowledge of both policy and the problem of enlightenment science with its presumption of progress, should make us wary of continuing to promise solutions if only we carry out more empirical research. Ultimately I reframe the familiar question of 'What has feminism to offer to criminology?'. If we ask 'What has criminology got to offer feminist scholarship?' we can suddenly see the relationship in a different light.

2

Criminological Theory: Its Ideology and Implications concerning Women

Criminological theories have rarely been concerned with the analysis of female criminality, being content to subsume women offenders under general theories or dealing with them exceptionally briefly in the way that most 'marginal' groups are treated. The reason offered for this overwhelming lack of interest is that within the population of known offenders, female offenders constitute a statistically much smaller proportion than male offenders. With the exception of offences like shoplifting and soliciting the numbers of female offenders nowhere exceed the numbers of male offenders known to the police. But statistical 'insignificance' alone cannot fully explain why so little work has been attempted in this area. Rather the absence of any work on crimes by women may be considered as symbolic of the nature of the discipline of criminology. Traditional criminology in both the UK and the USA has always had close links with social and penal policy making bodies with the result that research has tended to be directed towards areas officially designated as social problems. Female criminality has not generally been treated as a particularly important or pressing social problem not only because of its comparative rarity but also because of the nature of the offences committed by women. Official statistics (which are themselves a problematical source of information in sociology and criminology – cf. Douglas, 1967; Wiles, 1971; Hindess, 1973) indicate that women engage mostly in petty offences and once apprehended women appear to be easily deterred – court appearances by women are mostly by first offenders not recidivists – therefore they pose no particular problem to the agencies of social control. As a consequence, academic research into female criminality has failed to attract much interest or to receive very much 'official' support or finance – hence the relative scarcity of studies in this area.

It may, of course, be argued that, given the nature of Home Office financed research into 'crime', particularly its policy orientation, the dearth of material on crimes committed by women and the treatment of female offenders may not necessarily constitute the most undesirable state of affairs. However, to argue in this way is to fail to recognize that the relative absence of statistical information or study reports on women offenders obstructs the development of an understanding of the situation in almost any terms (Home Office, liberal or radical criminological perspectives). The lack of attention devoted to the question of crimes committed by women, their characteristics (marital status, social class, numbers of children, etc.) and treatment has given rise to the present unsatisfactory understanding of female offenders and the offences they commit. There has been no development of our knowledge in this area with the result that ideologically informed works have been allowed to stand uncriticized. Recognition of the underdevelopment of criminology and sociology in this area is explicit in Ward's statement to the US National Commission on Crimes of Violence (1968) that: 'Our knowledge of the character and causes of female criminality is at the same stage of development that characterized our knowledge of male criminality some thirty or more years ago'.

As a consequence of this lack of development the ideology and methodological limitations inherent in some of the earliest works on female criminality still permeate contemporary studies and furthermore is reflected in the treatment of female offenders. This is not to say that some studies of male offenders are not of equally poor quality but there does exist, in the case of studies of male offenders, different schools and traditions which are concerned to provide critiques of 'official' perspectives, policy and conventional understanding of crime. For example the societal reaction or labelling approach, in spite of all its failings (see Gouldner, 1973) has acted as a catalyst in the development of the sociology of deviance and yet with the possible exception of some works on prostitution, which integrated well with the sexual marginality and 'underdog' ethos of these theorists, this 'trend' has had no perceivable influence on the mainstream theories of female criminality.

In this paper I will be looking at the conception of women informing the work of particular theorists who have attempted to offer an explanation of crimes by women. I will be concentrating on the work of Lombroso and Ferrero (1895) and Pollak (1950), both of whom have attempted to account for female criminality in general as well as the work of Cowie et al. (1968) whose focus is upon female delinquency. I will attempt to reveal the underlying assumptions inherent in their conception of women which form the foundations for their respective accounts of the nature of female criminality. The paper is divided into two sections, one considering the ideological basis of the works of Lombroso, Pollak and Cowie et al., and the other concentrating on the implications of such work for the treatment of female offenders.

The ideology of theories of female criminality

The ideology which informs both classical and contemporary accounts of female criminality is a sexist ideology. It is sexist not because it differentiates between the sexes but because it attributes to one sex socially undesirable characteristics which are assumed to be intrinsic characteristics of that sex. Sexism, and occasionally racial and class prejudice, stem from the unscientific nature of this criminological theorizing. These problems arise because the socially structured and culturally given nature of the assumptions informing these theories are not treated as subjects for analysis, rather common-sense understandings are taken for granted as a suitable platform from which to commence theorizing. Working within the natural attitude, adopting culturally given understandings of the nature of sexual differences and in particular the characteristics attributed to women, the theorists concerned provide merely a scientific gloss for common-sense understandings. Reality becomes confused with its appearance and science submerged by ideology.

The most pervasive theme which emerges from the uncritical attitude adopted by Lombroso and Pollak, and which is to be found in the majority of studies on female offenders, is that of biological determinism. Biological determinist accounts take two forms. First, women who have committed offences are perceived to have been motivated by fundamental biological bodily processes. For example, menstruation or the menopause, through affecting the hormonal balance in the body, are taken to be precipitating factors leading some women to commit criminal acts. In this instance action is seen to be directly related to hormonal or biological imbalance. Second, and more significantly, the female biology is perceived to determine the temperament, intelligence, ability and aggression of women. In the case of Lombroso the adoption of the latter position leads him to postulate that biologically women are unfitted for criminal activity and therefore the women who do commit offences are perceived by him to be pathological.

As biology is treated as the most important influence in determining behaviour it follows that the female sex may be treated as a homogeneous group. Such factors as class, status, power, age, culture and so one are not considered as pertinent to an understanding of female criminality even though these variables are now accepted as relevant to the study of male criminality. As a result of the creation of a stereotypical perception of women which relies upon culturally constituted understandings of the nature of female sexuality and its determination of action by women, those women who do commit offences are judged to be either criminal by nature (cf. Lombroso and Pollak) or pathological because they deviate from the 'true' biologically determined nature of woman which is to be law abiding (cf. Lombroso and Cowie). The latter perspective which treats female offenders as pathological is prevalent in both classical and contemporary criminological theories, one consequence of this being the continuing implementation of policy decisions predicated upon an understanding that criminal activity by women is a product of pathology located within the individual rather than exemplifying meaningful action, for example, the transformation of Holloway from a prison to a psychiatric hospital. Indeed it has become a 'popular' belief that women who commit criminal offences are 'sick' and in need of psychiatric treatment; it is to a much lesser extent that this 'sick' analogy has been adopted in the treatment of men because men are generally assumed to be rationally responsible for their actions while women are not.

This theme of the biological basis of female criminality which has become so entrenched in official and academic explanations was first fully formulated by Lombroso and Ferrero in the work entitled *The Female Offender* published in 1895. It is, of course, true that Lombroso employed biological factors to account for male criminality but with few exceptions this school of thought has been repudiated. As Shoham maintains, 'Today . . . the Lombrosian myth in criminology, and the few contemporary adherents to the biophysiological approach to the genesis of crime, are considered a sad episode which retarded the development of the field by almost half a century' (1974: 117). This is undoubtedly the case with most of Lombroso's theories and yet the ideological content of his work on female criminality persists in contemporary explanations. I will briefly outline his theoretical position, focusing upon the ideological content, and hope ultimately to display its continued presence in contemporary theories and its influence on policy decisions.

Lombroso's major work on women's crime is mainly based on the now discredited concept of atavism although he did revise this hypothesis in later years. His theory maintained that criminals are in fact biological mutations or throwbacks to an earlier evolutionary stage. This fact, it was assumed, accounted for the 'uncivilized' or aggressive behaviour of criminals. Lombroso judged the existence and degree of atavism by the signs of degeneration he found among convicted criminals, for example he looked for small craniums, dark skin, excessive hairiness, and the presence of moles and tattoos. He found, however, that female offenders did not appear to have many of these signs of degeneration and so he concluded that the 'true' criminal type is rare among women. He argued that this was due to 'the undoubted fact that she is nearer to her origin than the male' and also to the fact that throughout the zoological scale physical anomalies are rarely a feature of the female of the species. In other words Lombroso maintained that women have evolved less than men and moreover that this is due to the sedentary nature of women's lives as compared with the challenging and stimulating existence of men.

But being more 'primitive' than men does not necessarily make women more criminal as one might assume. On the contrary, Lombroso argues that women's ancestors were less 'ferocious' than their male counterparts and therefore contemporary women are also less ferocious. The relationship between ferocity and crime is not in fact spelt out in Lombroso's work, nor indeed is the link between evolutionary stages and criminal behaviour which is one of his major assumptions. Clearly these relationships are taken by Lombroso to be self-evident and indeed if we accept these features of his work uncritically his conclusion that women are 'congenitally . . . less inclined to crime' appears quite logical. The belief that women's 'natural' passivity and conservatism robs them of the initiative to break the law has in fact become a predominant part of the ideology in criminological and sociological theories. Lombroso argued that women's biologically determined constitution is caused by 'the immobility of the ovule compared with the zoosperm'. It may be noted in passing that similar theories have been proposed elsewhere, for example Thomas's (1907) concepts of the 'anabolic' female (that is, storing of energy and therefore conservative) and the 'katabolic' male (that is, destructive of energy and therefore creative) which constitute resources for his account of male–female differences.

Significantly these theories still exist and theorists still resort to explanations comparable with those employed by Lombroso. The work of Cowie et al. (1968) is perhaps the best contemporary exemplar of a modified form of the ideology inherent in Lombroso's work. In analysing the differences between male and female delinquency they state, 'Differences between the sexes in hereditary predisposition [to crime] could be explained by sex-linked genes. Furthermore the female mode of personality, more timid, more lacking in enterprise, may guard her against delinquency' (1968: 167). Clearly Cowie et al., and other theorists who adopt similar positions, have taken no cognizance of cross-cultural studies nor of historical data which might suggest that, rather than there being only one 'female mode of personality' there are a multitude of culturally and historically based sets of attitudes and expectations that influence the consciousness or personalities of women, thus producing gender-related behaviour. To suggest, for example, that women are 'more lacking in enterprise', or in the case of Lombroso, lead more sedentary lives because of their genetic structure, is to ignore the social situation facing many women which gives no opportunity or outlet for active or creative behaviour. Inherent in this argument also is the belief that if women are normally or naturally passive and law abiding those who are not must be abnormal or unnatural. The consequences of this are discussed below.

Another belief in the nature of female criminality which has emanated from the work of Lombroso and which is reflected in particular in the work of Pollak (1950; see below) is the belief that when women become criminal they are far more cruel and sinister than men. Lombroso argued that the reason for this is that women are naturally less sensitive to pain than men and, as compassion is seen to be the offspring of sensitivity, the lack of this quality means that women cannot feel compassion for their victims. He also maintained that like children their moral sense is deficient. We may note that this 'paternalistic' attitude lives on in contemporary accounts, for example, promiscuity in girls or women is regarded as a consequence of the absence of morality. Thomas (1923) infers that such girls are amoral rather than immoral and Cowie et al. (1968) argue that girls in 'moral danger' should be placed in institutions for their own protection. However, Lombroso argued that, 'In ordinary cases these defects are neutralised by piety, maternity, want of passion, sexual coldness, by weakness and an undeveloped intelligence'. Should these neutralizing factors be removed, however – perhaps by educating women – the 'innocuous semi-criminal' present in all women would emerge.

Interestingly Lombroso maintained that one strong proof of the degeneration of the female criminal is the lack of a maternal instinct. This deficiency was perceived to mean that 'psychologically and anthropologically' the delinquent woman belongs more to the male than the female sex. But this belief, which is echoed in Cowie et al.'s work, is based on not only biological determinism but also on confusion between sex and gender. As Oakley (1972) has pointed out sex is a biological term and gender a social, cultural and psychological term such that for a woman to act in a socially defined 'masculine' way does not mean that she is sexually or biologically abnormal. However, where gender appropriate behaviour is seen as biologically determined women who adopt 'masculine' forms of behaviour become labelled 'masculine' themselves and this has connotations of 'maleness' which are seen to be linked to hormonal or genetic abnormalities. Cowie et al. in fact failed to distinguish between sex and gender at all; they state, 'Is there any evidence that *masculinity or femininity of bodily constitution* plays any part in predisposing to delinquency and in determining the form it takes?' (1968: 171; emphasis added). In response to this question they maintain, 'Delinquents of both sexes tend to be larger than controls, and overgrown by population standards. . . . Markedly masculine traits in girl delinquents have been commented on by psychoanalytic observers. . . . *we can be sure that they have some physical basis*' (1968: 172; emphasis added).

The point is that female delinquents are not perceived to be merely adopting behaviour more usually associated with males, they are portrayed as being chromosomally or genetically abnormal. This means that the 'treatment' of such offenders becomes justifiable, the aims, intentionality and rationality of the deviant act are overlooked and the social and cultural conditions under which the act took place can be neglected to the vague status of 'environmental' factors whose only role is to occasionally 'trigger' the inherent pathology of the deviant. Crime and delinquency can thereby be treated as an individual, not social, phenomenon.

The way in which Cowie et al. present their evidence is also worth noting for they attempt to appeal to the reader's 'senses' rather than intellect or critical faculties. They have a tendency to invoke 'common sense' and concepts of the 'natural' to support their claims rather than relying on credible, scientific evidence. Rather than reducing the influence of their work, however, their anti-theoretical and anti-intellectual approach may be conducive to acceptance by policy makers who perceive themselves to be concerned with 'practical' issues and not theoretical ones. For example, Cowie et al. (1968) state, 'Common-sense suggests that the main factors are somatic ones, especially hormonal ones', and again later '*It is more natural to suppose* that the male–female difference, both in delinquency rates and in the forms that delinquency takes, would be closely connected with the masculine or feminine pattern of development of personality' (1968: 170–1; emphasis added).

This debunking of a theoretical and intellectual approach to the topic may be seen as the witting embrace of ideology. An even more outstanding example of this tendency is to be found in Konopka's work, *The Adolescent Girl in Conflict* (1966). Konopka maintains that a theory is 'an arrangement of findings in a systematic form' and argues against commencing a study with any theoretical orientation for fear of introducing bias or prejudging the findings. But her concept of theory, which appears to be no more than an organizational technique, and her understanding of its significance in research exemplifies a misconception of scientific activity. Taken in its broadest sense scientific work proceeds through a mode of conceptualizing that is rationally or critically based on existing knowledge. To engage in a study without any theoretical orientation would be to attempt to understand without any rational powers of comprehension. There can in fact be no theory-free mode of observation or interpretation. Konopka's position, which is similar to that of Cowie et al., and which is common to the positivistic school, is that the observation of 'facts' is unproblematical and self-evident, requiring no theoretical orientation. By 'applying' theory after the event is observed she maintains that bias is overcome. However, the observation of 'facts', and indeed the existence of 'facts', is not unproblematical and understanding and even mere description is impossible without preconceptualization or 'knowledge that is always already a product of some means of production of knowledge' (Hindess, 1973: 40). The 'understanding' of female delinquency that Konopka has achieved is not based on an explicit sociological theory, it is constructed from implicit common sense which constitutes an unreflexive form of theorizing. In fact Konopka's enterprise is merely a process of rigidly 'applying' sociological theories to 'make understandable' facts which she has already unwittingly made comprehensible through common-sense theorizing. In other words she requires sociological theory to give coherence to her own understandings which are economically and culturally bound. This ultimately becomes, therefore, an exercise in providing a scientific gloss on an account predicated upon unexplicated cultural assumptions concerning female delinquency.

The theories so far discussed have in common not only an unscientific and uncritical approach to the study of female criminality, they also accept the assumption based on official criminal statistics that fewer women than men are involved in what is legally defined as criminal behaviour. The exception to this is Pollak whose book *The Criminality of Women* (1950) is largely concerned with the hidden or 'masked' nature of female criminality. His argument is basically that women are equally as criminal as men but that the type of offences they commit and their social roles protect them from detection. His fundamental analysis of the nature of women is, like Lombroso's and Cowie's, dependent on a concept of biological determinism. His theory is different only in that he sees the characteristics of women to be well suited to certain types of offences. Women are, he argues, more cunning and deceitful than men. These characteristics are related to the physiological fact that in the sphere of sexual relations, a woman, unlike a man, can hide her 'lack of positive emotion' because '[a] woman's body . . . permits such pretense to a certain degree and lack of orgasm does not prevent her ability to participate in the sex act' (1950: 8). By nature, therefore, women are deceivers and to compound this Pollak argues that social mores require them to practise deceit by concealing the fact that they menstruate. Thus by nature and by practice women become cunning and deceitful and grow accustomed to a different attitude towards 'veracity' than men. But Pollak is in fact generalizing from the particular in the above hypothesis. That is, he accords all women the master-status of liars and deceivers by extrapolating from his understanding of women as potential deceivers within the 'sex act'. This belief in the cunning nature of women is in fact a part of our common-sense perception of the female sex and Pollak gives no indication of how his account differs from the culturally given.

Pollak attempts to show, in contrast to Lombroso, that women are not predominantly passive, conservative and law abiding by nature but rather that their ability to deceive and to manipulate men has meant that they can conceal their crimes and avoid detection. In addition women's traditional roles are considered to enable them to enact their crimes in relative privacy. For example, Pollak argues that as preparers of meals women are able to administer poisons to their victims without fear of detection, while as mothers or childminders they are able to mistreat or neglect their children. Whether the extent of 'hidden' female crime referred to by Pollak actually means that offences committed by women are in 'reality' in excess of those by men is, however, highly controversial. Self-report studies (see Morris, 1965; Wise, 1967) indicate that in the case of juvenile offenders the differences revealed by official statistics between the sexes in criminal activity do not necessarily represent 'real' differences in delinquency. Indeed these self-report studies are frequently methodologically unsound, hence any conclusions must remain tentative. Additionally there are no self-report studies on adult female offenders and no grounds for extrapolating from self-report studies of female juvenile offenders to female adult offenders. Hence Pollak's statements concerning the scope and scale of female criminality remain highly speculative.

An important implication of Pollak's theory is the extent to which he has perpetuated the belief that women are treated more leniently by the legal and penal systems than men. He states:

One of the outstanding concomitants of the existing inequality between the sexes is chivalry and the general protective attitude of man towards woman. . . . Men hate to accuse women and thus indirectly to send them to their punishment, police officers dislike to arrest them, district attorneys to prosecute them, judges and juries to find them guilty and so on. (1950: 151)

Before fully outlining the implications of this belief in the existence of male chivalry I will summarize briefly the most significant aspects of the theories of female criminality discussed above.

Summary

The most significant feature of these theories, which is common to the work of Lombroso, Pollak and Cowie et al. is their mutual conception of women predicated upon an acceptance of the culturally given character of female sexuality. In other words, they treat the behaviour of women within a specific culture as exemplifying the 'true' and 'natural' character of Woman and by failing to distinguish between sex and gender they conceptualize the basis of these respectively female and feminine characteristics in biological terms. Consequently, in accounting for female criminality they invoke biological 'causes' rather than considering the possibility that criminal action may be cognitively rational action. The meaning of action to the actor, and to others involved in social situations, is not considered, in fact biological determinism renders action virtually meaningless to the actor because it relies on concepts of drives, impulses and instincts which are outside the actor's understanding and sphere of cognition.

There is a significant difference between the position of Pollak and that of Lombroso and Cowie et al., however, over the question of the frequency of occurrence of crimes by women. In Lombroso's and Cowie et al.'s work there is an implicit assumption, which is 'confirmed' by the official statistics, that women do commit fewer offences than men. Indeed, it is the comparative rarity of female offenders among the female population which authorizes their observation that female offenders are 'pathological' or 'abnormal'. Pollak on the other hand, basing his analysis upon the existence of 'hidden' crime, perceives the nature of women in general to be well suited to the criminal enterprise. In fact he argues that their ability to deceive and manipulate men makes them extremely successful criminals as they can avoid detection. However, we must be cautious in overstressing the differences between Lombroso and Pollak for the former infers that by nature women can be criminal. For example, Lombroso does maintain that, although relatively rare, women can be of the 'born criminal' type and that within every woman there is hidden an 'innocuous semi-criminal'. The important distinction to be made between these theorists, however, is that Lombroso maintains that societal norms repress the opportunities for these inherent tendencies in women to emerge while Pollak proposes that ample opportunities for crime to be committed and concealed exist within women's traditional role of wife, mother and housekeeper. The difference between the positions adopted by Pollak and Lombroso rests therefore with their respective perceptions of the availability of illegitimate opportunity structures for women rather than in any fundamental differences in the understanding of the nature and characteristics of women. The common theme inherent in these analyses of female criminality involves, therefore, an understanding of female crime in terms of unexplicated socially structured and culturally constituted beliefs about the relationship of female biology to deviant action. Even where there is an indirect attempt to consider the significance of sex role differences (cf. Pollak) these are subordinated to the status of a vehicle for inherent biological determinants. The question of the implications of these theories for the treatment of female offenders remains to be considered.

The implications of the above theories of female criminality

The implications of theorizing have frequently been overlooked by those sociologists or criminologists who perceive themselves merely to be observers or recorders of everyday life. Yet social theories do have indirect social implications either by confirming common-sense and culturally located beliefs or by altering the consciousness of people in their everyday lives through a criticism and demystification of accepted values and beliefs. Allen recognizes this when he argues that:

> Theories enter into the ideological process and emerge in an abbreviated, often vulgarized, sloganized form embedded in language and thought processes alike. They form the basis of common-sense attitudes. They are transmitted through the family, enter into folklore, get expression through the mass media. In a variety of subtle ways conventional theoretical explanations enter the consciousness of individuals and provide them with instant explanations. (1974: 10)

Although this process by which theories are translated into common conceptual currency will influence the actor's own perception of self, our concern here is more with the way in which particular 'scientific' theories of female criminality, operating with conceptions of social science which indicate an interest in technical control rather than emancipation or liberation and emphasizing the biological and pathological nature of criminal offences, may have influenced and/or legitimized the conceptualizations of policy makers such that female criminality is, or continues to be interpreted as, a biologically-rooted sickness.

Indeed there is a clear trend within the English penal system towards adopting a concept of 'treatment' for offenders rather than, or in association with, punishment. The development may be simply indicative of an 'official' recognition of more 'efficient' means of controlling criminals than have been available in the past but it may also indicate a change in the conception of the motivational basis of criminality away from the classical concept of responsibility to a more positivistic orientation (cf. Cowie et al.) which emphasizes individual pathology. This development is most marked in penal policies relating to female offenders. For example, one consequence of the adoption of the 'sick' analogy for understanding what is defined as criminal motivation, is the transformation of Holloway from a prison to a psychiatric hospital in which women will receive psychiatric treatment related to their perceived individual psychological 'needs' rather than to their offence (Faulkner, 1971).[1] The assumption underlying this policy is that to deviate in a criminal way is 'proof' of some kind of mental imbalance in women. This position is quite consistent with other assumptions about the mental health of women in general employed to explain or account for the mental health statistics which indicate that women suffer from mental illness more frequently than men. In fact mental illness has been perceived as an alternative to crime for women (Bertrand, 1973) – both crime and mental illness being treated as phenomena emerging from common causes. This hypothesis can be treated in two ways, however. Either action which is defined as criminal or as resulting from mental illness may be said to have a common aetiology in terms of representing rational solutions to certain untenable or stressful social situations (Laing, 1968). In addition to which the labelling process can be said to confirm the deviant identity (Becker, 1963; Scheff, 1974). Or action defined as resulting from mental illness can be perceived to be, by definition, irrational and caused by individual pathology such that by equating crime with mental illness, criminal activity will be perceived in a way similar to activity by the mentally ill. In practice it would appear that the latter position is adopted, especially in the case of female offenders. Walker lends some credance to this hypothesis when he states that:

> Certainly in practice women offenders have a higher chance of being dealt with as mentally abnormal. . . . We cannot however exclude the possibility that psychiatrists' diagnoses . . . are being influenced by the . . . proposition . . . that there is probably something abnormal about a woman delinquent. (1973: 302)

Even if we are unable to show that criminological theories of female criminality have precipitated these changes in the treatment of female criminals it can be argued that the ideological basis of such works offers a 'scientisitic' legitimation of social policy orientated towards an adoption of the 'sick' analogy and the development of more effective techniques of control. Legitimation follows from the confirmation of certain cultural understandings of female sexuality in general and criminal behaviour in particular and is consequential upon the failure of criminological theorists to explicate or treat as topics for analysis the understandings which they share with those engaged in the formulation of social policy.

The implications of Pollak's theories of female criminality are specifically relevant to the treatment of female offenders by the police and the courts rather than to the treatment imposed in penal institutions. Pollak argues that due to the nature of the relationship between men and women, which is, in his terms, one of oppressor to oppressed, men come to fear women. This male fear is a direct consequence of the unfair treatment of women and leads men to seek to placate women by acting chivalrously towards them. Because of this chivalry and a naïve belief in the virtues of womanhood it is maintained by Pollak that agents of social control are deluded about the real nature of women, which he notes is inherently deceitful. One important consequence of this situation for Pollak is that female offenders receive relatively lenient treatment at the hands of the police and the courts. However, while it may be agreed that sexual discrimination plays an important part in differential arrest and sentencing policy, it is misleading to assume, as Pollak does, that this discrimination is always in the favour of the female sex. It is difficult to reconcile the view that the police and legal system are staffed by 'chivalrous' men with research reports on the treatment of female political prisoners (see Davis, 1971), prostitutes (Davis, 1966; Millet, 1972) and raped women (Griffin, 1971). It would seem that if sexual discrimination is a determining factor in the treatment of women it is not a simple variable that always leads to greater leniency. This virtually unsubstantiated assumption, namely that women are rarely prosecuted and then rarely imprisoned, has become a part of our understanding of the operation of the legal system and has in fact concealed the existence of unfavourable attitudes towards, and practices involving, women held by and implemented by the agents of social control. Only recently have studies been carried out which refute the assumptions upon which Pollak's position is predicated.

Two studies which have attempted to deal with this issue of discrimination have been carried out by Terry (1970) and Chesney-Lind (1973). Unfortunately both of these studies are American and focus upon juvenile offenders. It is, therefore, not possible to generalize from such studies to the treatment of adult offenders in the UK. However, certain parallels may be drawn concerning the treatment of adolescent girls in the UK. In the first study by Terry it was discovered that, within his sample, girls suspected of sex offences and incorrigibility were more likely to have charges brought against them than males for whom comparable actions would not constitute criminal offences. Furthermore, he showed that although these offences constituted only 17.9 per cent of all cases known to the police to have been committed by girls, in fact 50 per cent of the charges brought against girls were for sexual offences. Moreover, Terry discovered that 70 per cent of these cases were then referred to social and welfare agencies with the result that girls stood a greater chance of being institutionalized even though they had less extensive records than male juvenile offenders. Chesney-Lind's study virtually replicates Terry's findings except that she emphasizes the way in which the courts operate with a double standard of morality and overemphasize the sexual nature of female juvenile offences. For example, the Children's Bureau in the USA in 1965 reported that 70 per cent of adolescent females were incarcerated for offences like 'running away' or curfew violation although self-report studies indicate that only 8 per cent of all offences by girls are of this nature. Chesney-Lind explains this discrepancy by arguing that the courts actually 'sexualize' the nature of female deviance due to their overwhelming concern for the sexual morality of young women – this is not a concern which is extended to young men. Having, by way of the double standard, created a category of offences used almost exclusively for female offenders, Chesney-Lind maintains that the courts proceed to punish more severely those found guilty of offences included in that category. This severe treatment is believed to be justified because those of bad 'moral' character are thought to be in greater need of control and guidance than juveniles who commit 'non-sexual' offences. Chesney-Lind states,

> These labels (immoral, incorrigible) allow for the same abuses that characterize the labels of 'sick' or 'insane' – that is, the 'saving' or 'helping' of a girl often justifies more radical and severe 'treatment' than does the punishment of a male law violator. (1973: 57)

Evidence of possibly similar treatment for girls in the UK is offered by Richardson (1969) who points out that girls in contrast to boys are frequently sent to Approved Schools for being found 'in need of care and protection' or for being in 'moral danger'. In fact Home Office statistics for 1960 reveal that while 95 per cent of boys are sent to Approved Schools for committing offences, only 36 per cent of girls are similarly committed. Consequently, 64 per cent of these girls are committed to penal institutions without having committed any criminal offence. The justification for this discrimination is often couched in humanitarian terms, for example as a form of protection or as an opportunity for moral guidance, but in practice it would seem that juvenile girls are punished severely for behaviour which is sometimes condoned, and at least expected, in boys.

In contrast to the studies discussed above Walker (1973) argues that in the judicial process, where it concerns adults, sex is a less significant variable than the length of criminal record. He refutes Pollak's argument that women are treated more leniently than men by the courts by presenting evidence which shows that women (particularly shoplifters) who come to court are most frequently first offenders who are therefore likely to receive a non-custodial sentence. On the other hand, a larger proportion of men have criminal records when they appear in court and are therefore more likely to receive a custodial sentence regardless of whether the offence for which they are being tried is very serious. Clearly there is a need for more studies on the possible effects of sexual discrimination on the treatment and processing of male and female offenders, but it should not any longer be simply assumed that women are more favourably treated by the penal and legal systems than men.

Conclusion

In this chapter I have attempted to describe and analyse aspects of the ideological basis of classical and contemporary explanations of female criminality. While a small number of studies have been produced which attempt to provide an alternative critical perspective to the prevailing hegemonic conceptions in this field of study (such as work produced by the School of Criminology, Berkeley), as far as current policy decisions affecting female offenders are concerned the influence of the type of work discussed above still predominates. Criminological theories of female criminality have tended to treat culturally given understandings of female behaviour as resources in accounting for women and crime. Such theories are readily compatible with policy decisions derived from a similar set of assumptions and orientated in turn towards the preservation or restoration of the given moral and socio-political order. These issues as they relate to male criminality have been addressed by radical and critical criminological theorists. However, radical and critical criminological theory, while providing a critique of conventional theorizing and the socio-political order for which conventional theorists offer either scientific legitimation or suggest ameliorating social reform to reduce rates of crime, fail to attend to the question of women and crime. Ironically critical theorists seem to have accepted the orthodox conception of female criminality as marginal to a general understanding of the nature of crime in contemporary society and its relationship to the socio-economic and political order. We need, therefore, to engage in more research into the aetiology, character and scale of female crime, and the treatment of female offenders by the legal and penal systems – but to do so by recognizing the critical significance of the cultural basis of sex and gender differentiation and the pervasiveness and consequences of cultural understanding of female behaviour.

Notes

This chapter was originally published in *The British Journal of Sociology*, 1977, 28(1): 89–100.

1   At the time of writing this paper Holloway was going to be transformed into a psychiatric hospital. However, during the rebuilding the policy changed and Holloway remained a prison, albeit with a psychiatric wing.

57494

3

Feminist Approaches to Criminology, or Postmodern Woman meets Atavistic Man

Some ten years ago it was *de rigueur* to start any paper on this topic with a reference to the dearth of material in the field. Now it is difficult to keep up with the production of papers and books. On the face of it this might seem a 'good thing' but on closer inspection we might begin to have some doubts since it is usually quality rather than quantity that counts. This is not to imply that there has not been a substantial amount of good work, rather it might be that valuable energies have been misdirected. In this chapter I want to explore schematically how feminist work in this field has developed and some of the problems that have been encountered. But first it is necessary to give some consideration to criminology – the atavistic man of my title. I shall argue that the core enterprise of criminology is problematic, that feminists' attempts to alter criminology have only succeeded in revitalizing a problematic enterprise, and that as feminist theory is increasingly engaging with and generating post-modern ideas the relevance of criminology to feminist thought diminishes.

It should be stressed of course that this is not exactly a novel exercise. Criminology seems to be *the* enterprise that many scholars desert or reject (Hirst, 1975; Bankowski et al., 1977). However, these notable rejections of criminology were based on a particular reading of Marx which led to the conclusion that Marxism and criminology were fundamentally incompatible. I am not interested in treating a text as a means of focusing and restricting thought so I shall not be appealing to a feminist orthodoxy with which criminology is incompatible. Rather, I shall draw attention to the rich variety of feminist scholarship at large when compared with the limited horizons of feminist criminology. I see criminology as something of a siding for feminist thought, with feminist criminologists risking something of a marginalized existence – marginal to criminology and to feminism.

The problem of criminology

The appliance of science

It is a story that has been told many times – although most effectively in *The New Criminology* (Taylor et al., 1974) – that criminology is an applied discipline which searches for the causes of crime in order to eradicate the problem. Admittedly criminology as a subject of scholarship embraces much more than this. For example, it tends to focus also on the operations of the criminal justice system, the relationship between the police and communities, or systems of punishment. However, such topics fit just as easily under the rubric of the sociology of law or even philosophy. What is unique about criminology, indeed its defining characteristic, is the central question of the *causes* of crime and the ultimate focus on the 'offender' rather than mechanisms of discipline and regulation which go beyond the limits of the field of crime. It is this defining characteristic I wish to take issue with here. Arguably it is this which creates a kind of vortex in this area of intellectual endeavour. It is the ultimate question against which criminology is judged. Can the causes of crime be identified and explained? Moreover, once identified, can they be modified?

Criminologies of the traditional schools have been unashamedly interventionist in aim if not always in practice. This goal was criticized by the radical criminologists of the 1970s for being oppressive, conservative, and narrowly partisan (that is, on the side of the state and/or powerful). Moreover, the radicals argued that the traditional criminologists had, in any case, got their theories wrong. Crime, it was argued, could not be explained by chromosomal imbalance, hereditary factors, working class membership, racial difference, intelligence and so on. So among the many errors of traditional criminology the two main ones to be identified were an inherent conservatism and inadequate theorization. The repudiation of these errors was condensed into the most critically damning term of abuse – positivist. To be positivist embodied everything that was bad. Positivism, like functionalism, had to be sought out, exposed and eliminated. Now, in some respect I would agree with this, but the problem we face is whether critical criminologies or the more recent left realist criminologies have transcended the problem of positivism or whether they have merely projected it onto their political opponents while assuming they are untainted.

I would argue that positivism is wrongly misconstrued if its main problem is seen as its connection to a conservative politics or a biological determinism. The problem of positivism is arguably less transparent than this and lies in the basic presumption that we can establish a verifiable knowledge or truth about events, in particular that we can establish a causal explanation, which in turn will provide us with objective methods for intervening in the events defined as problematic. Given this formulation, positivism may be, at the level of political orientation, either socialist or reactionary. The problem of positivism is, therefore, not redeemed by the espousal of left politics. Positivism poses an epistemological problem not a simple problem of party membership.

It is this problem of epistemology which has begun to attract the attention of feminist scholarship (the postmodern woman of my title). Feminism is now raising significant questions about the status and power of knowledge (Harding, 1986; Weedon, 1987) and formulating challenges to modes of totalizing or grand theorizing which impose a uniformity of perspective and ignore the immense diversity of subjectivities of women and men. This has in turn led to a questioning of whether 'scientific' work can ever provide a basis for intervention as positivism would presuppose. This is not to argue that intervention is inevitably undesirable or impossible, but rather to challenge the modernist assumption that once we have the theory ('master' narrative, Kellner, 1988[1]) which will explain all forms of social behaviour we will also know what to do, and the rightness of this 'doing' will be verifiable and transparent.

The continuing search for the theory, the cause and the solution

It is useful to concentrate on the work of Jock Young as a main exponent of left realism in criminology. His work is particularly significant because unlike many other left thinkers he has remained inside criminology and, while acknowledging many of the problems of his earlier stance in critical criminology, has sustained a commitment to the core element of the subject. That is to say he addresses the question of the causes of crime and the associated problems of attempting to devise policies to reduce crime. For example, he states:

> It is time for us to *compete* in policy terms, to get out of the ghetto of impossibilism. Orthodox criminology with its inability to question the political and its abandonment of aetiology is hopelessly unable to generate workable policies. . . . Let us state quite categorically that the major task of radical criminology is to seek a solution to the problem of crime and that of a socialist policy is to substantially reduce the crime rate. (Young, 1986: 28; emphasis in original)

This is compelling stuff, but it is precisely what I want to argue is problematic about the new forms of radical criminology for feminism. It might be useful initially to outline Young's position before highlighting some of the problems it poses.

As part of his call for a left realist criminology Young (1986) constructs a version of the recent history of postwar criminology. He sees it as a series of crises and failures (and in this respect we are at one). He points to the positivist heritage of postwar criminology in Britain which, in his account, amounts to a faith in medicine and cure and/or a reliance on biologically determinist explanations of crime. He sees the influence of North American criminology in a positive light (for example, Cloward and Ohlin, 1960; Cohen, 1965; and Matza, 1969) and then turns to the work of the New Criminologists in Britain who constructed a political paradigm in which to reappraise criminal behaviour. He is, however, critical of the idealism of this work and interprets it as the 'seedbed' of more radical work to come rather than a real challenge to mainstream orthodoxy or an adequate account in and of itself.

The failures of the criminological enterprise overall that Young identifies are in the main twofold. The first is the failure 'really' to explain criminal behaviour. The theories are always flawed either ontologically or politically. The second is the failure to solve the problem of crime or even to stem its rise. These are not two separate failures, however, as the failure to stop crime is the 'proof' of the failure of the theories to explain the causes of crime. Young argues,

> But in the post 1945 period, official crime rates continued to rise remorselessly, year by year, even accelerating as we entered the affluent sixties. Real incomes became the highest in history, slums were demolished one by one, educational attainment rose, social services expanded in order to provide extensive welfare provisions and safety nets, and yet the crime rate continued to doggedly rise! *All of the factors which should have led to a drop in delinquency if mainstream criminology were even half-correct, were being ameliorated and yet precisely the opposite effect was occurring.* (Young, 1986: 4–5; emphasis in original)

It is through this linkage between theory and policy that the positivism of the left realists comes to light. The problem is not that there is a commitment to reducing the misery to which crime is often wedded, nor is the problem that socialists (and feminists) want policies which are less punitive and oppressive. The problem is that science is held to have the answer if only it is scientific enough. Here is revealed the faith in the totalizing theory, the master narrative which will eventually – when sufficient scales have fallen from our eyes or sufficient connections have been made – allow us to see things for what they really are.

To return to Young's story, we pick up the unfolding of criminology at the point of intervention by the new criminologists. Young points out that while this intervention may have excited the academic criminologist there was simultaneously another revolution in mainstream criminology. This revolution was the transformation of traditional criminology from a discipline concerned with causes and cures, to one concerned with administrative efficiency and methods of containment. Young argues that mainstream criminology has given up the search for causes, the goal of the metanarrative of criminal causation. It has gone wholeheartedly over to the state and merely provides techniques of control and manipulation. Again it is important to highlight the linkages in Young's argument. On the one hand he is critical of what he calls administrative criminology because it has become (even more transparently?) an extension of the state (or a disciplinary mechanism). But the reason for this is identified as the abandonment of the search for the causes (a search which was according to Young in any case misdirected). The thesis therefore is that to abandon the search for the causes is to become prey to reactionary forces. This, it seems to me, is to ignore completely the debates which have been going on within sociology and cultural theory about the problems of grand and totalizing theories. And such ideas are coming not from the right but precisely from the subjects which such theoretical enterprises have subjugated, that is, lesbians and gays, black women and men, Asian women and men, feminists and so on. I shall briefly consider aspects of this debate before returning to the specific problem of feminism in criminology.

The debate over postmodernism

There is now a considerable literature on postmodernism and a number of scholars are particularly concerned to explore the consequences of this development for sociology (Bauman, 1988; Kellner, 1988; Smart, 1988) and for feminism (Harding, 1986; Weedon, 1987; Fraser and Nicholson, 1988). The concept of postmodernism derives from outside the social sciences from the fields of architecture and art (Rose, 1988). Bauman (1988) argues that we should not assume that postmodernism is simply another word for postindustrialism or postcapitalism. It has a specific meaning and a specific significance, especially for a discipline like sociology (and by extension criminology), one which challenges the very existence of such an enterprise. Postmodernism refers to a mode of thinking which threatens to overturn the basic premises of modernism within which sociology has been nurtured.

Briefly, the modern age has been identified by Foucault (1973) as beginning at the start of the nineteenth century. The rise of modernity marks the eclipsing of Classical thought and, most importantly, heralds the centring of the conception of 'man' as the knowing actor who is author of his own actions and knowledge (that is, the liberal subject) and who simultaneously becomes the object of (human) scientific enquiry. Modernism is, however, more than the moment in which the human subject is constituted and transformed. It is a world view, a way of seeing and interpreting, a science which holds the promise that science can reveal the truth of human behaviour. The human sciences, at the moment of constituting the human subject, make her knowable – a site of investigation. What secrets there are will succumb to better knowledge, more rigorous methodologies, or more accurate typologizing. Implicit in the modernist paradigm is the idea that there is progress. What we do not know now, we will know tomorrow. It presumes that it is only a matter of time before science can explain all from the broad sweep of societal change to the motivations of the child molester. And because progress is presumed to be good and inevitable, science inevitably serves progress. Knowledge becomes nothing if it is not knowledge for something. Knowledge must be applied or applicable – even if we do not know how to apply it now there is the hope that one day we will find a use for it (space travel did after all justify itself for we do now have non-stick frying pans).

Modernity has now become associated with some of the most deep-seated intellectual problems of the end of the twentieth century. It is seen as synonymous with racism, sexism, Euro-centredness and the attempt to reduce cultural and sexual differences to one dominant set of values and knowledge. Modernism is the intellectual mode of western thought which has been identified as male or phallogocentric (see, for example, Gilligan, 1982; Duchen, 1986) and as white or Eurocentric (see, for example, Dixon, 1976; Harding, 1986). It is also seen as an exhausted mode, one which has failed to live up to its promise and which is losing credibility. As Bauman argues:

> Nobody but the most rabid of the diehards believes today that the western mode of life, either the actual one or one idealized ('utopianized') in the intellectual mode has more than a sporting chance of ever becoming universal. . . . The search for the universal standards has suddenly become gratuitous. . . . Impracticality erodes interest. The task of establishing universal standards of truth, morality, taste does not seem that much important. (Bauman, 1988: 220–1)

Clinging to modernist thought, in this account, is not only antediluvian, it is also politically suspect. It presumes that sociology (which for brevity's sake I shall take to include criminology in this section) is a way of knowing the world is superior, more objective, more truthful than other knowledges. However, it is easier said than done to shake off the grip of a way of knowing which is almost all one knows. In turn this reflects a dilemma which has always plagued sociology, if we say we do not know (in the modernist sense) then we seem to be succumbing to the forces of the Right who have always said we knew nothing – or at least were good for nothing.

The irony is, as Bauman points out, that we are damned if we do and also if we don't. He points to the way in which sociology has little choice but to recognize the failure of its originating paradigm. On the one hand doubts cannot be wished away and we cannot pretend that sociology produces the goods that the postwar welfare state required of it. On the other hand governments already know this. We cannot keep it a secret. State funding of sociological research is already much reduced and what will be funded is narrowly restricted to meet governmental aims. It may have been possible in the past to claim that more money was necessary, or a larger study was imperative before conclusions could be drawn, but now we know (and they know) that conclusions, in the sense of final definitive statements, cannot be drawn. The point is whether we argue that all the studies that have been carried out to date have been inadequate or whether we reappraise the very idea that we will find solutions. Young, for example, is scathing about a major study carried out on 400 delinquents by West (1969). He points out that this was one of the largest and most expensive pieces of criminological work to be carried out in Britain. Yet, he argues disparagingly, it could only come up with a link between delinquency and poverty and no real causes. For Young the problem is the intellectual bankruptcy of the positivist paradigm. From where I stand he is right but, as I shall argue below, the problem is that he locates himself inside exactly the same paradigm.

The vortex that is criminology

It is, then, interesting that Young acknowledges many of the problems outlined above, although he does not do so from a postmodern stance. Rather, he is situated inside the modernist problematic itself. He acknowledges that mainstream criminology has given up the search for causes and the 'master' narrative. He also recognizes the power of governments to diminish an academic enterprise which they no longer have use for. Hence to keep their jobs criminologists have had to give up promising the solutions and knuckle down to oiling the wheels. He is rightly critical of this, but rather than seeing the broad implications of this development these criminolog*ists* are depicted as capitalist lackeys while criminology as an enterprise can be saved from such political impurity by a reassertion of a modernist faith. While applauding Young's resistance to the logic of the market which has infected much of criminology (and sociology) I am doubtful that a backward looking, almost nostalgic *cri de coeur*, for the theory that will answer everything is very convincing. Yet Young can see nothing positive in challenging the modernist mode of thought, he only sees capitulation. The way to resist is apparently to proclaim that suffering is real and that we still need a 'scientific' solution to it.

In so doing Young claims the moral high ground for the realists, since to contradict the intellectual content of the argument appears to be a denial of misery and a negation of the very constituencies for whom he now speaks. So, let me make it plain that the challenge to modernist thought, with its positivistic overtones which are apparent in criminology, does not entail a denial of poverty, inequality, repression, racism, sexual violence and so on. Rather it denies that the intellectual can divine the answer to these through the demand for more scientific activity and bigger and better theories.

The problem which faces criminology is not insignificant, however, and arguably its dilemma is even more fundamental than that facing sociology. The whole *raison d'être* of criminology is that it addresses 'crime'. It categorizes a vast range of activities and treats them as if they are all subject to the same laws – whether laws of human behaviour, of genetic inheritance, of economic rationality or development and so on. The argument within criminology has always been between those who give primacy to one form of explanation rather than another. The thing that criminology cannot do is deconstruct 'crime'. It cannot locate rape or child sexual abuse in the domain of sexuality, nor theft in the domain of economic activity, nor drug use in the domain of health. To do so would be to abandon criminology to sociology, but more importantly it would involve abandoning the idea of a unified problem which requires a unified response – at least at the theoretical level. However, left realist criminology at least does not seem prepared for this:

> We must develop a realist theory which adequately encompasses the scope of *the criminal act*. That is, it must deal with both macro- and micro-levels with the causes of criminal action and social reaction, and with the triangular inter-relationship between offender, victim and the state. . . . It must rescue the action of causality whilst stressing both the specificity of generalization and the existence of human choice and value in any equation of criminality. (Young, 1986: 27–8; emphasis added)

It is not just that this appears to be a fairly tall order, it is a quest for a grail which will divert energies into the theoretical vortex which now constitutes left realist criminology.

Feminist interventions into criminology

I have argued that the core enterprise of criminology (which is the search for a cause of the category of behaviour called crime) is profoundly problematic. However, it is important to acknowledge that it is not just criminology which is inevitably challenged by the more general reappraisal of modernist thinking. So my argument is not that criminology alone is vulnerable to the question of whether such a knowledge project is tenable. But criminology does occupy a particularly significant position in this debate because both traditional and realist criminological thinking are especially wedded to the positivist paradigm of modernism. This makes it particularly important for feminist work to challenge the core of criminology and to avoid isolation from some of the major theoretical and political questions which are engaging feminist scholarship elsewhere. It might therefore be useful to consider schematically a range of feminist contributions to criminology to see the extent to which feminism has resisted or succumbed to the vortex.

Feminist empiricism
Sandra Harding (1986, 1987) has provided a useful conceptual framework for mapping the development of feminist thought in the social sciences. She refers to feminist empiricism, standpoint feminism and postmodern feminism. By feminist empiricism she means that work which has criticized the claims to objectivity made by mainstream social science. Feminist empiricism points out that what has passed for science is in fact the world perceived from the perspective of men, that what looks like objectivity is really sexism and that the kinds of questions traditional social science has asked have systematically excluded women and the interests of women. Feminist empiricism, therefore, claims that a truly objective science would not be androcentric but would take account of both genders. What is required under this model is that social scientists live up to their proclaimed codes of objectivity. Under this schema empirical practice is critiqued but empiricism remains intact. Such a perspective is not particularly threatening to the established order. It facilitates the study of women offenders to fill the gaps in existing knowledge, men can go on studying men and the relevances of men as long as they acknowledge that it is men and not humanity they are addressing.

In criminology there has been a growth in the study of women offenders (see, for example, Heidensohn, 1985; Eaton, 1986; Carlen, 1988). It would be unjust to suggest that these have merely followed the basic tenets of mainstream empirical work but a motivating element in all of these has been to do studies on women. Because of the dearth of studies on women (in sociology as well as criminology) the desire to do such studies was and is entirely understandable. But as Dorothy Smith pointed out in 1974, to direct research at women without revising traditional assumptions about methodology and epistemology can result in making women a mere addendum to the main project of studying men. It also leaves unchallenged the way men are studied.

Harding sees a radical potential in feminist empiricism, however. She argues that the fact that feminists identify different areas for study (that is, domestic violence rather than delinquency) has brought a whole range of new issues on to the agenda. It is also the case that feminists who subscribe to empiricism have also challenged the way we arrive at the goal of objective knowledge. Hence different kinds of methods are espoused, note is taken of the power relationship between researcher and researched and so on (see Stanley and Wise, 1983). The move towards ethnographic research is an example of this (although this is not of course peculiar to feminist work).

It is perhaps important at this stage to differentiate between empiricism and empirical work. Harding's categories refer to epistemological stances rather than practices (although the two are not unrelated). Empiricism is a stance which proclaims the possibility of objective and true knowledge which can be arrived at, and tested against, clearly identified procedures. Mainstream criminology, having followed these tenets, claimed to have discovered valid truths about women's criminal behaviour (and of course men's). The initial reaction of feminism to this claim was to reinterpret this truth as a patriarchal lie. It was argued that the methods used had been tainted with bias and so the outcome was inevitably faulty (Smart, 1986). This left open the presumption that the methods could be retained if the biases were removed because the ideal of a true or real science was posited as the alternative to the biased one.

Empirical research does not have to be attached to empiricism, however. To engage with women, to interview them, to document their oral histories, to participate with them does not automatically mean that one upholds the ideal of empiricism. So to be critical of empiricism is not to reject empirical work per se. However, some of the empirical studies generated under the goal of collecting more knowledge about women which feminist empiricism engendered presented a different sort of problem for the project of a feminist criminology.

This problem was the thorny question of discrimination. The early feminist contributions did not only challenge the objectivity of criminological thought, they also challenged the idea of an objective judiciary and criminal justice system. Hence there grew a major preoccupation with revealing the truth or otherwise of equality before the law in a range of empirical studies. Some studies seemed to find that the police or courts treated women and girls more leniently than men and boys. Others found the opposite. Then there were discoveries that much depended on the nature of the offence, or the length of previous record, or whether the offender was married or not (see, for example, Farrington and Morris, 1983). As Gelsthorpe (1986) has pointed out, the search for straightforward sexism was more difficult than any one imagined at first. It was of course a false trail in as much as it was anticipated that forms of oppression (whether sexual or racial or other) could be identified in a few simple criteria which could then be established (or not) in following a ritual procedure. The irony is perhaps that the supposed failure to find the objective truth of sexism leads to a denial of feminism rather than of empiricism. So in this respect the (with the benefit of hindsight) overly simplistic approach of early feminist work in this field has created an obstacle to further developments. For a question which can now be posed is 'if feminist work cannot show that there is discrimination is there any justification in studying women as a separate or distinct group?' Or worse, 'If there is no empirical proof of discrimination do we need feminism?'

The other drawback to this type of research is the one which has been highlighted by MacKinnon (1987). She argues that any approach which focuses on equality and inequality always presumes that the norm is men. Hence studies of criminal justice always compare the treatment of women with men and men remain the standard against which all is judged. This has led to two problems. The first is a facile, yet widespread, reaction that if one has the audacity to compare women with men in circumstances where men are more favourably treated, then in those instances where they are treated less favourably one must, ipso facto, also be requiring the standard of treatment of women to be worsened. Hence, in comparing how the courts treat men and women, the response is inevitably the threat that if women want equality they must have it in full and that feminists want women to be sent in their droves to dirty, violent and overcrowded prisons for long periods of time. This is what Lahey (1985) has called 'equality with a vengeance'. It is intended to punish the audacity of the original request and to imply that it is feminism which will make matters worse for women and not the patriarchal order.[2]

The second problem goes beyond the transparent difficulties of treating women as if they were men to the level of the symbolic. Basically the equality paradigm always reaffirms the centrality of men. Men continue to constitute the norm, the unproblematic, the natural social actor. Women are thus always seen as interlopers into a world already organized by others. This has been well established in areas like employment law where the equality argument has been seen unintentionally to reproduce men as the ideal employees, with women struggling to make the grade (Kenney, 1986). Underlying such an approach in any case is the presumption that law is fundamentally a neutral object inside a liberal regime, thus wholly misconstruing the nature of power and the power of law (Smart, 1989). Law does not stand outside gender relations and adjudicate upon them. Law is part of these relations, and is always already gendered in its principles and practices. We cannot separate out one practice – called discrimination – and ask for it to cease to be gendered as it would be a meaningless request. This is not to say we cannot object to certain principles and practices, but we need to think carefully before we continue to sustain a conceptual framework which either prioritizes men as the norm, or assumes that genderlessness (or gender blindness) is either possible or desirable.

Standpoint feminism

The second category identified by Harding is standpoint feminism. The epistemological basis of this form of feminist knowledge is experience. However, not just any experience is deemed to be equally valuable or valid. *Feminist* experience is achieved through a struggle against oppression, it is therefore argued to be more complete and less distorted than the perspective of the ruling group or men. A feminist standpoint is therefore not just the experience of women, but of women *reflexively* engaged in struggle (intellectual and political). In this process it is argued that a more accurate or fuller version of reality is achieved. This stance does not divide knowledge from values and politics, but sees knowledge arising from engagement.

Arguably standpoint feminism does not feature strongly in feminist criminology except in quite specific areas of concern like rape, sexual assault and domestic violence. It is undoubtedly the influence of feminists engaged at a political level with these forms of oppression that has begun to transform some areas of criminological thinking. Hence the work of Rape Crisis Centres (for example, London Rape Crisis, 1984) have been vital in proffering an alternative 'truth' about rape and the experience of the criminal justice system. However, as far as mainstream criminology is concerned we should perhaps not be too optimistic about this since the accounts provided by such organizations have only been partially accepted and then as a consequence of substantiation by more orthodox accounts (Chambers and Millar, 1983; Blair, 1985).

So taking experience as a starting point and testing ground has only made a partial entry into criminology, and interestingly where it has has been in the domain of left realism. It is here we find the resort to experience (that is, women's experience of crime) a constant referent and justification. Women's fear of rape and violence is used in this context to argue that rape and violence must be treated as serious problems. The question that this poses is whether we now have a feminist realist criminology or whether left realism (and consequently criminology as a whole) has been revitalized by the energies and concerns of a politically active women's movement. If we consider texts like *Well-Founded Fear* (Hanmer and Saunders, 1984), or *Leaving Violent Men* (Binney et al., 1981) we find that the motivating drive is the desire to let women's experiences be told. These experiences are not meant to stand alongside the experiences of the police, or violent men – they represent the expression of subjugation which will replace the dominant account. Hanmer and Saunders outline methodological procedures for tapping into this experience and produce what Harding has referred to as a 'successor science'. As she argues, 'the adoption of this standpoint is fundamentally a moral and political act of commitment to understanding the world from the perspective of the socially subjugated' (1986: 149). In fact it goes beyond this as the researchers, as feminists, also inhabit the world of the socially subjugated. So it is not an act of empathy as such but a shared knowledge.

The real issue remains unresolved, however. For while feminist work is generating another sort of knowledge (for example, other ways of accounting for violence) feminist work which left realist criminology attempts to fit under its umbrella does not embrace the full scope of what Young has called for (see, for example, Gregory, 1986[3]). This is because standpoint feminism has not taken masculinity as a focus of investigation. Precisely because standpoint feminism in this area has arisen from a grassroots concern to protect women and to reveal the victimization of women, it has not been sympathetic to the study of masculinity(ies). Indeed it would argue that we have heard enough from that quarter and that any attempt by feminists to turn their attention away from women is to neglect the very real problems that women still face. So the feminist realists (if we can use this term for the sake of argument) are on quite a different trajectory to the left realists. It may be convenient to the left to support the work of feminists in this area, but it is unclear to me where this unholy 'alliance' is going analytically. Like the protracted debate about the marriage of Marxism and feminism, we may find that this alliance ends in annulment.

Feminist postmodernism

It would be a mistake to depict feminist postmodernism as the third stage or synthesis of feminist empiricism and standpoint feminism.

Feminist postmodernism does not try to resolve the problems of other positions, rather it starts in a different place and proceeds in other directions. Much postmodern analysis is rooted in philosophy and aesthetics (Lyotard, 1986; Rorty, 1985; Fekete, 1988), but in the case of feminism it started in political practice. It began with the separate demises of sisterhood and of Marxism.

By the demise of sisterhood I mean the realization that women were not all white, middle class, and of anglo-saxon protestant extract. Feminism resisted this realization by invoking notions of Womanhood as a core essence to unite women (under the leadership of the said white, middle class etc?). However, black feminists, lesbian feminists, 'Third World' feminists, aboriginal feminists and many others simply refused to swallow the story. To put it simply, they knew power when they saw it exercised. So feminism had to abandon its early framework and to start to look for other ways of thinking which did not subjugate other subjectivities. But at the same time feminism came to recognize that individual women did not have unitary selves. Debates over sexuality, pornography and desire began to undo the idea of the true self and gave way to notions of fractured subjectivities. These developments were much influenced by the work of Foucault and psychoanalysis, but they cannot be dismissed simply as a 'fad' because the recognition of the inadequacy of the feminist paradigm was not imposed by the intellectuals but arose out of a series of painful struggles for understanding combined with a progressive politics.

The other key element in this development was the demise of Marxism as a rigorously policed grid of analysis to which adherence had meant the promise of the total explanation or master narrative. Again feminist practice revealed the inadequacy of the grand theoretical project of Marxism quite early in the second wave. But the struggle to retain the paradigm lasted much longer. None the less, it is now realized that we cannot keep adding bits to Marxist orthodoxy to try to explain all the awkward silences. So while many Marxian values may be retained, the idea and the promise of the totalizing theory have gradually loosened their grip.

The core element of feminist postmodernism is the rejection of the one reality which arises from 'the falsely universalizing perspective of the master' (Harding, 1987: 188). But unlike standpoint feminism it does not seek to impose a different unitary reality. Rather it refers to subjugated knowledge*s*, which tell different stories and have different specificities. So the aim of feminism ceases to be the establishment of the feminist truth and becomes the aim of deconstructing Truth and analysing the power effects that claims to truth entail. So there is a shift away from treating knowledge as ultimately objective, or at least the final standard, and hence able to reveal the concealed truth, towards recognizing that knowledge is part of power and that power is ubiquitous. Feminist knowledge therefore becomes part of a multiplicity of resistances. Take for example feminist interventions in the area of rape. This is an area which I have explored in detail elsewhere (Smart, 1989) but for the sake of this discussion I wish to rely on the work of Woodhull (1988). Woodhull, in an article on sexuality and Foucault argues against a traditional feminist mode of explanation for rape. She concentrates on Brownmiller's (1975) approach which seeks to explain rape in terms of the physiological differences between men and women. Taking biology as a bottom line Brownmiller asserts that because men have a sexual organ that can penetrate and women have a sexual organ that can be penetrated men have been able to create an ideology of rape. Woodhull's argument is that in explaining rape in this way, Brownmiller puts sex and biology outside the social, as preceding all power relations. Thus women are always already disempowered because men carry a built-in weapon and women a built-in vulnerability. What is missing is an understanding of how sexual difference and the meanings of different bits of bodies are constructed. Woodhull argues:

> If we are seriously to come to terms with rape, we must explain how the vagina comes to be coded – and experienced – as a place of emptiness and vulnerability, the penis as a weapon, and intercourse as violation, rather than naturalize these processes through references to 'basic' physiology. Instead of sidestepping the problem of sex's relation to power by divorcing one from the other in our minds, we need to analyze the social mechanisms, including language and conceptual structures, that bind the two together in our culture. (Woodhull, 1988: 171)

So it becomes a concern of feminism to explore how women's bodies have become saturated with (hetero)sex, how codes of sexualized meaning are reproduced and sustained and to begin (or continue) the deconstruction of these meanings.

This is just one example of how postmodernism is influencing feminist practice (for others see Jardine, 1985; Weedon, 1987; Fraser and Nicholson, 1988; Diamond and Quinby, 1988) and it is clear that the ramifications of the epistemological crisis of modernism are far from being fully mapped or exhaustively considered as yet. So we are in no position to judge what shapes feminism will be taking in the next decade or so. However, it might be interesting to consider, albeit prematurely, what all this means for criminology.

Conclusion

It is a feature of postmodernism that questions posed within a modernist frame are turned about. So for a long time we have been asking 'what has feminism had to contribute to criminology (or sociology etc.)?' Feminism has been knocking at the door of established disciplines hoping to be let in on equal terms. These established disciplines have largely looked down their noses (metaphorically speaking) and found feminism wanting. Feminism has been required to become more objective, more substantive, more scientific, more anything before a grudging entry could be granted. But now the established disciplines are themselves looking rather insecure (Bauman, 1988) and as the door is opening we must ask whether feminism really does want to enter.

Perhaps it is now apt to rephrase the traditional question to read 'what has criminology got to offer feminism?' Feminism is now a broadly based scholarship and political practice. Its concerns range from questions of philosophy to representations to engagement; it is, therefore, no longer in the supplicant position of an Olivia Twist. On the contrary, we have already seen that a lot of feminist work has revitalized radical criminology. It might be that criminology needs feminism more than the converse. Of course many criminologists, especially the traditional variety, will find this preposterous but perhaps they had better look to who their students are, and who their students are reading.

It is clear that if mainstream criminology remains unchanged it will follow the path that Young has outlined into greater and greater complicity with mechanisms of discipline. However, the path of radical criminology seems wedded to the modernist enterprise and is, as yet, unaffected by the epistemological sea changes which have touched feminism and other discourses. Under such circumstances it is very hard to see what criminology has to offer to feminism.

Notes

This chapter was originally published in L. Gelsthorpe and A. Morris (eds) (1990) *Feminist Perspectives in Criminology*, pp. 70–84, Milton Keynes, Open University Press.

1   Kellner has argued that there is some confusion between terms like 'master narratives' and 'grand narratives'. By the former is meant 'that attempt to subsume every particular, every specific viewpoint, and every key point into one totalising theory' (1988: 253). By the latter he means the attempt to tell the Big Story such as the rise of capitalism or patriarchy. Criminology has necessarily been more concerned with the former.

2   I have argued against equality feminism elsewhere (Smart, 1989). However my criticism is that equality feminism misunderstands the nature of the law and the state, and naïvely asks for equal treatment on the assumption that it will improve things. Evidence indicates that equality legislation only improves things for men (MacKinnon, 1987; Fudge, 1989).

3   Jeanne Gregory's paper in the Matthews and Young (1986) collection is an
    interesting example of what I mean here. Located alongside Young's call for a
    re-emphasis on criminology and deviance is Gregory's paper which starts within a
    criminological perspective but moves rapidly outside this field as she progresses on
    to a discussion of the future direction of feminist work.

PART II
SEXUALITY

Introduction

In this section on sexuality and law, I focus principally on what is said about sexuality and how these discourses and narratives (I use both terms) are constitutive of certain social processes or incite certain social consequences. In Chapter 4, which was originally published in 1985, I focus on prostitution and its relation to ideas about female sexuality in general. In substance I explore magistrates' constructions of 'normal' and 'deviant' female sexuality, and the way in which the prostitute is constantly defined as Other or outside the boundaries of the acceptable. I argue that the conceptualizations deployed by magistrates arise from, but also perpetuate, normalizing discourses (although I do not use this terminology). By this I mean, following Foucault, that certain discourses create a norm of behaviour or personality type against which other behaviours or types are judged and calibrated. This gives rise to mechanisms to change or reform the behaviour or type and the individuals who behave in this fashion are judged according to their nearness to or distance from that which is defined as the norm.

This normalizing discourse is, in turn, linked to the perpetuation of outrageous methods of regulating prostitute women which are deemed to be culturally acceptable because the discourses which construct the prostitute always construct her as outside the boundaries of decent treatment (or even civil rights). I dwell on how this outlawing of prostitutes has failed to generate much of a response from feminism because in seeking to ameliorate the situation facing prostitutes there is a fear that prostitution itself – a mode of sexual exploitation of women – is condoned and perpetuated. In concluding I call for a feminist strategy to challenge the law both as a means of assisting prostitute women to escape the surveillance and punishment of criminal sanctions and also as a way of challenging wider discursive (normalizing) constructions of female sexual behaviour. As will become evident, my work is often less hesitant in inviting a feminist response to law when it involves decriminalization than when it involves an extension of law's domain or further criminalizations. The strategy I propose is not therefore a programme or set of policies, but a way of trying to escape from a normalizing discourse which has become concretized in law and legal practice.

The remaining three chapters in this part of the book all address more explicitly this issue of engaging with law. What unfolds across the three chapters is a growing concern about *how* to engage with law as a feminist. There is little of this 'uncertainty' in the papers originally published in the early 1980s but it does come to predominate in the 1990s. In Chapter 5 I focus on rape and the way in which the rape trial constructs men and women as naturally different, from which presumption the core problems of the rape trial are argued to follow. I suggest that in tackling the problem of the trial, feminism has also tended to construct men and women as naturally different and to presume an essential experience of rape. This essential experience is drawn from narratives on rape which have emphasized the horror of rape, its very assault on the self and the way that it victimizes women. I explore why both many feminist accounts of rape and the law's version of rape are so similar – at least epistemologically and ontologically – and suggest that this may be a serious problem. On the ontological level the problem resides in the assumption that men have a natural sex. Thus law tends to assume men are *naturally* sexually aggressive while feminism tends to assume that men have the *natural* equipment to rape and learn how to use this aggressively.

In seeking to condemn rape and to allow women to speak out about their experiences, much feminist work in this area has left aside any consideration of the sexing of the male body. Some reference may be made to socialization processes, but typically men are simply depicted as being sexually atavistic. In sharing this perspective with law, feminism often ignores the role that law plays in sexing the male body. Thus I suggest that both law and much feminism shares the same ground on male sexuality (and to a lesser extent on female sexuality). The only difference is that feminism wants to change the outcome of this acknowledged and agreed upon difference between men and women. It is, however, my argument that we cannot move to a complete reconceptualization of rape and policies on rape as long as we hold to a belief in this essential difference – and this is the epistemological point. This is because this very belief in essential difference is what is generative of the possibility of rape in the first place. We need to understand the construction of male and female sexuality and how they are rendered fundamentally different rather than taking this difference as our starting point. In this way we can try to avoid concretizing male sexuality in violence and aggression and female sexuality in vulnerability and trauma. If we continue to do this, I argue that we merely confirm law's construction of sexual difference rather than subverting it. We also, metaphorically, leave women rapable.

Chapter 5 concludes with a discussion of how a particular narrative of rape has come to dominate and how this reinforces the idea of women as sexually vulnerable. Chapter 6 takes up this idea of dominant feminist narratives in the realm of pornography and law. My argument suggests that certain (longstanding) narrative forms which allow women to speak openly of sex (at least in the domain of law) tend towards a regulatory imperative (that is, a self-evident assumption that more law is needed to resolve the problem). I discuss the confessional mode of address used in feminist lobby politics and how this ignores the moral overtones (which I distinguish from content) of the personal testimony. I explore why the personal testimonies of women can be regarded as so sacred to feminism and here I revisit the issue of standpoint feminism and the power of experience.

In Chapter 6 I also discuss the separation of the idea of politics from the idea of morality in feminist work on sexuality. For a long time British feminism has ignored questions of values and morality/ethics and has found a more fruitful way of challenging orthodoxies by concentrating on questions of power and oppression. While acknowledging the usefulness of this orientation, in Chapter 7 I go on to focus more explicitly on the need now to think in terms of feminist ethics. It may help, therefore, if I distinguish here between what I now mean when I use the terms morality and ethics since I do not do so in the following chapters and I discover that in places I have used them somewhat interchangeably. I use morality in Chapter 6 mainly to refer to a set of values which 'creep' into certain kinds of feminist work even when it is most vociferous about excluding moral issues. This morality is akin to normative expectations about sexual behaviour found commonly expressed in western Judaeo-Christian cultures and is sometimes referred to as 'moralism' as a way of indicating that it has a narrow remit. When I speak of ethics, however, I am referring to a reflexive and deliberate consideration of values which can frame decisions about forms of behaviour quite aside from the sexual. Much feminism has turned to a consideration of ethics with the demise of a faith in absolute scientific truths which could determine political choices. We may thus be said to be entering a phase of ethical feminism, having moved away from phases of political feminism and scientific feminism.

In many ways Chapter 7, which is the last in this part and written most recently, seeks to clarify a lot of the emergent themes in the previous three chapters. It takes time to discuss the related concepts of sex, gender and sexuality, and suggests that the understanding of these concepts which have developed in psychoanalytic and post-structuralist feminist work need to be imported into the field of feminist theory of law. One reason why many feminists are reluctant to do this, I argue, is linked to a concern that such approaches are not politically useful in a legal forum. While I acknowledge the power of this, I suggest that such approaches need to be developed alongside discussions about feminist ethics. This means that we can gradually let go of a politics based on (now shaky) essentialisms and epistemological and ontological certainties. However, we need to do this alongside debates about ethics, responsibility and harm. In Chapter 7 I pursue these ideas in relation to rape and sado-masochism. The point I always seem to reiterate, however, is that law is never a stable ally, indeed it is hardly an ally at all. If feminism identifies harms in the domain of sexuality I suggest that we should recognize that law is more a part of the problem (in the way that it genders, sexes and sexualizes the female and male body) than part of the solution.

4

Legal Subjects and Sexual Objects: Ideology, Law and Female Sexuality

Much has been written on the subject of law and female sexuality (for example, Brownmiller, 1975; Clark and Lewis, 1977; Edwards, 1981) and specifically on the question of prostitution (Jaget, 1980; Walkowitz, 1982; McLeod, 1982). The vast majority of this contemporary work has been inspired by the women's movement and the development of feminist theory which has begun to analyse problems, long familiar to feminists, such as the double standard of sexual morality and the division of women into categories of whores and madonnas. The laws governing prostitution have consistently been identified as a source of oppression of women because in the UK these laws have always directed their punitive surveillance towards women (see Bland, 1985).

Our current laws on soliciting and loitering (1959 Street Offences Act) is a prime example of straightforward legal sexual discrimination because only women can be defined as common prostitutes and so only women become subject to the particularly repressive regime of regulation that follows from this definition (Smart, 1976). It is not, however, these visible and well-documented features of law relating to prostitution that I wish to explore here. Rather, I wish to examine the ideological content of the views of judicial actors, who routinely adjudicate in cases of soliciting and related offences, and to go on to consider how similar ideologies inform policy making and law reform in the area of prostitution. In other words, I want to shift concentration away from elements of self-evident discrimination in legislation towards the less self-evident question of ideologies of female sexuality which inform the enforcement and the development of law. Although I would argue that legislation does identify a special class of women (in this case common prostitutes) and therefore constructs some women as specific 'legal subjects' with fewer rights than other citizens, I would also wish to argue that it is legislation and legal practice informed by specific ideologies of female sexuality which serves to construct prostitute women as mere 'sexual objects'. In turn this sexual objectification of prostitute women reinforces their special status as denigrated legal subjects and helps to preserve legislation which, by most standards, must be regarded as unusually harsh and repressive.

That there is great resistance to changing the law in this area is evidenced by the number of fruitless attempts to introduce reforms in recent years. There have been five private members bills in the House of Lords since 1967 and two in the Commons in 1979 and 1981. Moreover, since the Wolfenden Report of 1957, which provided the basis for the subsequent rationalization of legislation on prostitution, there have been two important Government reports: one produced in 1974 by the Home Office, entitled *Working Party on Vagrancy and Street Offences Working Paper*, and the other produced by the Criminal Law Revision Committee in 1982, entitled *Working Paper on Offences Relating to Prostitution and Allied Offences*. In addition, at the time the Criminal Law Revision Committee (hereafter CLRC) was considering the law on prostitution, the Policy Advisory Committee on Sexual Offences was set up to give advice to the CLRC. Yet, in spite of all these efforts and documents, the law remains basically unchanged and the major criticism of the law which was expressed over fifty years ago (Macmillan Report, 1928) is still valid today, namely that the law constructs a specific category of women called common prostitutes which it then subjects to a unique form of prosecution and regulation.

It is therefore the aim of this chapter to look at how it is that such legislation is either defended and justified or, in those instances where it is found wanting, how it is that even more draconian measures are proposed as ways to reform the law. I hope to show that ideas about women's sexuality, women's bodies and women's place in the family as wives and mothers are central to these debates on the law, and how the specific 'sexual objectification' of prostitute women provides the basis for retaining or 'reforming' the law along lines which are based on a very direct control[1] over women's bodies. Consequently, in the first section of this chapter I shall document what magistrates had to say about prostitute women and the 'problem' of prostitution. This is based on tape-recorded interviews with 25 randomly selected magistrates (14 men and 11 women) who were sitting regularly in the Sheffield Magistrates' courts in the winter of 1981. In the second section I shall briefly examine their views on the law as it stood in 1981 and on potential law reforms, and finally I shall consider some of the official policy documents on prostitution which outline the established position on the legal regulation of prostitutes and which frequently reflect the values expressed by the magistrates.

Sexuality, ideology and the bench

When discussing women's sexuality it is important to recognize that it is extremely difficult to avoid talking at the same time about marriage, love, the family and children. Although feminist work on sexuality attempts to produce an analysis of it which does not impart ideas on how female sexuality can *only* be fulfilled inside a monogamous, heterosexual, legally sanctioned union, this is not the common-sense view of women's sexuality. Women and girls who have sex outside marriage are still regarded as promiscuous, or more colloquially as slags and sluts; unmarried mothers are still unable to legitimize their children without getting married. So unless we concentrate solely on the physiology of sex, discussions of female sexuality almost always invoke the determining context of marriage and the family. Consequently, most discussions of prostitution also invoke the cultural ideals of heterosexual love, monogamous marriage and the sanctity of the family. Take, for example, the following statement by the Reverend Ian Paisley during the debate on Maureen Colquhoun's Private Member's Bill to reform the laws on soliciting in the House of Commons in 1979.

> I rise to oppose the bringing in of this Bill. I do so because I believe in the sanctity of our women folk. . . . In all parts of this House and in all sections of the community there is concern that the standards that have made this nation and protected its women folk in the past are in serious jeopardy. . . . The person who has been caught up in prostitution . . . has lost the greatest thing in life – the purpose for which she came into the world. All of us here today remember our own mothers. . . . We all remember the sanctity of the family and joy and peace that flows from family life. . . . This is only the beginning of a scheme to undermine what lies at the very heart of our society. (Parliamentary Debates, 7 February 1979, Vol. 962, Cols 1096–7)

There are two main elements to Paisley's statement which deserve to be drawn out. The first is that any relaxation of the law which diminishes legal control over prostitution is a threat to the family and the nation. The second is a pity for the women concerned who can never know the joy of women's *real* purpose in life. These elements of dread and pity which coincide in Paisley's speech are commonly invoked in relation to so-called promiscuous women and they were a consistent theme in the remarks made by the Sheffield magistrates. Consider the following three statements:

> 'It is a social problem because it tends to undermine marriage and I believe that stable marriage is fundamental to the well-being of any

nation. That is quite apart from the fact that it can spread venereal disease. It is a clear and very obvious social evil in my opinion.'

'Well I think I'd be old fashioned enough to say there is a better fulfilment in a stable relationship which is either a contractual one like marriage or something which does instead of.'

'It's a problem in that, you know, without wanting in any sense to condemn the women, I find it absolutely tragic and very hard to understand why they want to use this most wonderful gift of sex in this way.'

Although other magistrates were not as explicit as this, it was none the less the case that prostitution was always discussed in a context which idealized marriage or monogamous relationships. Marriage always remained the point of comparison and departure. What the magistrates had to say about female sexuality outside the regulated and authorized boundaries of the legal contract of marriage therefore also spoke volumes about what may constitute 'acceptable' forms of female sexuality. Hence, although magistrates were speaking only about prostitute women, the content of their statements has ideological significance for all women. Consider the following statements:[2]

'Well I think that detectives in the vice squad are so very familiar with this sort of problem that they would never put that sort of a handle on a woman who was *anything near decent*.' (emphasis added)

'I think one would be reluctant to send a girl to prison when she had children. *I'm told by probation officers that some of them make very good mothers*.' (emphasis added)

'Even though they are *undesirable ladies* they are not bad mothers.' (emphasis added)

'No *decent* man will have anything to do with them afterwards. They can't get boyfriends.' (emphasis added)

The theme running through these comments, and many more which littered the speech of almost all the magistrates, is that prostitute women are quite beyond the pale. They may have some redeeming features but these are cause for remark and, not infrequently, even astonishment that they may still have some 'human qualities'. Yet *all* that prostitute women have done is to offend a sexual taboo. Surprisingly, the magistrates were not talking about serious criminals but about women who earn a living with their sexuality. Moreover, the dividing line (allowing for the sake of argument that such a division exists)[3] between prostitute women and other women is extremely narrow. It would take very little for any woman to slip beyond the pale into the almost non-human species referred to by the magistrates. It may simply hang on a police*man*'s ability to distinguish between the category of 'indecent' women and '*near decent*' women or, equally, some probation officer's remarks on their capacity for child care. So when magistrates (or indeed any persons) speak so disparagingly of prostitute women, their remarks are, in some form, meant for all women. Either they constitute a coded warning (to remain decent, monogamous or married) or they reflect a simple misogyny which does not in any case distinguish between women.[4]

It would be a mistake, however, to assume that all magistrates spoke from a unified position or set of values. Although all shared a view that some coercive intervention into the lives of prostitute women was necessary (for example, to salvage them, to help them, to guide them, to control them, to regulate them more efficiently, to educate them and so on), the nature of that intervention varied according to the magistrates' perceptions of the *problem*. How the magistrates understood the problem tended to fall into three main categories or ideological positions which were influenced by three different discourses on sexuality. These discourses I have identified as liberal/permissive (the largest category), puritan/authoritarian (the second largest) and welfarist. Not all magistrates remained located within a discrete world view and some (about one-third) expressed views which were a mixture of two discourses. None the less, the majority consistently used one of the three discourses to explain prostitution and to justify their policy regarding prostitutes.

The liberal/permissive discourse
This discourse was probably most clearly articulated in the Wolfenden Report (1957) which argued that what consenting adults did in private should not be the concern of the criminal law. The magistrates who adopted this view also felt that what adults did in private was their affair and, like Wolfenden, argued that prostitution was only a matter for the criminal law when it became visible on the streets. The solution, they tended to argue, was a pragmatic recognition of the need for licensed brothels where people could get on with it without causing a nuisance. The following are some examples of this position:

> 'In the present climate a lot of younger girls, because they can't find employment, are going onto the street because it is a very lucrative source of income. It's a matter of opinion whether it is a desirable one or not – I don't think it is but you know to me they're selling their own bodies and it's theirs to sell if they wish.'

> 'I cannot see why there should be such a fuss over a natural act. Basically, I can see no reason why you couldn't have a brothel that's perfectly legal. . . . It is a perfectly natural, absolutely basic urge and if you can satisfy that urge in a civilized manner, where you're not groping about in

the dark, frightened to death that the police are coming, it surely must be to everyone's benefit.'

While being 'permissive' about certain forms of sexuality, this discourse, like the views expressed in the Wolfenden Report, could, none the less, prove to be very repressive in its consequences for those who would not fit into the liberal forms of regulation. For example:

'I think there's a need for sexual services to be given to males. I'm also in favour of having one for women as well. . . . And it would take the offence as it stands now off the streets and then, if people did continue to hang about the streets looking for clients, *you could really crack down on them.*' (emphasis added)

The puritan/authoritarian discourse

This category of magistrates were concerned to control not just prostitution but also prostitutes; they tended to be in favour of imprisoning women, felt the police 'did a good job' and saw no reason to reform the laws on soliciting. They were the group which displayed most overt hostility towards prostitute women, namely:

'Oh yes, unquestionably [soliciting should be a criminal offence]. There are many reasons. Number one is that it's a form of obscenity which is offensive to the ordinary, respectable citizen. And secondly, it's a temptation to foolish men, usually in drink, to waste their money and perhaps contract venereal disease. And thirdly since prostitutes usually operate in a well defined area it is extremely offensive to the respectable residents in that area and tends to deprecate the whole moral value and tone and standard of living of that district.'

'Very often I think they're lazy, they don't want regular work, and many start almost straight from school. . . . There's a sort of friendship amongst them of course but I think they find it an easy way of getting money.'

The puritan/authoritarian discourse relied significantly upon three main axes: a Christian morality which sees prostitution as immoral and undermining of the value of family and social life; a puritan ethic which condemns prostitution because it is assumed (mistakenly) to be a way of making easy money without really working for it; and an exaggerated concern over disease. This concern over disease was not, however, limited to this group of magistrates although it was an important element constituting the puritan/authoritarian position. The following are examples of this particular concern:

'I think the jail sentence . . . is a good thing you know, because if they are really bad prostitutes and don't look after themselves it's a way of them being at least examined now and again.'

'There's a health hazard of course, which might or might not be controlled. A lot of them have cervical cancer or suggestions of it.'

'I think it would save the country a lot of money and time in court if prostitution was legalized, if we had legal brothels that were controlled, that the prostitutes in the brothels had to live up to standards, they had to live up to health standards . . . up to hygiene standards. I think it would save a lot of time in court, monies in court, and probably *pain and suffering to some unfortunate men.*' (emphasis added)

The second component of the puritan/authoritarian discourse was evidenced by the frequent comments about easy money, while the elements of a Christian morality were reflected in statements about a lack of moral upbringing, salvaging individuals, prostitution constituting a social evil, and so on. In a small minority of instances this moral stance elided quite clearly with racism and chauvinism. That strong moral objections to prostitution should be linked to a dislike of other racial or ethnic groups is not a new phenomenon (see Smart, 1981) but it continues to enhance a form of moral disgust which is directed towards groups outside the privileged circles inhabited by white, Christian English*men*:[5]

'There are, from time to time, people who are married – I hate to say it – often to coloured gentlemen who send them on the streets.'

'You'll have gathered from my remarks that I believe [prostitution] has been stimulated in Sheffield by the inflow of coloured immigrants who bring here social practices which are not common in England. . . . Well it's a way of life of course in former colonies of ours.'

'First of all the girls are forced into doing things they wouldn't naturally do themselves, even with the worst intentions. Secondly, you find the girls get very seriously abused, sometimes physically by these people. . . . There again the courtesy towards women amongst black people is not as good as even among the bad whites. They treat their women much more brutally.'

The welfarist discourse
This third discourse articulated by the magistrates is based on vague psychoanalytic theories of child development which are much influenced by a *mélange* of welfare concerns and a good deal of 'common sense'. This constituted the smallest category and was made up almost exclusively of women magistrates. Basically this position held or presumed that there was something psychologically amiss with prostitute women, and this was frequently explained in terms of childhood development. Prostitution was not usually seen as resulting directly from economic need or greed as with the two previous categories. Rather it was perceived of as the result of some

unresolved personality problem. In one instance the problem was seen to extend to the client and even the client's wife.[6]

'I think a lot of them do it because they come from a very poor family unit, especially young girls in a sort of advanced adolescent state. It seems to me that at the very time that a girl needs back up, if during this period she becomes promiscuous then a strong fatherly hand or even a mother's hand, would do her a world of good, and they're not getting this. I think a lot of them seem to lack love, and they get it from clients.'

'I think one of the main things is that you find that very often they come from disturbed family backgrounds. You also often find that they have been in some ways under achieved. I don't necessarily mean academically, although that could be part of it. They seem to find some fulfilment . . . from their sexuality.'

'I think also inadequate girls – girls who probably come from broken homes, well perhaps not necessarily broken homes, but homes where life is not good and perhaps – you know – problem families.'

Although it was only within the puritan/authoritarian discourse that prostitutes were constituted as completely undesirable and as social parasites, all the magistrates, even those with a welfare orientation, located prostitutes in a distinct social category which was at some distance to 'normal' or 'respectable' people. The magistrates continually referred to *these* people or *these* women thus constructing a special category of persons. *These* people might have been described as pathetic, lazy, stupid, hard, unfortunate, or as just earning money, but the construction of the category of *these* people, regardless of what characteristics were then attributed to them, was enough to separate out this group of women. It is of course quite probable that magistrates would tend to speak of a wide range of people who come before them in these disparaging terms, but with prostitute women this tendency coincides with the specific and separate legal classification of 'common prostitute'. This legal category in turn lends some rigidity to the conventional wisdom on prostitutes and permits the development of further methods and measures which can be justified because they deal exclusively with this legally and common-sensically identified group of errant women. In other words, the magistrates' views on prostitute women are legitimated and sustained by the legislation which is in turn deeply rooted in a conventional (misogynist) morality. This is not to suggest that all the magistrates always agreed with the law but, as I shall point out, disagreement with specific features of current legislation does not mean that some other form of regulation, informed by equally disparaging views of prostitute women, will not be embraced. I shall turn now to what the Sheffield magistrates had to say about the law, in particular the Street Offences Act 1959.

Magistrates and the law

One of the first things that must be appreciated when discussing magistrates' views on legal matters is that they have virtually no legal training and frequently do not know the law in detail. Consequently, our discussions tended to be based on notions of fairness and natural justice rather than on the meaning and consequences of specific legislation. Although the interviews with the magistrates covered a wide range of issues, I shall concentrate here on some of the most heavily criticized aspects of the Street Offences Act 1959. These major criticisms point out that on the basis of two cautions from a police officer a woman can be permanently classified as a common prostitute, and that she can then be charged in court as a common prostitute who has been soliciting or loitering for the purposes of prostitution. Because the charge is formulated in this way the bench is implicitly informed of a woman's 'previous record' prior to a finding of guilt. Moreover, all that is required to convict a common prostitute is the uncorroborated evidence of a police officer. At the time of the Sheffield interviews in 1981, a woman could also be sent to prison for soliciting or loitering[7]. Critics of the existing law tend to argue that it should not rest with the police to define women as common prostitutes, and that in any case this category of persons should be removed from the legislation so that persistent or annoying soliciting or loitering would become an offence if committed by anybody. Other critics argue that there is sufficient legislation to deal with nuisances on the street without having one law especially framed to deal with sexual matters, while yet others argue that it is inequitable to find a person guilty on the evidence of a police officer alone as this is open to abuse. On most of these matters the magistrates tended to side with the critics (see Tables 4.1, 4.2 and 4.3).

Table 4.1 *Magistrates' views on whether the cautioning system by which a woman becomes known as a common prostitute is 'fair and just' (%)*

	Women magistrates (N = 11)	Men magistrates (N = 14)	Total (N = 25)
Yes	18	71	36
No	46	29	48
Don't know	36	0	16

Table 4.2   *Magistrates' views on whether being known as a common prostitute in court disadvantages prostitute women* vis-à-vis *other defendants (%)*

	Women magistrates (N = 11)	Men magistrates (N = 14)	Total (N = 25)
Yes	64	64	64
No	36	36	36

Table 4.3   *Magistrates' views on whether they would be in favour of abolishing the term common prostitute (%)*

	Women magistrates (N = 11)	Men magistrates (N = 14)	Total (N = 25)
Yes	100	43	68
No	–	50	28
Don't know	–	7	4

As these tables show the majority of the sample of Sheffield magistrates were, on average, unhappy with these controversial sections of the 1959 Street Offences Act. There was, however, a distinct difference between the women and men magistrates on the question of cautioning and removing the label of common prostitute. Of course we must be cautious about drawing comparisons or making generalizations when using such small numbers as these,[8] but for the Sheffield sample, at least, it would appear that the women magistrates were less satisfied with the provisions of the 1959 Act than the men. (This held good for other features of the law too such as the use of imprisonment and fines.)

As I have already suggested, however, a disenchantment with current legislation did not lead the magistrates to the view that the problems inherent in the law arose from its aim to control extensively the lives of prostitutes who work outside the invisible networks of saunas, hotels and escort agencies. Instead, their discontent led to proposals for more rational systems of regulation and surveillance, namely legalized brothels (see Table 4.4).

This predominant view in favour of legalized brothels did not stem from a concern for prostitute women. The considerations which motivated the magistrates tended to be a concern for the tone of residential areas of the city (one magistrate suggested that the brothel

Table 4.4 *Magistrates' views on whether they would be in favour of the introduction of legalized brothels (%)*

	Women magistrates (N = 11)	Men magistrates (N = 14)	Total (N = 25)
Yes	64	86	76
No	18	7	12
Don't know	18	7	12

could be located outside the city limits in the Derbyshire country-side), a concern for clients to meet prostitutes without causing a nuisance, and a belief that women working in the brothels could be more closely regulated. For example, two magistrates commented:

> 'I think if it were legalized you'd have to have some controls – medical inspections and so forth. I don't know enough about medical inspections but I'm satisfied in my own mind that a lot of disease results from this, and if there were some legislation then that legislation could include some control including medical control.'

> 'Well I'm a socialist me, I'm in favour of nationalizing them. To run them would be easy, the girls could be medically checked regularly. But again it's the staffing of them that's the difficult part.'

The men magistrates (71 per cent of them) were much more concerned about controlling disease than the women (36 per cent), but their concern was in almost all cases extremely naïve and displayed a fundamental ignorance about VD. Such medical checks could have little value unless they were carried out after every sexual encounter or on every man prior to intercourse (which is unlikely in practice). In effect, such checks would simply be a further enforced harassment of women. They also raise the question of what would happen if women refused to submit to the compulsory medical examination. Would it, for example, lead to a revival of the nineteenth-century Contagious Diseases Acts in which women could be held in detention in lock hospitals? Or would such women be forced back into the unlicensed market on the streets where they would face much harsher penalties than exist under current legis-lation? The legalized brothel may appear to be the rational, permissive, sanitized answer to what is perceived as the problem of prostitution, but it imports many more repressive measures than those currently employed.

Yet while the legalized brothel is no less a form of regulation than existing measures, it does represent a break with the established approach towards prostitution. While most criminal laws on soliciting, brothels and similar activities have been formulated as negative sanctions which regulate and condemn, the legalized brothel is a positive form of regulation designed to direct prostitution into controllable channels rather than putting it outside state regulation by outlawing it. This method has not won universal support,[9] however, because while legal brothels may be efficient they imply an official condonation of prostitution which is not forthcoming. The legalized brothel is therefore rejected – but not on the grounds of its repressive potential.

Very few of the magistrates considered the desirability of legalized brothels from the point of view of the prostitute women involved. Only two women magistrates said they would suspend judgement until they knew what prostitute women felt about them, and two others rejected them on the grounds that they would simply constitute forms of lawful exploitation or harassment. For most of the magistrates prostitute women did not even merit consideration, they would simply be obliged – in the public interest – to fit into the new scheme. The plan for legalized brothels does not therefore reflect any change in the common perception of prostitute women, on the contrary, it simply reflects a different dimension of the same view, namely that prostitutes are sexual objects which constitute a health hazard unless properly regulated.

Policy and law reform

As I have noted above there have been two major reports on prostitution during the last decade. In 1974 the Home Office produced its report and in 1982 the CLRC also made suggestions for reform. Both documents are extremely conservative and stay very close to the proposals outlined in the earlier Wolfenden Report (1957). These documents are not identical, however. For example, the CLRC suggests that kerb crawling should become an offence while the Home Office Working Paper would not agree to such a proposal. But both working papers make proposals which will only slightly modify the law as it affects prostitute women. Neither of them recommend that the term common prostitute should be removed nor that the system of cautioning should be abolished. The arguments put forward by both reports are remarkably consistent and both depend on a circularity of logic which ultimately rests upon the law's prior ability to construct prostitutes as a special class in relation to law. Consider the following extracts:

> It has also been suggested that to define an offence by reference to the category of persons who commit it, where the same act might be

committed with impunity by others, is a legal impropriety. But that is a matter of opinion. The conduct with which the law seeks to deal is conduct which *people find offensive precisely because it is committed by prostitutes* in pursuing their calling. (Home Office, 1974: 74; emphasis added)

Lastly, those of our members who favour the retention of the expression [common prostitute] argue that the object of the law in this area is purely regulatory: *Prostitutes as a class* cause nuisance in the way that they conduct their business in the streets and the law is designed to reduce the nuisance *caused by that class of person.* (CLRC, 1982: 30; emphasis added)

In spite of declarations that our modern law on prostitution is not concerned with morality but simply with nuisance, these two statements make it quite clear that certain activities can only be legally defined as a nuisance if they are committed by a special, morally defined category of persons. Of course a moral dimension is present in the majority of criminal laws, but what is interesting about the laws on prostitution is the attempt, since the Wolfenden Report of 1957, to separate questions of morality from questions of nuisance. Having suggested that these are two separate matters, all the post-Wolfenden reports have then justified the retention of a special law to regulate the nuisance caused by prostitution by reference to the fact that people find this kind of nuisance especially repugnant. What they fail to acknowledge is that 'nuisance' caused by a prostitute is more objectionable than 'nuisance' caused by a street vendor precisely because she is regarded as immoral. In other words 'nuisance' is just a moral category by another name.

I am not trying to develop a pedantic argument here, nor am I illustrating how devious policy makers can be. Rather I am trying to show that although the arguments put forward by Wolfenden, the Home Office and the CLRC contain a faultless logic, they are based upon certain attitudes towards prostitute women, and ultimately towards all women, which are invisible because they are taken so much for granted. These are the sort of attitudes, expressed by the sample of magistrates in Sheffield, which located prostitute women outside the usual bounds of consideration. Even less conservative policy makers than the Home Office or the CLRC, who support more radical reforms in this area, fall into the same practice of denigrating prostitutes. For example, Robert Kilroy-Silk, MP for Ormskirk, remarked during the Committee stage of the Criminal Justice Bill in March 1982, that,

'In the main, the picture which is painted of the street prostitute who gets herself arrested and imprisoned is one of someone who is physically – mentally in some cases – disabled or suffering from some disability, but

very largely disadvantaged, inadequate and frequently inarticulate.'
(Parliamentary Debates, 11 March 1982, Vol. 19, Col. 515)

On the basis of this, Kilroy-Silk was arguing that prostitute women
should not be imprisoned for soliciting or loitering, but at the same
time he was confirming the status of many prostitutes as subnormal,
inadequate and deserving of pity.

These views of prostitute women do appear to be remarkably
consistent across party political lines, across socio-economic class
and across gender. Moreover, they appear to have become particularly rigid in the UK in the post-Second World War period (Smart,
1981). Although prostitutes may never have been popular folk
figures there have certainly been moments in history when legislation
has been less oppressive (Storch, 1977). For example, prior to the
1959 Street Offences Act prostitution was governed by the Vagrancy
Acts which were not always applicable, or by local Police Acts and
by-laws which did not always carry the sanction of imprisonment and
which sometimes required proof of annoyance before a woman could
be convicted of soliciting. Moreover, the major report on prostitution
which pre-dated the Wolfenden Report and which has largely been
overshadowed by it, namely the Macmillan Report (1928), was far
more progressive in its approach than all subsequent reports have
been. This Report recommended that there should be a single law
which would be directed against *every person* soliciting a person of
the opposite sex for immoral purposes. The Report also went as far as
to recommend that: loitering should no longer be an offence unless it
was established that it caused a nuisance; the term common
prostitute should be abolished because it disadvantaged a woman in
court; and that police evidence alone should not provide a basis for
conviction in these cases.

The Macmillan Report was by no means a progressive document in
its entirety but the fact that in 1928 it recommended measures which
appear to be totally unacceptable in the 1980s does raise questions
about why a law of such singular importance to women has remained
so repressive and has become increasingly rigid. It may be that one
reason is the failure of the women's movement as a whole to identify
this as an important women's issue. There has been no contemporary
version of the 1860s campaign against the Victorian Contagious
Diseases Acts, which could challenge the prevailing ideological
stance on prostitution (Walkowitz, 1982), and it may be that
contemporary feminism has even contributed towards a view of
prostitutes as no more than sex objects. But it should also be
recognized that our perception of the social context in which
prostitution now occurs has been influenced by the so-called sexual

revolution of the 1960s which concealed the continuing existence and tenacity of prostitution, by the growth of the women's movement itself with its anger over the sexual objectification of women's bodies, and by an ideological climate which makes ideas that women might prostitute themselves simply to earn money quite unacceptable.

All of these factors contribute to views on prostitution which paralyse political action. We are uneasy with the idea of selling sex because it makes sex a commodity and hence women's bodies become commodities. We are uncomfortable with prostitute women who symbolize an overt form of female sexual slavery (even though we know all about women's poverty). And we do not know how to support prostitutes without promoting prostitution. At the same time we cannot fail to recognize how, as legal subjects, women defined as prostitutes have fewer rights and are less adequately protected by (and from) the law than other women. The laws on soliciting, which are so concrete in their effects on prostitute women, also carry an ideological message to all women and so create an unavoidable issue for the women's movement. But they also make it impossible for the women's movement to absorb prostitution into the wider campaigns on women's poverty, equal pay, day care facilities and so on because the criminal law makes prostitute women into a special category which constantly calls for the attention of a single issue campaign (that is, to end imprisonment, to decriminalize, to resist brothels). These contradictions faced by feminists working on the issue of prostitution are not new (see Walkowitz, 1982; Bland, 1985) and there are no simple solutions.

Working in any area of law reform raises the possibility of perpetuating the cause of the problem by ameliorating its symptoms. But we have to recognize that working for reforms is not always an attempt to ameliorate a static situation, but is frequently an attempt to stop a situation deteriorating further. In this respect there is little option for feminists but to confront the law, even though working on specific campaigns around prostitution sustains the very distinction between prostitute women and non-prostitute women which is so divisive. Arguably, a major priority must be to remove the legal category of common prostitute which, as we have seen, lends support to conventional wisdom about divisions between moral classes of women. If the law ceased to be able to define the issues around which the women's movement should organize it would be far easier to concentrate on the issues that unite rather than those that have always successfully divided women.

Notes

This chapter was originally published in J. Brophy and C. Smart (eds) (1985) *Women in Law*, pp. 50–70, Routledge.

1   In this instance the term control is used advisedly, and I argue that a useful distinction can be made between a specific control and a more generalized function of regulation. While the law in general may be a mechanism of regulation of sexuality, the criminal law on soliciting is (and the proposal for legalized brothels would be) a direct method of controlling the sexual behaviour of women who are defined as common prostitutes. It is therefore a specific mechanism which can be removed or relocated. This is a different argument to that expressed in an essentialist position which might imply that regulation of sexuality *in general* can be eliminated to expose a true and natural sexuality which has been repressed. The struggle to resist these mechanisms of control is therefore not an idealist one but one that is linked to feminist projects in a range of areas. Ultimately, the feminist position on prostitution is not a liberal, permissive one which would argue that women must be free to be prostitutes, it aims to remove oppressive legal constraints in the first instance and to remove, in the long term, wider, social, political and economic constraints which make prostitution one of the few lucrative ways for women to earn a living and which construct women's sexuality as a marketable commodity.

2   There were so many statements like these that it is impossible to record them all here. But at the same time it is important to realize what an impact the summation of all these comments has. It is this totality which is important and not just the examples. For this reason I include a few quotations here.

> 'I think it's something to do with not being able to get jobs. . . . I must say that with the ones I've met on the bench I've never met any who are kind of bursting at the seams with O levels or A levels. *They all seem a little bit thick*, it seems a strong word to use but that is how I feel about it.' (emphasis added)

> 'There are some *ladies – shall we call them –* who appear before us on the bench who you feel that it is through, probably, domestic circumstances.' (emphasis added)

> 'I think that if there's an opportunity of *salvaging the person* back into the standards of what we would term *civilian life*, then the probation officer has the best chance of doing it.' (emphasis added)

3   I would in fact argue that there is such a dividing line. This is not based on some moral stance but on the pragmatic recognition that the activities of the criminal law (in labelling some women as common prostitutes, in fining them, and so on) does separate out women by creating a group who are subject to very specific forms of oppression.

4   This misogyny frequently manifested itself in statements about women (but hardly ever men) who were carriers of diseases. Somehow it was always women infecting men as if women produce disease autonomously, namely:

> 'There's a health hazard of course, which might or might not be controlled. A lot of them have cervical cancer or suggestions of it. . . . And the second thing of course is that by the anatomy of a lady it is very difficult to spot the disease in its early stages. . . . Well, there are ways girls can conceal it if they suspect anything you see?'

5   All of the magistrates who articulated the puritan/authoritarian discourse were men.

6   One magistrate held the following view:

> 'I think married men who go with prostitutes have got a real big problem. I think more so than a single bloke who goes with a prostitute. A single bloke who goes with a prostitute goes for a bit of excitement. A married man – he's got a problem because if he's prepared to take that risk when he's married then God he's got a problem. *And I think his wife has got a problem as well that should be looked at.*' (emphasis added)

7   The Criminal Justice Act 1982 removed the penalty of imprisonment for soliciting or loitering from the 1959 Street Offences Act. Magistrates can no longer send women guilty of soliciting or loitering straight to jail, but they can fine them so severely that they cannot pay the fines and so go to prison for defaulting.

8   The magistrates were selected for interview by a system of stratification according to sex. Magistrates who were new to the bench or who sat very infrequently were excluded in the initial stage. As the ratio of men to women on the bench was 3 : 2, the sample was selected to reflect this. However, slightly more men than women declined to be interviewed so this ratio was not sustained, becoming 2.5 : 2. Thirty-five magistrates were contacted and the refusal rate was 29 per cent, leaving a final sample of 25.

9   Interestingly, the Criminal Law Revision Committee (1982) would not accept the proposal to introduce legalized brothels on the grounds that legitimation meant a form of condonation. They preferred to support the more traditional course of imposing negative forms of regulation.

5

Law's Power, the Sexed Body and Feminist Discourse

In this chapter I shall explore a key problem facing feminist legal scholarship. This problem concerns the nature and validity of knowledge, and it is an issue which is being widely debated throughout feminist scholarship (see, for example, Harding, 1986; Smith, 1988; Garry and Pearsall, 1989; Griffiths and Whitford, 1988). Many of us who work as feminist scholars can be said to be facing a period of intense uncertainty where taken-for-granted assumptions about knowledge and about the relationship between knowledge and politics no longer hold. For example, the comfortable correlation between theory and practice where one justified the other now seems unreliable. Moreover, there is uncertainty as to what 'correct' politics are, and the well-founded criticisms by working-class and black women that feminism (as currently constituted?) does not speak for or to them, has shattered a naïve confidence in an emotionally based sisterhood. In intellectual work the challenge to the commonality of womanhood has undermined the assumption that empirical enquiries into 'women's experience' would reveal the epistemological failings of malestream social science (Harding, 1986, 1987). This is not just because women's experiences are so varied but because we have come to recognize that challenging men's truth with women's truth may have political purchase but it leaves us on shaky ground when truth itself is no longer an absolute – outside the fray – to which we can appeal (Weedon, 1987). If feminism cannot speak for or to all women; if it engages with the traditional epistemologies only to find that postmodern and poststructuralist thought has moved the goalposts; if it can no longer respond to intellectual problems with political answers (Braidotti, 1989) then it is time to try to reformulate the problematic that feminism addresses and to re-evaluate taken-for-granted feminist truths and practices.

This is, of course, much easier said than done. We need, for example, to transcend the all too familiar practice of categorizing feminism into radical, socialist, cultural and liberal feminisms because these conceptual straitjackets now conceal more than they reveal.[1] We need to abandon the craving for a metanarrative which will (at last) explain the oppressions and subjectivities of race, class and gender. And, if we are to give up certain orthodoxies, we need to consider from what position(s) we can continue to speak out against those oppressions and to give voice to our subjectivities. If we argue that the category of woman is constructed (by language, culture, symbolic law) do we still have an authenticity from which to speak and be heard (Riley, 1988)? This is both an intellectual and political dilemma. It is particularly problematic in the field of law because legal discourse is so powerful and so silencing of feminist inter-ventions. Indeed, the only purchase that feminism has had in relation to law has been based on a claim that feminism can reveal the truth of women's experience and can give voice to something legitimate which has otherwise been silenced (Dahl, 1987). If we show any (apparent) self-doubt in the face of the legal monolith; if we cannot justify our claim on acceptable terms (irrespective of the acceptability of their content); if we critique traditional jurisprudence without (to the traditionalists) solid epistemological and ontological foun-dations, do we not give up the battle before it has begun? Or should we seek to move the battle to another terrain?

In this paper I shall work through a number of issues. First, I want to elaborate on the idea that law is a particularly powerful discourse because of its claim to truth which in turn enables it[2] to silence women (who encounter law) and feminists (who challenge law). Tradition-ally feminists have been concerned with the silencing of women: this concerns me too, but in this paper I want to give some attention to both forms of silencing. Then I want to examine how women are sexed by law; how specific, sexualized meanings are attributed to the corporeality of women. I shall then use the example of rape to show both the silencing of women and the projection of a patriarchal vision of female sexuality onto the body of the woman. The feminist response to this has been to claim that law cannot do 'justice' to women's *real* experience but this now needs further thought if we are beginning to doubt the taken-for-grantedness of the categories of 'woman' and of 'experience'. I shall then raise the question of whether we can still challenge the power of law in this field without slipping back into liberalism (that is, the battle over consent, intent and volition), and/or biologism (that is, men – the owners of the penises – make the laws).

Law's claim to truth

Scholars of law from a wide range of backgrounds and disciplines have long been interested in questions of the legitimacy or the authority of law. Explanations have been as diverse as those which lay claim to law as a reflection of natural justice or divine intervention, to those which see law as a reflection of normative values, through to those who see it as a tool of class interests or the capitalist state. Feminism has added its own accounts to this list, arguing that law is a reflection of male interests or values, or that law is part of the patriarchal state. But whatever the mode of explanation, the central question has focused on the power of law to occupy a given position in culture, to enact a range of measures and to define rights and wrongs.

I shall depart from the parameters of this traditional debate to focus on the question of the power of law in a different way. Relying substantially on the work of Foucault (Gordon, 1980), I shall concentrate on law as a form of discourse which can make claims to scientificity and hence truth. This, in turn, positions law on a hierarchy of knowledges which allows for the disqualification of 'subjugated knowledges' and hence gives rise to the power of law.

It is perhaps useful to be reminded that Foucault's notion of power is quite distinct from that of Marxism's conceptualizations. First, Foucault has argued that power has changed; modes of power exercised in the eighteenth century are quite different from those deployed in the late twentieth century (Gordon, 1980). In addition, power is not perceived by him to be a manifestation of an economic system whereby owners of capital also have exclusive ownership of power. For Foucault power is much more systematic and decentred; it is not the property of one class. Moreover, for him power is not simply that thing which the ruling classes use to restrict and punish other classes. He argues:

> power would be a fragile thing if its only function were to repress, if it worked only through the mode of censorship, exclusion, blockage and repression. . . . If, on the contrary, power is strong this is because, as we are beginning to realize, it produces effects at the level of desire – and also at the level of knowledge. Far from preventing knowledge, power produces it. (Gordon, 1980: 59)

Central to Foucault's analysis, therefore, is the relationship between power and knowledge. This is not the old (even if valid) idea that knowledge is power, but rather the converse that power is productive of knowledge which necessarily enhances given modes of power. This in turn gives rise to his argument that the deployment of power is facilitated when the knowledge produced can also make a claim to truth. In other words, it is a feature of modernism that knowledge which can claim to be true (rather than belief, superstition, opinion, and so on) occupies a place high up in the hierarchy of knowledges. The claim to truth is therefore a claim to deploy power.

In using the term 'truth', Foucault does not of course mean 'the ensemble of truths which are to be discovered and accepted'. On the contrary, he uses it to refer to 'the ensemble of rules according to which the true and the false are separated and specific effects of power attached to the true' (Gordon, 1980: 132). Foucault is not, therefore, concerned with what is considered to be the usual quest of science, namely to uncover the truth. Rather, he is interested in discovering how certain discourses claim to speak the truth and thus can exercise power in a society that values this notion of truth. The exercise of power is, in fact, manifested in the claim to be a science, because in claiming scientificity other knowledges are accorded less status and less value. Other knowledges can exercise less influence; they are subjugated or disqualified. Defining a field of knowledge as science is, according to Foucault, to claim that it speaks a truth which can be favourably compared with partial truths and untruths which epitomize non-scientific discourse.

In this discussion of knowledge and power Foucault is talking about the rise of science (including behavioural and psychological sciences) in the post-Enlightenment period in the West. He specifically discussed the claims – made by Marxism and psychoanalysis – to be scientific, and similar parallels can be drawn with the claims of sociology to be a science. The question Foucault asks is 'Why do these discourses wish to be seen as science? What power will thereby accrue to them?'

The problem for my analysis is that Foucault does not include law in his discussion. In fact, he argues that law pre-dates the modern episteme in which truth (as grounded in science) becomes the dominant mode of knowledge. Is it possible, therefore, to extend or stretch Foucault's ideas to meet this case?

I would argue that in spite of the problems of periodicity, and in spite of the fact that law does not make an express claim to truth as such, law makes claims which are sufficiently similar to the claims of science for us to see that power is being deployed in a similar way. For example law has its own method, its own testing ground, its own specialized language and system of results. Law sets itself apart from and above other discourses in the same way that science does. As Goodrich has argued:

> The school of glossators (of the twelfth century) . . . had a foundational impact upon legal studies in Europe. It provided for the first time a science of law based upon the *Corpus Iuris*; it established an independent discipline of legal study and provided it with a meticulously worked-out set of legal techniques. (1986: 101–2)

Legal method, which purports to reveal the original meaning and authority of legal texts, has therefore been central to law for many centuries. The fact that this legal method is not the same as later forms of scientific method is neither here nor there. What is important is the claim that a given method gives rise to a correct interpretation or even a direct access to the truth which avoids the problem of human interpretation. Moreover, behind the legal text is the presumption that it is the written form of a rational will. In other words, the text always already occupies a space inside rationality and objectivity. This space is also the space which later science has claimed to occupy.

Consequently, the fact that law pre-dates science does not exclude it from the analysis of truth/power/knowledge which is Foucault's project. To be sure, it means that law has not had to enter into the contemporary scrum to try to call itself scientific in order to be taken seriously. But this is because the foundations of law's claim to truth were laid centuries before. Indeed, we can see that law's status is enhanced by the fact that it is not a 'johnny-come-lately' like Marxism, sociology or psychoanalysis.

So far we have been discussing law as a discourse which, by reference to its method, makes claims which are similar to the effects of making claims to truth and scientificity. But we should not overlook a more routine or mundane aspect to law. On a daily basis members of the public go to lawyers for advice, and the lawyers they consult may never occupy themselves with seeking the correct interpretation of the legal text. It might be argued, for example, that the claim to truth has little to do with the routine of the ordinary legal aid practice. Yet it underlies this practice, even if routine obscures it. Primarily the job of the solicitor is to translate everyday affairs into legal issues (Cain, 1979: 331). On hearing the client's story, the solicitor sifts it through a sieve of legal knowledge and formulations. Most of the story will be chaff as far as the lawyer is concerned, no matter how significant the rejected elements are to the client. Having extracted what law defines as relevant, it is translated into a foreign language of, for example, ouster injunctions, unfair dismissals, constructive trusts. The parts of the story that are cast aside are deemed immaterial to the case and the good solicitor is the one who can effect this translation as swiftly as possible. This is the routine daily practice of law in which alternative accounts of events are disqualified. The legal version becomes the only valid one. The barrister and the judge may then proceed to the stages of interpreting legal texts in order to reach the correct legal decision on each individual case. Of course, most cases never go this far and many individual practitioners fall short of this 'ideal'. However, the system is constantly reproduced each time legal advice is sought. As with medicine where there may be inadequate medical practitioners but where a reliance on *medicine* as a science is retained, so with law its claim to truth (and hence power) is not diminished by local failings. On the contrary its status is reaffirmed by the mere tendency to turn to law as if it did indeed hold rightful/correct or efficacious solutions.

Power, knowledge and gender

Thus far we have discussed knowledge and power as if gender was in some way irrelevant. However, feminism in the last two decades has expressly addressed and undermined the idea of knowledge (in form as much as content) as neutral and ungendered. There are two main elements to this body of work. The first addresses questions of universality, neutrality and objectivity and seeks to reveal that dominant forms of knowledge are always specific, gendered and subjective (see Smith, 1988; Hartsock, 1987). It is this perspective that I shall concentrate on below. The second concerns the reconstruction of knowledge through values rather than a new form of truth. Hence there is a tendency to seek out feminine values to construct a different ontological basis for knowledge (Griffiths, 1988; Jaggar, 1989; Whitbeck, 1989). Both of these strands of feminist epistemology are called into question by poststructuralist feminism on which I shall base my argument.

The first strand is well represented by Dorothy Smith (1988). Smith has carefully documented what she sees as the eclipsing and silencing of women in culture generally and in sociology specifically. She argues:

> Being excluded, as women have been, from the making of ideology, of knowledge, and of culture means that our experience, our interests, our ways of knowing the world have not been represented in the organization of our ruling nor in the systematically developed knowledge that has entered into it. (Smith, 1988: 17–18)

Women have therefore been marginalized and what passes for knowledge under such a regime necessarily reflects the one-sided interests of men. Smith then argues that knowledge from the point of view of men has been presented as universal and fed back to women as a neutral and objective stance of the world.

Smith is not, however, arguing that this partiality can be corrected by the addition of knowledge from the point of view of women. As a feminist in the Marxist tradition her analysis points to structures of power through which men are able to define the world but, because of their position of power, their knowledge is not merely partial but incorrect. Members of the patriarchy, like members of the capitalist class, cannot see how their point of view (their ability to know, theorize, provide accounts and so on) is dependent upon the essential, but invisible, labour of women or the working classes. It is only women who can see how patriarchal relations actually work because they are doing the labour which sustains it. Hence house-work and child care is invisible, yet without it men could not occupy positions free of such concerns which enable them to conceptualize the world as they do.

Smith's analysis does not stop here, however. She goes on to argue that it is not just that women see the world differently, but that it is only women who can see the truth of patriarchy. In other words only women, as an oppressed group, can see the 'reality' of the system and can provide the valid, correct or true analysis. But again, following Marx, Smith is aware that not all women can 'see' this reality. The reality becomes visible only through struggle, or when women can collectively realize that their experiences of the world do not coincide with the masculine accounts (that is, through consciousness raising). Thus Smith is able to argue that the feminist standpoint can provide a correct analysis of patriarchal relations as long as women's experi-ences are collectivized and politicized. From the standpoint of men, knowledge will always be superficial and biased.

Standpoint feminism has now become a major form of feminist epistemology. It celebrates the existing politics of the women's movement; the key concept of experience gives the theory a much-desired materiality or concreteness, and, perhaps most im-portantly, it can claim a validity or scientificity which competes with most dominant theories of knowledge. So, it is a form of politically sound truth; a scientific feminism.

In the field of law, standpoint feminism might seem to be almost unassailable. Feminist legal scholars have argued that law operates with a partial or incorrect vision of the reality of women's lives. For example, it might be argued that family law treats all women as dependants of men when in reality: men fail to support their wives and children; women's wages are vital to the household economy; most married women return to the labour market, and so on. Dahl's work on women's law fits most exactly with this model (Dahl, 1987). Her project is dedicated to revealing how law's vision of women and women's lives is utterly distorted and how only by interviewing women and capturing the reality of their lives and their priorities can law begin to be less oppressive and inequitable towards women.

Catharine MacKinnon's (1987) work (albeit very different from Dahl's in terms of feminist politics) also fits into the standpoint feminism mould. Like Smith she has pointed to the hidden gendering of concepts like neutrality and objectivity which are cornerstones of legal philosophy. She states:

> When [the state] is most ruthlessly neutral, it will be most male; when it is most sex blind, it will be most blind to the sex of the standard being applied. . . . Once masculinity appears as a specific position, not just the way things are, its judgements will be revealed in process and procedure, as well as adjudication and legislation. . . . However autonomous of class the liberal stance may appear, it is not autonomous of sex. (1983: 658)

MacKinnon also argues for consciousness raising as a way of producing alternative knowledge. In particular she sees it as a way of generating new legal norms or legislative activity which will be generated from the needs and perspectives of women (for example, laws against pornography or sexual harassment).

Women's experience has therefore been perceived as a lever which can be used against law whether in the form of legislation, legal and criminal procedure, or legal method, values and jurisprudence. The concept of experience operates at a number of levels. First, it claims to be real. In this mode it is thought to escape ideology and to be a direct and unmediated expression of an event(s). At this level it can compete with law's claims to be outside ideology. The claim to reality is further enhanced if large numbers of women are said to share the same experience. So if one woman has an experience it will be treated as real, but if many women do, it is (oddly) more real. This brings us to the second level. The reality of experience is linked to a statistical formulation thus appealing to a genre of quantification and hence scientificity. But the term experience operates on yet one other level. It appeals to hermeneutics because experience invokes the fluidity of social interaction and the importance of interpretation and meaning. The term 'experience' can, so to speak, have its cake and eat it. It can appeal to a range of conflicting constituencies and, like virtue, seem above reproof.

Should we, therefore, abandon women's experience as a concept when it seems to create a sense of political collectivity among women and provides an epistemological grounding to challenge the patriarchal lie? And, if we abandon it, how can we critique the rape trial, the legal treatment of child sexual abuse, the attempt to limit legal abortions, and so on? As Riley has argued:

> There is a wish among several versions of Anglo-American feminism to assert the real underlying unities among women, and of the touchstone of 'women's experience'. It is as if this powerful base could guarantee both the integrity and survival of militant feminism. (1988: 99)

But the orthodoxy of this experience is already being challenged. The most crucial criticism has come from black women who are tired of being included in the sweep of white women's experience. They are also tired of being tagged on as in 'and of course this state of affairs is even worse for black or working-class women.' Women's experience has become fragmented, and once fragmented it loses its power to claim a universal validity or truth. Precisely because standpoint feminism does not challenge the idea of this truth, it cannot handle the concept of multiple realities, or deconstructionist ideas. However, it is not my intention here to mount a critique of standpoint feminism (Weedon, 1987; Harding, 1987; Riley, 1988). Instead I want to attempt to analyse law in a way which recognizes the power of law to disqualify or silence, yet does not seek to posit an alternative truth as the main strategy to resist legal discourse. I shall use the example of rape which is a familiar narrative in feminist writing. But before doing so I need to establish a series of arguments.

The context of legal discourse: phallocentric culture

Phallocentrism is a term which is now familiar in feminist psycho-analytic literature and which is becoming widely adopted. It is deployed to refer to a culture which is structured to meet the needs of the masculine imperative. However, it is a term which is meant to imply far more than the surface appearance of male dominance which is all that is captured by concepts like inequality and discrimination which, in turn, are the standard (inadequate) terms used where law is concerned. The term 'phallocentrism' invokes the unconscious and raises profound questions on the part that the psyche and subjectivity play in reproducing patriarchal relations. Phallocentrism attempts to give some insight into how patriarchy is part of women's (as well as men's) unconscious, rather than a superficial system imposed from outside and kept in place by social institutions, threats or force. It attempts to address the problem of the construction of gendered identities and subjectivities. Law must, therefore, be understood both to participate in the construction of meanings and subjectivities and to do so within the terms of a phallocentric culture.

The value of the concept is that it conveys the deep structure of the meaning of sexual difference. It conveys that they way we think, and the way we desire, cannot be separated from the cultural meanings attributed to gendered difference. But these meanings are not simply imposed upon us: we continuously reconstruct them to make sense of the world; they explain, validate and create our experience and subjectivity.

This leads to the argument that it is not the biological category called men who simply make the meanings for women (as Smith, 1988, might suggest); nor is it men's experience which always already defines women – although in certain important instances it might. Masculinity is constructed by these meanings as well as constructing them. However, this construction occurs under specific historical and cultural conditions (for example, patriarchy, neocolonialism, and so on). In other words, masculinity is prioritized and the deployment of power in its multiple forms is gendered. It is,therefore, important for feminist theory to go beyond analyses of law which stop at the point of 'recognition' that men (as a taken-for-granted biological category) make and implement laws while women (as a taken-for-granted biological category) are oppressed by them. We need instead to consider the ways in which law constructs and reconstructs masculinity and femininity, and maleness and femaleness, and contributes routinely to a common-sense perception of difference which sustains the social and sexual practices which feminism is attempting to challenge.

The concept of phallocentrism has, of course, a particular significance for an understanding of sexuality and desire, and consequently for my discussion of rape below. To state it briefly, within phallocentric culture sexuality is always presumed to be heterosexuality and thus heterosexuality achieves a spurious universality against which 'deviations'(which are called by special names) are judged. In turn this (hetero)sexuality is overdetermined by the prioritized activity of intercourse and its satisfactions become synonymous with the pleasures of the phallus. As Campbell (1980) has argued, the phallus is constructed as the organizing principle of sex. Sex simply becomes penetration, and pleasure is defined in terms of duration of tumescence, or simultaneous orgasm, or ejaculation *in vaginam*. Under this regime, female pleasure can be said to be relatively unimportant and/or mysterious. One has only to consider the debate starting with Freud and continuing into the 1970s which rendered mysterious the site of the female orgasm, and produced volumes of text on whether it should be situated in one place or another (Koedt, 1970). Female sexual pleasure is constructed as unreliable or incomprehensible (or even voracious and insatiable) in a phallocentric culture. Usually, however, it is presumed to coincide with the pleasure of penetration and intercourse. The presumption in favour of the pleasure/intercourse linkage makes it virtually impossible for alternative accounts to emerge – unless in a medical/psychological context where such confessions are excused by the quest for a 'cure'.

Because women's sexual pleasure is constructed as mysterious and as something that women themselves do not really know (that is, the 'frigid' woman; Jackson, 1987), while men's sexuality is constructed around the supposedly more straightforward (honest?) and obvious imperative of erection, penetration and ejaculation, women are often understood to be guardians of what men most want, but of which they have little understanding. (Take, for example, the warnings issued to girls and women that they must be careful lest their behaviour unwittingly inflames the desires of men.) This in turn constructs sexual encounters or relationships in terms of how men can gain control of, or access to, their pleasure which is inconveniently located in women's bodies. Figuratively speaking, women are seen as having charge of something which is of greater value to men than to themselves. It is within this dominant regime of meanings that law presides over contested accounts of rape and seduction. But before examining the rape trial it is necessary to consider more widely how law constructs sexed (and not simply gendered) subjectivities.

Law and the sexed subject

I want to start by asking what happens when a woman encounters law. Is she seen and treated the same way as a man is seen and treated? The answer must be yes and no, and even maybe. But all these responses are equally problematic from a feminist perspective. For example, family law now addresses 'spouses', and both spouses have the same legal rights to custody of children, maintenance, the matrimonial home and property. Yet should husband and wife be treated the same we are fully aware that the wife will be disadvantaged (Smart, 1984). On the other hand, in the area of welfare benefits and employment protection, women have different rights because of their capacity for pregnancy. We know in turn that these 'special' rights disadvantage women in the labour market. Finally, legislation governing sex discrimination or equal pay resides in the anomalous position of recognizing women as women in order to ensure they are treated the same as men.

The problem with this discussion (which has exercised the minds of feminist legal scholars for too long) is that it does not begin to tap the depth of the problem the law presents. As Eaton (1986) has shown in the field of criminal law, it is not a matter of whether law (or in her case the courts) treats men and women equally or differently, it is the way in which law constructs women as family members, wives, divorcees, mothers or daughters that matters. I want to take this analysis a step further to argue that it is not just these gendered identities that count, but also the sexed body which can rarely be escaped and which is constantly reproduced in law. By sexed body I do not only mean the body which is saturated (or totally encoded) with sex – although this is an important aspect of a woman's body – I mean also biological womanness.

Having drawn a distinction between sex and gender in the 1970s, feminists were largely willing to see gender as something to do with culture and sex as something to do with nature (biology). The main debate was over which element had pre-eminence. But this apparently clear-cut distinction is now being rethought to the extent that it is increasingly argued that nature is a discursive construct just as much as gender. This has in turn given rise to reinterpretation of the apparently self-evident categories of woman and man. Where once we could see the limitations of being consigned to a feminine gender, we now know that escaping these trappings does not mean we escape the female body and the meanings which are associated with it.

The biological category of woman depends on the significance given to body parts and in particular those parts which concern reproduction and sex. These parts are identified as different from the organs possessed by men. Hence we have the taken-for-granted, mutually exclusive and presumably natural opposites man/woman. Within this frame there is no room for other types, no matter that not all 'women' can or do become pregnant or that not all 'men' are sexually attracted to women. The categories are overdetermining no matter how people actually live their lives.

Now of course we are aware that being a man or woman is also part of our subject position. We feel ourselves to be women or men; we 'know' that as women or men we experience the world differently, and so on. We 'know' this because the language that we use, which is also the expression of our identity, facilitates – even ensures – that we know it. In language there is no other space to occupy other than man or woman. Even early expressions of lesbianism in terms of being a man inside a woman's body (Radclyffe Hall, 1950) do not escape this dualism.

Some forms of feminism have taken this dualism for granted. Others have celebrated it, calling for the construction of gynocentric values and language or invoking notions of connectedness and the ethics of caring (Daly, 1979; Gilligan, 1982; West, 1988). But for others, the naturalness of woman as biological category poses problems (Eisenstein, 1988; Riley, 1988). Part of the problem has been identified as the way in which the concept of natural woman preserves an edifice of meaning based on dualisms. In this form of thinking, which is identified with the deconstructionist mode, there is a rejection of a basic concept of western thought, namely that the signified precedes the signifier (Derrida, 1978; Culler, 1981). Hence traditionally we have thought that sex differences exist in the real (unmediated) world and that language merely names or labels these differences. However, it is now possible to think otherwise, namely that natural sex differences do not exist before being brought into consciousness through language. There is no natural pre-linguistic existence/reality which is a constant given to which we attach labels and then, in turn, to which we can appeal as if it were outside culture.

There is no knowledge which is unmediated by language and this language is, in turn, constitutive of our subjective positioning as women and men.

It follows, therefore, that discourses which reproduce the taken-for-granted natural differences reinforce our 'experience' as men and women. They are also constantly drawn into a dualistic frame of reference whereby the concept of woman is meaningful only so long as there is a concept of man against which it can be formulated. Woman becomes what man is not. The problem for feminist discourses which take women for granted is that they too preserve this dualism – in spite of the political goal of overcoming the consequences of this dualism. The point is that self-evident difference is presupposed even though it may be the overcoming of this difference which is the goal. But the difference cannot be overcome because it is always already part of our conceptual framework. (Hence the seemingly endless discussions within feminist legal scholarship on equality and difference, and whether it is better to treat women as if they were men or as if they were non-men.)

Law is one of the discourses which constantly reproduces self-evident and natural women. In addition law reproduces her in a sexualized and subjugated form. This is again related to the issue of dualism in the construction of meaning. As many feminists (starting with the French post-Lacanians; Duchen, 1986) have argued, binary opposites such as male/female, masculine/feminine, good/bad, rationality/emotionality, objectivity/subjectivity, culture/nature, active/passive, truth/falsehood do not simply construct an understanding of difference, they construct different values (Cixous, 1985). Hence rationality, objectivity, culture, activity and truth are good and are associated with the male and masculine. On the other side of the divide emotionality, subjectivity, nature, passivity and falsehood are undesirable and are associated with the female and feminine. The female and feminine are always on the downside of the divide along with all the other undesirable attributes. Moreover, as there is little room for a discursive escape from female embodiment (that is, from being a biological woman) there is little room to escape the other attributes.

Law may benevolently or malevolently confirm us in our discursive place as woman; the point is that it does so. Moreover, it does so within the context of a powerful discourse; one which is positioned high on the hierarchy of knowledges and which is able to disqualify other or 'subjugated' knowledges. As Eisenstein has argued:

> This process becomes most true and most problematic when political discourses, such as law, assume the stance of the 'real' biological (sex) 'difference' of woman's body as fact. Instead of recognizing the part that

cultural interpretation plays in the designation of woman as 'different', these discourses make woman's body masquerade as scientific proof that she is, and is meant to be, 'different'. (1988: 81)

Alternative accounts can hardly compete with such powerful and also commonsensical discursive statements. Take, for example, the following:

No matter how you may dispute and argue, you cannot alter the fact that women are quite different from men. The principal task in the life of women is to bear and rear children. . . . He is physically the stronger and she the weaker. He is temperamentally the more aggressive and she the more submissive. It is he who takes the initiative and she who responds. These diversities of function and temperament lead to differences of outlook which cannot be ignored. But they are, none of them, any reason for putting women under the subjection of men. (Lord Denning, 1980: 194)

The power of such statements is undoubtedly enhanced where there is reference made to reproduction or sexuality. I shall, therefore, turn to the example of rape to try to draw together the various strands of this essay, namely law's claim to truth and hence power to disqualify other knowledges, the problematic use of women's experience as a mode of resistance, and the construction of the sexed body (that is, woman) in legal discourse, and how in a phallocentric culture this sexed body might have unwelcome or uncomfortable resonances with feminine subjectivities.

Rape, law and the sexed subject

Much has been written on rape in the last decade and I do not wish to go over familiar critiques of law and the criminal process (London Rape Crisis Centre, 1984; Adler, 1987; Temkin, 1987; Lees, 1989; Smart, 1989). We know that a woman's account of her abuse is always filtered through a mesh of legal relevances about, for example, consent, intention, corroboration and so on. Her story is reconstructed into a standard form of sexual fantasy or even pornography in which she becomes the slut who turns men on and indicates her availability through every fibre of her clothing and demeanour. The only difference between the rape story and the standard fantasy is that in the former she complains. With this turn of events her story is then transcribed into another account which has considerable currency. She becomes the spiteful, avenging harpie. She is no longer just the slut, but she takes on the mantle of the 'woman scorned'. It has been stated over and over again by feminists and by women who have been raped that it is the victim who becomes the prime suspect.

The process of the rape trial can be described as a specific mode of sexualization of a woman's body – a body which has already been sexualized within the codes of a phallocentric culture. Her body becomes literally saturated with sex. She is required to speak sex, and figuratively to re-enact sex; her body and its responses become the stuff of evidence. As she occupies the metaphorical sexual space which is allocated to her during the trial, she simultaneously invokes woman as a sex; the biological woman. The natural/sexed woman is always already known to be more emotional, less rational, more subjective, more mendacious, and less reliable than man. The utterances of judges constantly reaffirm this.[3]

Almost every rape trial tells the same story; it is like the Original Story being re-enacted on a daily basis. It confirms what is known about women – by women and men. In other words, women's sexual subjectivity has already been framed by the language of rape. Women 'know' they are to blame for rape. (Rape crisis centres routinely report that women blame themselves and that their task is to try to reduce or eliminate this blaming.) The rape trial also confirms what we already 'know' about (hetero) sex, namely that men have uncontrollable urges and natural desires and that women may only passively consent.

Against the story that is constructed in the legal context of court proceedings, police interrogation, legal rules and the adversarial system, feminists have posed women's experience. The personal accounts of what women and children have endured remain deeply shocking, no matter how familiar they become. The aim of this strategy has been to reveal the truth of rape and how it is treated and thus to challenge the myths and lies of law. But law's deployment of power is not in fact reduced by this strategy; indeed it might be argued that it is extended. This extension is achieved by silencing all but one account of rape, an account which in turn produces the rapable (biological, sexed) woman of legal discourse. It is necessary to formulate this argument carefully.

The story of rape which is told is of a humiliating, degrading, depersonalizing and terrifying ordeal. The trial is virtually the same ordeal but with witnesses.[4] This account eclipses all others in feminist discourse (although I have heard others). The question to pose, therefore, is how and why has this become the dominant account? The 'why' is not difficult to answer. This is the language many women use. Looking at it one way this language merely 'gives voice' to the experience. From a deconstructionist position, however, the experience is already constructed in language – a language which is part of the formation of the subjectivity of womanhood. It is a language that wins moral support and empowers the speaker. It is the language of the moral crusades of the nineteenth century which constructed women and children as the victims of the lusts of debauched and unrestrained men. It is therefore an account that has a specific history and culture.

The issue of 'how' this mode of account has come to predominate in the late twentieth century is more complex. Explanation necessarily must focus on the meaning of sex. Foucault (1981) has identified the body and sex(uality) as sites for the deployment of power in the emerging disciplinary societies of the eighteenth and nineteenth centuries. One of the mechanisms of power was the construction of sex (and sexual desires, perversions, repressions and so on) as central to identity. Sex became the ultimate truth of a person; it became each individual's most secret yet telling property. In the twentieth century this deployment of power took the form of the politics of sexual liberation in which this truth had to be revealed through extensive practice and an 'immense verbosity' on the subject of sex (Brunt, 1982). The individual was encouraged to demand sexual rights (that is, the right to orgasm or multiple orgasms; the right to serial monogamy or multiple partners and so on). Sex as identity also became central to the gay and lesbian movements (Weeks, 1987).

Feminists challenged the idea of sexual liberation as a liberation for women because of its phallic imperatives and heterosexism (Campbell, 1980). However, much feminist work of the 1970s and 1980s still rested on the notion of sex as identity. This sex was seen as natural in the sense that it was something pre-cultural and hence outside the patriarchy. At least, if it could be freed from the limitations imposed upon it by patriarchy, it could emerge as the living evidence of what women really are. MacKinnon has formulated this idea thus: 'Sexuality is to feminism what work is to Marxism: that which is most one's own, yet most taken away' (1982: 515). This is an ontological statement about women which presumes that there is a natural state of desire and sexual 'beingness' which could exist in a non-alienated condition.

This form of feminist theorizing builds upon already powerful understandings of sex as something which can occupy a space outside culture. It adds to this an extra dimension of the meaning of sexuality for women because, as MacKinnon so ably demonstrates, it has tended to be women's sexuality which has been commoditized, exploited and reviled in patriarchal cultures. Feminist discourse on sexuality therefore builds upon the Victorian construct of sex and the development of sex as identity; it thereby combines a powerful moral discourse with a political discourse. In this form it can address two quite distinct constituencies besides the women whose lived experience it 'gives voice to'. The first constituency is the liberal one which strives to protect the individual from any violation of individual rights and to preserve self-determination usually through the gender-blind mechanism of law. The language of defilement and degradation invokes in many (myself included) a visceral reaction and anger, which in turn is frequently reduced to a fruitless debate over competing legal rights. The second constituency is the conservative one, which tends to hear the moral elements without the politics and likewise expresses outrage. This outrage is that innocent women (wives and mothers) should be abused – but few measure up to the imposed standards of innocence and purity and the many are deemed deserving. The two forms of outrage may also give rise to different remedies (that is, more protection for women and more policing, rather than more rights for victims) but the point is that both constituencies can be moved by such appeals. The discourse therefore appears 'successful'.

The problem is that this form of feminist discourse does not allow for the de-sexuating (Diamond and Quinby, 1988) of women's bodies. As Diamond and Quinby argue, 'to accept this [discourse] is to promulgate the larger culture's belief that sex is the measure of identity and the instrument of truth' (1988: 200).

Returning to the specifics of law, this discourse shares with legal discourse the construction of woman as her sex, and in turn a sexed body open to/vulnerable to the 'desires' and designs of men. In both the sexed body is victimized. In the former the body becomes the eternal victim, in the latter the deserving victim. Neither discourse empowers. This construction is remarkably close to feminism's construction. Take, for example, the following statement:

> Feminist consciousness is consciousness of *victimization*. . . . One is victimized as a woman, as one among many, and in the realization that others are made to suffer in the same way that I am made to suffer lies the beginning of a sense of solidarity with other victims. (Bartky, 1972: 26; emphasis in original)

Woman becomes the eternal victim because of her sex which is, in turn, a natural and self-evident attribute.

My point is that there may be other accounts of rape which could become forms of resistance rather than sources of victimization.[5] The accounts that law gives and which feminism gives fit too uncomfortably with our feminine subject position against which we should resist. Yet feminism may not be able to articulate alternative accounts because of the real fear that law will snatch back the minimal protection it offers. If women were to give up their victim status, could law proclaim that all along it knew that women were 'really' mendacious, irrational bodies overdetermined by their sex? Could it claim that law had been right to believe only a tiny minority of complaints of sexual abuse? I suppose the answer is probably 'yes'. In other words, a feminist discourse which might attempt to construct rape differently, which might attempt to deconstruct the biological/sexed woman, is silenced by the apparition of law's sexed woman to whose survival it is unwillingly tied. This means that the more we focus on law as the problem and solution, the more we are drawn into a paradox.

Solutions to such paradoxes are not easy to find. As Foucault argued, 'it is not that everything is bad, but that everything is dangerous. . . . If everything is dangerous, then we always have something to do' (quoted in Gandal, 1986: 129). So, although there are risks, I think it is time to resist the twin straitjackets of liberalism and biologism which law invites us to wear in order to hear us. This may mean giving up our standard strategy of opposing law's truth with women's experience and moving out into uncharted territory. But if it allows us to start thinking outside the confining concept of the natural/sexed woman we may be able to deconstruct law's truth rather than unwittingly colluding with it.

Notes

This chapter was originally published in *Journal of Law and Society*, 1990, 17(2): 194–210.

1   Here I am not suggesting a new Utopian sisterhood which can be achieved by fiat – but rather an abandoning of old conceptual categories which were developed in the 1970s but are no longer appropriate to feminist thought in the 1990s.

2   I refer to law in the singular here. This is not because I regard law as a unity with unitary goals, but because this unitary appearance, which is achieved through a linguistic device, further empowers legal discourse and is therefore part of the effect I am discussing here.

3   There are many examples of judges' utterances on the mendacity of women where sexual matters are concerned (see Patullo, 1983). These are perhaps so familiar now that they will not stand further repetition.

4   In case I should be misunderstood, let me make it clear that I am *not* saying that women say they experience fear, degradation, and so on, when really they do not. My point is about how these modes of experience are constructed through language and then, through repetition, are taken up as the only truth of rape.

5   It would be unjust to give the impression that such accounts do not exist at all in feminist discourse. The abandonment of the term 'victim' in relation to rape and child sexual abuse is, for example, very significant. But the dominant mode, and the one which occurs routinely in the field of feminism and law, is the victim-orientated conceptualization (for example Clark and Lewis, 1977; Adler, 1987; Lees, 1989).

6

Unquestionably a Moral Issue: Rhetorical Devices and Regulatory Imperatives

I have been intrigued for some time by the power of the rhetoric of the feminist anti-pornography pro-censorship lobby. In consequence, in this chapter I want to explore issues of form more than content of speech or, perhaps more accurately, how form dictates a certain cluster of meanings which may not be the 'intention' of the speaker. I am not so much concerned with arguing whether or not activists like Catharine MacKinnon or Andrea Dworkin are *really* sexual conservatives; rather my focus will be the form of argumentation they use and the power that this form exercises in feminist circles. I shall argue that this form of argument uses powers of persuasion and logic which are already too grounded in specific meanings about sexuality to be wrenched out of their overdetermining historical context. I shall also suggest that as a consequence of insisting on a distinction between politics and morality, with feminist arguments being presented as addressing politics and traditional anti-feminist positions being presented as imbued with a given sexual morality, we have become blind to the moral underpinnings of much of the feminist response to pornography. It is precisely this (denied) underlying morality which gives strength to the rhetorics of feminists like MacKinnon and Dworkin.

A moral issue?

One of the major strengths of feminist analyses of pornography has been the insistence that pornography is not 'outside' power. By this I mean that pornography has been recast in terms of power relations between men and women, between multinational cooperations and women, and between the state, law and women. In taking (hetero)-sexuality out of the sphere of the natural, many feminists from a range of quite different theoretical stances, began to see that pornography was a form of deployment of power. Not all may agree that it represents a simple deployment of power by men against women, but at least the issue of power, and hence politics, became central.

Once the issue of power was addressed the liberal moral argument that only the public sphere should be the realm of legitimate political (legal) intervention, while the private should be free of any form of investigation (analytical, legal or otherwise), became suspect. The conservative moral argument had been less of an obstacle to the development of a feminist stance on matters of sexuality. The form that this moral argument took in the 1960s and 1970s was so clearly pro-monogamous heterosexuality and anti-women's sexual autonomy (let alone lesbianism) that feminists were able to deconstruct this rhetoric and reframe it as a form of anti-feminist politics in the guise of a humanitarian morality.

So the argument went that (all?) moral positions are merely politics in disguise and, while these politics obscure the oppression of women, feminist politics reveal not only the truth of oppression but how its obfuscation occurs. Now, I do not exactly dissent from this argument but it may be that we have taken the force of the critique too far and have come to imagine that, because feminism speaks of politics it is not imbued with a wide range of values on the question of sexual morality. In observing the mote in our opponent's eye we may have become blind to the beam in our own. But this is perhaps an unhelpful analogy because it sees morality as a sort of ideological blemish in the purity of politic's vision and thus perpetuates the feminist aversion (which is perhaps beginning to wane) to addressing questions of morality. But my point is that much feminist work in the field of sexuality has seen questions of morality as automatically meaning the reintroduction of reactionary politics. This makes an error on two levels. First, it equates morality fixedly with a narrow Judaeo-Christian, Victorian version of sexual morality or as a ruse for something equally problematic. Second, it ironically imbues assertions of politics with a moral superiority (because they at least are clear and open about questions of power) while seemingly embracing a politics without morality. Traditions of moral philosophy may not have been informed by feminist thinking but does this mean we reject all questions of morality quite so smoothly? But, more importantly for my discussion here, have we deceived ourselves in thinking that because we are talking of (sexual) politics we have transcended (sexual) morality?

To pursue this line of argument I want to consider two speeches (which later became articles) by Catharine MacKinnon (1987). The first is entitled 'Not a moral issue', the second which I shall discuss later in this chapter, is entitled 'On collaboration'. The former article deals in detail with the separation of morality and politics. She argues:

> Obscenity law is concerned with morality, specifically morals from the male point of view, meaning the standpoint of male dominance. The feminist critique of pornography is a politics, specifically politics from women's

point of view, meaning the standpoint of the subordination of women to men. Morality here means good and evil; politics means power and powerlessness. (1987: 147)

This argument is part of a specific strategy to distinguish between criminal laws based on issues of obscenity (good and evil) and civil laws based on issues of civil liberties and harm (politics). Thus what MacKinnon, and other feminists who are not necessarily pro-censorship, are doing is distinguishing between the feminist objection to pornography and the traditional moral objection that all sex outside marriage is dirty, representations of sex are smut and so on. She goes on to argue that disputes over what constitutes obscenity have always been fights between men over the best means to perpetuate the male system of power over women. Thus debates between liberals and conservatives which dominated the question of pornography in the 1960s and 1970s are interpreted as questions between men. The feminist insistence on politics is seen as avoiding the trap of perpetuating this form of debate.

Now, my point is not that we can never distinguish politics from morality on an analytical level (although I am not sure that an amoral politics would be desirable in practice) but that in having made this initially useful distinction, much feminist discourse has ignored the way in which fairly traditional moral ideas and rhetoric have entered into feminist speech. It is as if we have come to assume that whenever a feminist speaks what comes out is politics not morals, no matter what she is saying. The distinction between politics and morality has meant that we felt we need not be rigorous about moral issues because morality was seen as a diversion and merely a question on the agenda of the reactionaries. Perhaps feminists just tend to assume that the espousal of feminist politics embraces good rather than evil (taking MacKinnon's definition of morality) such that we need give it no further consideration. However, as debates over abortion, new reproductive technologies, pornography and sexuality in general have deepened, it seems we may be coming up against a sort of atavistic core, an unreconstructed element in much feminist thinking which is unreconstructed precisely because we have ignored it for so long.

It is this unreconstructed, or at least unchallenged, element to which I think much of the anti-pornography pro-censorship rhetoric appeals, *while publicly disavowing questions of morality*. Thus, while the content of the speech denies the traditional moral dimension, the form speaks directly to this traditional, unreconstructed moral paradigm. In saying this I am not saying that it is a deliberate strategy but, deliberate or not, it has very serious consequences. I shall now give some consideration to examples of the form of rhetoric deployed in the pro-censorship lobby.

Speaking from the heart?

A vital strategy of the pro-censorship lobby has been the personal testimony. This should hardly surprise us given that this form of argument appears to be powerful in both mainstream politics and marginal pressure group politics. I stress that it only *appears* to be successful in mainstream politics because we should by now be aware that a broad and complex socio-political canvass all but determines which personal testimonies will be heard and when. Yet in spite of the fact that it is not always successful many campaigners have realized that you do not get to first base without some kind of personal account. Pressure groups, for example, know that there is little point complaining about benefit levels or housing policies unless they can produce at least one individual or family who will speak from 'personal experience' of poverty or homelessness.

The personal testimony as a form of political intervention has, or can have, an authority denied the theorist, statistician or demographer. (Personal testimony also has a special place in feminist politics, but I shall return to this later.) The personal testimony is given the status of a truth, unless the speaker can be disqualified effectively.

As second wave feminist politics has moved increasingly towards the pressure group model of lobbying, litigation and legislation making, so it has gradually deployed the personal testimony in an instrumental way. I am using the term instrumental here not as a criticism but as a way of distinguishing between personal testimony in consciousness raising situations which are or were (ideally) safe, women-only and 'private', and personal testimonies used in highly public situations with a predetermined political goal in view. Moreover, the distinction I wish to make is not simply one which sees the same account in two different fora; rather my argument is that these become two very different accounts. As Valverde (1985) has so succinctly pointed out, a story about sexual experiences in one context (a limited publication for women only) takes on a very different meaning when it appears in another (such as an established 'girlie' magazine). It is not just that the author may lose control of the meanings attributed to the statement (as this can never be guaranteed anyway) but the speech occupies a different symbolic space. I want to suggest that the symbolic space, and hence meaning, of the personal testimony (in general, but particularly concerning sexual matters) is overdetermined by an already established framework of meaning which comes into play as the narrative begins. The whole symbolic and actual framing of the narrative, usually given in the form of spoken or written evidence to a special committee, or given indirectly through 'experts' who can speak for those too distressed to speak for themselves, contributes to how we can understand what is being said. Moreover, the simple repetitiveness of this strategy (it is one that has been repeated over and over again since the purity and temperance campaigns of the nineteenth century combined with the development of lobby politics) ensures that we place accounts within a specific framework of meanings. The point is that we not only know we will be shocked and horrified, we also know that real villains will be unambiguously exposed, and that we will conclude that something must be done. This is what I refer to as the 'regulatory imperative' of this form of rhetorical orchestration. The very framing of the issues and the obviousness of the harm, renders the value of intervention and regulation self-evident. To challenge this outcome is, of course, to side with the villains who rape, maim and exploit the innocent.

It is in this strategy that I see pro-censorship feminism embracing a very traditional form (if not content) of morality. Sharp dichotomies of good and evil are established, there is no nuance at all. Moreover, only the evil or wilfully misguided will stand in the way of putting matters right. This is precisely what MacKinnon (1987) does in her article 'On collaboration'. She states, for example,

> Why do women lawyers who identify as feminists buy and defend the pornographers' view of what a woman is for, what a women's sexuality is? Why, when they look in the mirror, do they see the image of themselves the pornographers put there? (1987: 200)

Thus, women lawyers who call themselves feminists (although MacKinnon implies they cannot be *real* feminists) in speaking against the legislation she wishes to enact, are portrayed as siding with the pornographers. This is the classic argument that 'those who are not for me are against me' and logically, as the 'I' of the statement occupies the moral high ground (being defender of the victimized) those who are opposed are *bad* people. This is an argument which depends on a heavily encoded set of moral messages which we know so well in a western Judaeo-Christian culture that we often fail to see its workings.

But this form of argument, which might otherwise be transparent, is protected when used in conjunction with the personal testimony. The point about the personal testimony in this context is that in speaking against proposed reforms one is effectively placed in the position of speaking not against a relatively powerful woman like MacKinnon, but against less well resourced women who have given testimony of abuse. Thus one appears to be denying their experience or suggesting that it is of no consequence. This is a particular dilemma for feminists as I shall try to argue later.

It might at this stage be useful to analyse a number of personal testimonies derived from different sources but following a virtually identical form.

> Formerly I had no complaints about my husband's conduct, but since the appearance of the sex films, he has changed. Now he is merely a 'bull performing to capacity', if you will, please, excuse the expression. . . . And because I can no longer respond to him with what he desires, he calls me a frigid, uninterested old grandmother. . . . I know with certitude that this change was caused in him by sex films because we were happily married for ten years before the films arrived. I hate to see him go to a sex film, for when he returns he falls upon me like a wild animal and I offer him too little. (Whitehouse, 1977: 214)

> Finally pornography took over and he stopped counselling. I continued on and on. . . . He was drawn to pornography even though I offered him a loving relationship and enjoyed sex with him before his involvement with pornography. Masturbation took over our sex life. I know for a fact that pornography destroyed our marriage. (Schlafly, 1987: 89)

> He called me on the telephone and he said that he had seen several short pornographic films and that he felt very horny. . . . So he asked if he could come over specifically to have sex with me. I said yes, because at that time I felt obligated as a girl friend to satisfy him. . . . This encounter differed from others previous, it was much quicker, it was somewhat rougher, and he was not aware of me as a person. I feel what I have to say here is important because I feel what he did, he went to this party, saw pornography, got an erection, got me to inflict his erection on. There is a direct causal relationship there. (Everywoman, 1988: 64–5)

Ms MacKinnon: Chairman White, might I be able to be permitted to read a letter which is written by Women Against Pornography?

> 'Although our work has not curbed the power and influence of the pornography industry, it has made us acutely aware of the magnitude and severity of the harm done to girls and women by pornography. We have received calls and letters from women whose employers and co-workers have used pornography to harass and intimidate them. We have heard from wives whose husbands have pressured them to act out their favorite pornographic scenarios. . . . Up to this point, however, there has been nothing we could do to help women victimized by pornography take action against those who victimize them. The proposed amendment to Title 7 would provide us with the means to help these women receive justice.' (Everywoman, 1988: 85)

These four extracts come from three different sources. The first was a letter written to a doctor friend of Mary Whitehouse at the height of her campaign against pornography (and also a much wider range of so-called permissive views on sexuality and the family). The letter is published in her book *Whatever Happened to Sex?* The second extract comes from the official transcript of proceedings of the US Attorney General's Commission on Pornography in 1985/6. The proceedings in this case were selected and edited by Phylis Schlafly, author of *The Power of the Positive Woman* and other anti-feminist writings. The edited collection is entitled *Pornography's Victims*. The last two extracts come from the transcripts of the Public Hearings on the MacKinnon and Dworkin pornography ordinances in Minneapolis in December 1983 and were published by the *Everywoman* magazine, under the title *Pornography and Sexual Violence: Evidence of the Links*, as part of a campaign to put new legislation against pornography on the political agenda in the UK.

My comments on these extracts are not of the usual sociological variety which might typically suggest that those who give evidence are never representative of a general population or that further selections from an already self-selected group hardly constitutes a meaningful sample. While these would be quite useful comments, I am more interested in the fact that over a span of some 10 years, from different sources and avenues of publication, the same story repeats itself. Harnessed to quite different political goals we have the same personal testimony. The personal testimony takes a specific narrative form with certain essential ingredients. A key ingredient is that without pornography these abuses would not happen or that prior to the individual's discovery of pornography all was well. Pornography is presented as a drug to which men become addicted, so we have the slippery slope element, as well as the idea of people falling into the grip of something alien.

What becomes blurred in the first three more 'personal' accounts is whether what is found to be objectionable is the arousal of desire in men or whether it is that their partners are ambivalent about, or quite appalled by, becoming the object of that arousal. This is an important distinction to make because accounts like these can produce a powerful, even visceral response, but it is not always clear whether this is to the idea of (male) sexual arousal or to the idea of using women (or other human beings) as means to an end. The question that then follows is that if our concern is about the 'use' of women and others as means to an end, then why do we only seem to become so alarmed about it in a sexual context?

Of course, there is an answer to this question from a radical feminist perspective. This would be that sexual oppression and exploitation are not only the source of all oppressions of women, but the means of disguising all sorts of other oppressions. But this is not what most personal testimonies say. These testimonies are much more likely to say that there is nothing wrong with (hetero)sex, the problem is unwanted (hetero)sex. (A distinction of which MacKinnon is particularly scathing.) Moreover, there is a strong theme in many of the testimonies given to the Attorney General's Commission and to the Public Hearing in Minneapolis, that there is a distinction to be made between natural and unnatural sexual practices. Pornography is seen to provoke unnatural sex. Once again, a distinction needs to be made between whether the horrified response occasioned by these accounts relates to hearing of 'unnatural' sexual practices or whether it is because these practices are inflicted on unwilling partners.

I would suggest that the 'harm' element based on assertions of coercion operates not to produce the outraged response, but to make the account tellable. Thus, while for feminism in general the problem with pornography and certain forms of sexuality is that they may be directly coercive or related in a more complex way to a general coercion of women, in this wider political and public context I want to suggest that the 'harm' issue does quite different 'work' to the work it performs within feminist discourses. References to force, being drugged, being overpowered or simply being obliged allow the speaker or her representative to tell the tale. If the tale were told without the harm dimension it would, of course, simply become a standard pornographic story in and of itself. What I am proposing is that ways of speaking about (hetero)sex are now thoroughly overdetermined and that only two forms seem open, one is the pornographic tale (I did it and enjoyed it) or the anti-pornographer's tale (They did it to me and it was terrible). Feminism in the West (both first and second wave) has largely eschewed the former, and left it with the latter which is unfortunately a narrative constructed on very different premises to feminism's.

These accounts are therefore heard and read by an audience that *already* knows that sex is harmful (even if ideas about who the real 'victims' are may vary). Thus the surprise is not in the rediscovery of what is already known. The visceral response comes from hearing about what is done. This is not simply a reiteration of the point that these accounts may be enjoyed as pornography is enjoyed, and therefore feminists should not be the vehicle for providing such accounts. My point is that in taking objections to pornography into the lobbying/evidence giving mode, the anti-censorship feminists have stepped into a hermeneutic circle where certain meanings already dominate. The whole issue almost inevitably becomes one of (narrow, Judaeo-Christian, sexual) morality, not one of a politics which has transcended morality. There is, therefore, an undesirable slippage from one frame of reference into another which is quite antithetical to most of feminism's aims.

The examples I have provided above may give the impression of too brief a history of the narrative mode I am discussing. Indeed, if I could only point to a decade or so of the deployment of such accounts regarding sexual matters and legal reforms, the power of such forms would be far less significant than I am claiming. However, it is possible to illustrate a much more firmly entrenched set of practices starting in the latter half of the nineteenth century. The 'confessionary' mode of talking about sex obviously pre-dates this historical moment (Foucault, 1981) but the harnessing of the confession with the context of coercion to make the tale publicly palatable and to give it the force to generate legislation, was a specifically Victorian development. The melodramatic form with extremes of good and evil, of innocence sullied and ruined lives was a widely used and understood form in Victorian writing. And indeed it is hardly surprising that it was journalists like W. T. Stead and publishers like Alfred Dyer who deliberately used this mode in their vigilance campaigns on issues of the so-called White Slave trade and the age of consent (Bristow, 1977).

In 1881 Dyer reported to the House of Lords Select Committee on the Protection of Women and Girls, that he had spoken to many women who had been 'taken' or decoyed to Belgium and had been forced into brothels. This is part of the text of one account he relayed to the Committee. It was extracted from a letter by a young woman named as Jones.

> When I left London six months ago I was as innocent as a child, but it was soon taken from me and through compulsion was obliged to take part in deceit and other things worse. . . . [B]y God's help, I will prove to them that I have been sinned against not sinned. I cannot express my feelings on this slavery . . . once free and able to act, I will leave nothing undone to rescue girls that are unfortunately placed in these dens. (Select Committee of the House of Lords on the Law Relating to the Protection of Young Girls, 1881: 464)

The Select Committee heard many such accounts and a large number of letters from young women were printed as part of the proceedings. They tell of promises of marriage from complete strangers, of charming men and helpful women who suddenly become cruel, of uncaring authorities and so on.

These accounts can be compared with an account given a century later by Linda Marciano who was a key witness to the Minneapolis hearings in 1983.

> I feel I should introduce myself and tell you why I feel I am qualified to speak out against pornography. My name today is Linda Marciano. Linda Lovelace was the name I bore during a two and a half year period of imprisonment. . . .
>
> It all began in 1971. . . . A girlfriend of mine came to visit me with a person by the name of Mr Charles Traynor. He came off as a considerate gentleman, asking us what we would like to do [etc.]. . . . Needless to say I was impressed, and started to date him.
>
> When I decided to head back north and informed Mr Traynor of my

intention, that was when I met the real Mr Traynor and my two and a half years of imprisonment began. He began a complete turnaround and beat me up physically and began the mental abuse; from that day forward my hell began. (Everywoman, 1988: 24–5)

The important question about these testimonies is not, it seems to me, whether they are 'true' or 'false'[1] but the way in which they draw the reader into a set of apparently logical connections which lead to the seemingly inevitable consequence that legislation must be introduced to end the abuse so graphically detailed. It is virtually impossible to resist this regulatory impulse without actually, or in appearance, denying the harm of the experience recounted by the narrator. All arguments which are based on grounds that new legislation will not work as intended, or that it will catch a wider, 'innocent' group in its sweep, or that it will be used by the wrong people for the wrong purposes is easily condemned as collaborative prevarication.

MacKinnon's second article 'On collaboration' is an example of this because she elides some feminists' concern with using the state apparatus against pornography, with being *for* pornography. Anti-censorship becomes transposed as pro-pornography. The way in which the argument has been structured allows of only two positions namely anti-pornography/pro-censorship and pro-pornography/anti-censorship. In creating this binary dichotomy the moral highground is located with the pro-censorship lobby. Good can be easily distinguished from evil in this formulation.

Speaking like a woman

I have suggested above that there are particular difficulties for feminists in responding to personal accounts and testimonies and I now propose to add this dimension to my argument. On the face of it one might imagine that feminists would 'see through' the device of using personal accounts to achieve a political goal. After all we have been scathing enough of accounts that suggest that pornography helps individual men to avoid raping women, or that pornography saves marriages. Could it be that our response to the personal testimony is dictated by whether we agree with the perceived political goals to whose service the account is put? While it would be sanctimonious to suggest that there is nothing in this suggestion, there is a deeper issue at stake.

Second wave feminism in the UK developed a core principle through the practice of consciousness raising which maintained that every woman's story was valid and should be acknowledged rather than silenced. This principle, which may have been honoured more in the breach than in its observance, has become even more elevated with the recognition that many women were indeed silenced by a largely white, middle class movement. But there is now a further dimension added to the status of 'speaking' one's personal story. This is the influence of standpoint feminism.

Standpoint feminism appears to be the place where the politics of the women's movement(s) meshes with the construction of knowledge in more academic terms. Standpoint feminism has been most clearly articulated by Dorothy Smith (1988) who is a proponent and by Sandra Harding (1986) who is more critical. Basically this theoretical argument suggests that the standpoint of women provides the most accurate or truthful account of the workings of patriarchal society. However, standpoint feminism does not celebrate the vision of all women, but only those who have collectivized and reinterpreted their experiences through processes of consciousness raising or similar political activity. Hence standpoint feminism does not actually claim that all women have the correct political analysis of patriarchy, but only women who have been politically transformed into feminists. There is therefore retained an implicit hierarchy of knowledge. I stress implicit because when standpoint feminism becomes rhetorical it fails to distinguish between women and feminists. Thus MacKinnon claims to speak from the standpoint of (all?) women, yet retains the distinction between feminists and other women when she suggests that her opponents cannot be real feminists.

Now the problem with standpoint feminism in the debate on pornography is that it claims that there is a *women's* position on pornography which has been arrived at through the *feminist* process of consciousness raising. Thus the feminist who speaks against this overly simplistic view commits two major sins. First, she speaks against the wishes of ordinary women, and second, she fails as a feminist. The reluctance to commit these 'sins' becomes particularly problematic when faced with personal accounts in a public forum where personal testimonies become forms of evidence. It is even more problematic when women are giving statements on their experiences of incest, sexual abuse, sexual harassment and are unproblematically linking these experiences to pornography. A rejection of this linkage becomes interpreted as a rejection of their experience.

The subsequent silencing of alternative analyses should not (or need not) be interpreted as a deliberate strategy. It appears much more likely to be an outcome of a series of initially unconnected but gradually related events such as the rise of the New Right, the increasing concern over sexual violence, and the availability of a form of lobbying/argumentation which seems to pay dividends. Moreover, the difficulty for anti-censorship feminists to speak against pro-censorship feminism once personal testimonies have been deployed, has its roots in a much deeper problem within feminist approaches to the construction of knowledge and the relationship between knowledge, truth and experience.

Conclusion

Sexuality has always been a site of contested meaning for feminists and we should hardly be surprised when differences erupt. But it seems to me that it is vital to be clear about what these differences are. The more forms of argument derived from strategies of moral panic and moral vigilance are used, or personal testimonies are deployed for instrumental reasons, the more we are forced to retreat into uncomprehending, opposing camps. While I am deeply concerned about the faith being placed in a legal solution to pornography (let alone women's oppression generally, see Smart, 1989) what I have attempted to do in this chapter is to draw attention to another development which I find equally worrying. This is the tendency to use pragmatic lobbying devices most particularly in controversial areas for feminism. Another example would be in the field of reproductive technologies where there are deep divisions between feminists, but where the device of turning personal testimonies into political evidence is becoming manifest. Many forms of feminism may have used this sort of strategy in the past (such as, asking prostitutes or lone mothers or battered women to speak to Select Committees) but if we are to continue to do this, especially in contested areas, we should perhaps become more acutely aware that the *content* of our message may be overlain by meanings already encoded in the *form* we are using. In such circumstances we may find we further empower precisely the wrong people regardless of our intentions.

Notes

This chapter was originally published in L. Segal and M. McIntosh (eds) (1992) *Sex Exposed: Sexuality and the Pornography Debate*, Virago.

1   The question of truth and falsehood has, of course, preoccupied many in this field. The Select Committee in 1881 pointed out how many of the women who gave evidence of coercion to Mr Dyer and his associates said the exact opposite to other investigators. Moreover, some of the women complained that Dyer tried to remove them forcibly from the 'houses' where they worked. Similarly Linda Marciano has given very different accounts of her period as Linda Lovelace. The problem with these competing accounts is that the teller can be disqualified as a known liar. But her accounts will live on to be harnessed to different political goals while she becomes little more than a pawn in the game of political rhetorics.

7

Law, Feminism and Sexuality: From Essence to Ethics?

In this chapter I am concerned to explore how sexuality is theorized from within feminist perspectives in the field of law. The approach to questions of sexuality to be found in areas of law which have been identified as central to feminist concerns (for example rape) are often far removed from feminist debates on sexuality which derive from cultural studies, lesbian and gay studies and film theory. Put simply, feminist work on law and sexuality often seems wedded to the idea of sexuality as essence, as a pre-given entity which needs regulation by a reformed legal system or system of laws. Yet this idea of sexuality as an object upon which culture, law, representations or education may act 'upon' is rigorously questioned elsewhere. Sexuality is no longer given an a priori status but is presented more in terms of discursive constructions of sexualit*ies*. It is interesting to consider why work on sexuality is now so diverse and why, with the exception of the field of pornography, there has been so little engagement between these competing understandings of sexuality found in legal analysis and elsewhere. I shall explore some of these issues but first I shall elaborate a little on what are often referred to as poststructuralist analyses of sexuality.

Sex, gender and sexuality

Feminist scholars such as Butler (1990), Martin (1992) and Pringle (1992) have recently pointed to the political and analytical need to distinguish between ideas of sex, gender and sexuality (which includes identity and orientation) and to challenge the foundational position of sex in relation to the other categories which are almost always seen as the cultural or psychic overlays to that which is pre-given, that is, sex.

Thus we need first to recognize the meanings that are attached to these crucial terms. Put quite simply for the moment, sex is the term which is used to signify a biological given. It is assumed to be a category into which we are born and which is determined initially by chromosomes and then the effects of different hormones (for example, testosterone and oestrogen). This presumed binary system of male and female is widely adhered to in western cultures and arguably has been a cornerstone of much feminist work until recently. Sex then is taken as the foundation, it is regarded as pre-cultural and unencumbered by history, language or society. Throughout the nineteenth century and much of the twentieth century in the West it was assumed that sex and gender were really indistinguishable. That is to say, in as much as a distinction was made between these concepts (and they were often used interchangeably), it was presumed that the male sex gave rise inexorably to masculine attributes and behaviour and that the female sex simply gave rise to the feminine. In Britain it was the pioneering work of Oakley (1972) which first articulated the feminist dis-ease with this immutable linkage. Using cross cultural studies she revealed that what constituted masculine attributes and characteristics varied according to culture rather than nature. Similarly different cultures regarded very different and quite contradictory forms of 'feminine' behaviour or orientation to be entirely natural. In so arguing Oakley loosened the link between sex and gender. She used the term sex to refer to 'biological sex' and the term gender to refer to cultural (and variable) attributes known as masculinity and femininity. This argumentation was vital to feminist work because it freed women, so to speak, from a biological determinism.

The relationship of the concept of sexuality to concepts of sex and gender has a more complex history. While the conventional wisdom prevailed that one's biological sex gave rise to one's sexual orientation (that is, men would naturally desire women and so on) the impact of lesbian activism and thought in the women's movement quickly challenged such simplistic ideas. New ways of thinking developed on the social construction of sexuality in which sexual desire was understood to be the outcome of cultural, psychic and/or political environments. Sexual orientation became to be seen as a matter of choice and sexual identity a matter of politics. Although these matters are now debated in much more nuanced terms (see, for example, Weeks, 1991; Connell and Dowsett, 1992; Stanton, 1992; Gibson and Gibson, 1993) such discussions loosened the apparent grip of the biological on the sexual.

Thus with the virtual autonomy of both gender and sexuality from sex there developed an immense discourse on femininity and masculinity and on heterosexuality, gay and lesbian sexuality. However, as relatively free-floating as these concepts were seen to be, Biddy Martin (1992) has argued that sexuality became closely associated with gender. This meant that in feminist work gender became the determining factor in both 'problematic' sexualities and in 'radical' sexualities. Thus aggressive, competitive, penetrative sexualities were seen as resulting from masculinity; gentle, caring, woman-orientated sexualities (lesbianism) were seen as arising from what is good in femininity. Under such regimes of meaning the butch and femme lesbians or S/M (sado-masochistic) lesbians were (at first?) regarded as gender traitors not as sexual radicals.

Sexuality was subordinated to gender. There were possibly two main reasons why this occurred. The first is because a great deal of lesbian writing in the 1980s came through the Women's Movement in which gender was the dominant paradigm. This dominant framing was challenged by lesbians who argued, initially, that their lesbianism pre-dated the second wave women's movement and thus they attributed different meanings to their sexual desire other than a recognition of gender oppression (Clark, 1982; Ardill and O'Sullivan, 1986). The second reason was the need to separate lesbianism from male homosexuality. The dominance of heterosexuality and heterosexism in conventional society rendered any denial of heterosex a mere perversion and thus lesbians and gay men would be lumped together as if the same, with the same histories and the same desires (see Pringle, 1992). Thus it became important for lesbian activists to identify their own history and the specificity of lesbian desire and politics. Such lesbians did not wish to be subsumed into the Gay Movement and thus rendered invisible again.

However important these elements were (and in some ways still are), there is now a move to reinstate lesbianism and male homosexuality as oppositional to heterosexuality and not merely as an aspect of gender or patriarchal oppression. Thus, for example, Martin writes of Joan Nestle in terms of how 'Nestle restores queerness to lesbianism in order to locate it again in the sexual orderings that its equation with gender (identification) has obscured' (1992: 109). This move is, of course, reminiscent of other earlier strategies where feminists refused to allow the category of gender to be submerged in class, or where black feminists refused to allow 'race' to be submerged in gender. The reassertion of 'queerness' does not deny gender difference, but it builds on this period of analysis and struggle and then insists on a new visibility for the sexual and questions of desire.

So far I have discussed how gender and sexuality have, in feminist work, been separated from the supposed foundation of biological sex. I have suggested that sexuality (at least women's sexuality) then became subordinate to gender and that this conceptual domination was eventually challenged. The problem is, however, that none of these developments has posed a challenge to the idea that sex (that is, one's maleness or femaleness) is given in nature nor to the idea that gender and sexuality have some relation to this binary arrangement even if this relationship is now seen as fairly tenuous. The problem is that, tenuous or not, the unchallenged foundation of biology (nature) to 'biological' sex is a constant obstacle to social constructionist or sociological thinking on sexuality and gender.

The idea that there are two sexes given in nature (and thus immutable) both structures and frames how gender relations and sexuality are understood. Feminists, to make the point rather simply, wish to transcend gender difference while basing their argument on the uniqueness and difference of women as a biological category. Women are taken to be a self-evident category, but they can only be so in opposition to some other differentiating category, that is, men. Thus arguments about women as a group constantly invoke men as a different and fixed category and thus give succour to both common-sense and reactionary perceptions of men and women as naturally different. In Butler's terms:

> Is the construction of the category of women as a coherent and stable subject an unwitting regulation and reification of gender relations? And is not such a reification precisely contrary to feminist aims? To what extent does the category of women achieve stability and coherence only in the context of the heterosexual matrix? (1990: 6)

In the field of sexuality the preservation of the idea of there being a natural binary sexual differentiation constantly prioritizes hetero-sexuality as the norm. Thus lesbianism and male homosexuality are almost always explained as some derivation of or (worse) deviation from this obvious symmetry. This presumption of binary sexual difference combined with the cultural imperative of biological reproduction, always already demotes non-heterosexual sexual expression and desire.

Judith Butler has, pre-eminently, challenged this dominant under-standing of biologically given binary sexual difference. However, before I discuss her work I wish to raise a few other related dissenting voices. Dissent can be found even within the field of biological science where ideas of sexual difference are often more nuanced than the common-sense appropriation of biology allows. Take, for example, the scientific basis of sexual difference as residing in one's chromosomal composition. It is argued that the female ovum carries an X chromosome and the sperm carries either an X or a Y chromosome. The combination of XX is said (conventionally) to give rise to a female foetus, and XY to produce the male. However, the recent controversy over the so-called sex testing of athletes at the Olympic Games has revealed that a number of women have XY chromosomal composition. These women who have breasts, female genitalia and who are within the range of height, build and strength usually associated with women have been declared to be men and disqualified. Equally hirsute, well-built men have been identified as having XX chromosomes thus rendering them women.

There are of course other well documented difficulties in 'discovering' the correct sex of individuals. There are those whose genitalia is identified as female at birth, but who have descended testicles at puberty. Or there are cases of the converse. Such cases of hermaphrodites have, since the dominance of medical science in the West and almost certainly before, been regarded as 'freaks of nature' (Foucault, 1980). But they are (were) freaks only because of the construction of a strict binary divide to which medical science has given credibility through overly simplistic models such as that of the X and Y chromosomes.

Thomas Laqueur's (1987) work is vital to the development of the critique of binary biological difference as essence. Laqueur puts forward the thesis that it is possible to identify two models of sexual difference in the history of medical science. The first, which stretches from the earliest form of medicine with Galen in the second century AD and possibly before, is the one sex model. The other, which comes about in the eighteenth century at the time of the Enlightenment and which takes on a particular ideological significance in the Victorian era, is the two sex model.

The one sex model understands the different anatomical structures of the reproductive organs of men and women in terms of male genitalia, which are suspended outside the body in men, being inverted and found on the inside of women's bodies. Thus the vagina and ovaries were understood merely to be the penis and testicles inverted or turned inside out within the body. It is Laqueur's argument that the one sex model did not produce, nor was it the product of, an assumption of equality or equal worth between the sexes. Women were seen as lesser men. However, they were not seen as *fundamentally* different. It is with the development of the two sex model that the idea of fundamental (that is, natural and biologically given) difference emerges as a scientific tenet of Victorian medicine and culture. In perceiving the uterus, ovaries, vagina and clitoris as structurally different the argument that women were essentially different to men was enhanced. Thus women's lack of intelligence, of achievement, of moral reasoning and so on could be placed at the door of the uterus. Women were understood to be the victims of their natures (biology). Thus Laqueur would point to the discursive construction of woman as hysterical and inadequate, but also to the assertion of binary biological difference as something fully empirically and scientifically established. He attempts to deconstruct this scientific truth by examining the language of science which he maintains is deeply cultural (as opposed to its proclaimed objectivity). The way in which women's bodies were spoken of was not a reflection of mere 'description' but an example of the cultural construction of the subject supposedly under investigation. Interestingly Laqueur points out that even where science itself has moved on and refutes its former ideas, they often remain rooted in conventional wisdom for much longer – especially where such ideas have been taken up strongly at the ideological level.

Emily Martin's (1989) work on women's perceptions of their bodies and their understanding of reproductive functions points precisely to the power of problematic scientific or medical constructions of women's bodies which are still perpetuated in biology classes and sex education lessons in schools. Her argument has a slightly different focus to Laqueur's but she points to how deeply embedded supposedly objective visions of women's bodies become through science education. Through such critical work we are increasingly able to appreciate the discursive construction of biology, rather than taking the biological for granted as if it were a foreign land for intrepid scientists to 'discover' and describe to us accurately and uncontroversially. To these contributions we need to add Butler's work.

Butler and the instability of binary sex

Butler (1990) articulates a many layered argument against the commonsensical idea that sex, or the sexed body, pre-dates or pre-exists culture and hence gender. While celebrating the feminist argument that gender should be seen as culturally and historically constituted (and thus variable) she is sceptical of feminist theories which have left the realm of sex or the sexed body as the domain of the natural scientist who discovers facts about a supposedly non-social entity.

She argues that this move to separate sex and gender had many benefits but ultimately that the exiled concept of sex restricts our thinking (and politics) around gender. Butler raises a difficult problem for feminist thinking by warmly welcoming the apparent freedom gained by understanding gender as free-floating and not bound by biological sex, but then asking why, given the immense potential variety there must be for the full range of genders, we still only have two. Why is it we still fit all our gendered attributes into either masculine or feminine? The suggestion that some men can be feminine and some women masculine does not challenge the binary regime which arguably feminist politics wishes to overcome. Moreover, Butler argues it reinforces what she calls the 'heterosexual matrix', namely the dominant understanding that 'normal' sexual desire arises out of difference. It also imports with it a presumption of reproductive sex which similarly reinforces the naturalness of heterosexuality.

Butler therefore invites us to think the unthinkable.

> Are the ostensibly natural facts of sex discursively produced by various scientific discourses in the service of other political and social interests? If the immutable character of sex is contested, perhaps this construct called 'sex' is as culturally constructed as gender; indeed, perhaps it was always already gender, with the consequence that the distinction between sex and gender turns out to be no distinction at all. (1990: 7)

To put Butler's thesis into rather simple terms, she appears to be arguing that while we have tended to read gender from sex (even while we disputed an exact causality), we should have been reading back from gender to sex. The sexed body is that which has been constituted by the practice and discourse of gender, it is not that which is given to us in nature.

In this move, Butler is inviting us to challenge the *doxa* or *doxic experience* to use Bourdieu's (1991) terminology. This conceptualization is useful here because doxa refers to the taken-for-grantedness of the social world, in which our experience seems to support what is held up to be objectively (scientifically) true. Thus we constantly observe that there are two sexes, we take for granted that there are two (excluding those we regard as unfortunate because nature has played a nasty trick), and we (most of us?) experience ourselves as either men or women. So taken for granted is this that we may become quite enraged if someone seriously suggests otherwise. Yet the concept of doxa does not presume that we are overdetermined cultural dupes who can only think as we are told to think, and only experience what we are allowed to experience. The usefulness of the concept of doxa is that it presumes that we take for granted many things because social life would be virtually impossible if we questioned everything all the time – but we are quite capable of questioning when issues are problematized. This is, arguably, what Butler is doing.

So Butler argues that we should not see the sexed body as a passive medium on which cultural and gendered meanings are inscribed. On the contrary she suggests that bodies cannot be said to have any meaningful existence prior to their 'mark' of gender. There is therefore no essence of sex which we should elevate to a revered position, allowing it to impose its binary meanings on the social world. Rather we sex the body as we gender it. And gender, for Butler, is not a thing but a performance – thus sex is not an a priori entity but an achievement of gender performance. Equally she argues that (sexual or gender) identity is 'the sedimentation of meanings, or the after-effect of repeated signifying practices' (quoted in Martin, 1992: 102). Thus identity is plainly real, but it is not the reflection of an essence.

Political action, law and competing theories of sex, gender and sexuality

I remarked at the start of this chapter that I was interested that feminist work on sexuality in the field of law does not (yet?) seem much influenced by the sort of thinking on questions of sexuality and gender that is offered by poststructuralist thinkers. In broad terms (and I shall explore these) there are possibly two main reasons. The first is that poststructuralism has become associated – wrongly – with a kind of apolitical stance which really wishes only to bandy words and not to engage in struggle. Because feminists in the field of law are often there precisely because of their interest in action, lobbying and legal reform, a theoretical orientation which problematizes these kinds of practices would hardly seem attractive. The second reason is that in the field of law feminists are, on the one hand, dealing with very pressing issues such as rape, child sexual abuse, violence and so on, and on the other, with a legal system which sometimes seems barely aware that women have gained the vote, let alone being receptive to ideas which seek to destabilize categories of sex and gender. I make no claims to be able to reconcile these differences; however, I do wish to explore them in a little more detail here.

Poststructuralism problematizes a certain type of political action. Unfortunately it is this style of politics which has become predominant in the twentieth century and is therefore now regarded as conterminous with feminist political action. This style is dependent upon the identification of an interest group with a shared identity who, it can be 'established' empirically, are denied their full and proper legal and/or human rights in the context of a liberal democracy. This approach (and here I speak mainly of developed capitalist societies such as Britain or Canada) presumes the existence of a welfare state and not simply a liberal democracy, which will extend rights and benefits once convinced of the need. A very powerful state is therefore the necessary basis of such a political style.

Equally crucial is the idea of shared identity. In this political structure it is vital to claim minority group status in order to be heard. The bigger the minority group of course the better, and the category of women in Britain was so big as to be a majority group. This irony of a majority group with minority group status was, of course, exploited fully. Through this mechanism claims were made and some important achievements were secured.[1] However as feminists, in Britain at least, were throwing themselves more actively into this kind of political action, the Conservative Government was dismantling the Welfare State both structurally and ideologically. As more and more was being demanded, the mechanism through which such reforms could possibly have been achieved was withering away. At the same time the Women's Movement, which had been so confident that it represented all women, came under sharp attack from women of colour, lesbians, working class women, women of differing religions, and women from developing societies for being so presumptuous. These issues are now well documented and do not need repeating here. However, I raise them to point to a certain irony. The women who attacked the Women's Movement and Feminist Theory for the presumption that there was a 'We' being properly represented and who pointed out that such representation was spurious and that gender should not obliterate race or ethnicity, or sexuality and so on, received none of the opprobrium that Butler and others have received for saying virtually the same thing. Arguably poststructuralist feminism does not abandon politics, but attempts to create a politics out of the recognition of difference, rather than striving to re-create the fictitious homogeneity much loved by some feminist activists, but rejected by many others.

The politics of poststructuralism is thus clearly different to that of minority or identity politics but a widespread resistance to such politics is, in my view, not only based on a refusal to give up representational politics. Much feminism is equally unhappy with giving up on liberal humanism. Yet this is what Butler invites us to do when she rejects the main tenet of liberal humanism, namely the individual as the source of social action and effects. She does not look for the doer behind social practices. It is therefore often presumed by her critics that in her rejection of the concept of the individual she is also abandoning political action – since action presumes an actor. It is here, I think, that a basic misunderstanding resides. In rejecting the *category* of the individual, Butler is rejecting a specific philosophical concept, one that carries the ideational baggage of the nineteenth century belief in pre-social beings and natural entities (see Hekman, 1990). One is not denying agency. On the contrary, Butler discusses various forms of political action which may destabilize the gender order, these actions may not be in the form of signing petitions, or joining trade unions (although they could be), but they are political activities none the less.

So far so good. We can talk of cultural politics and of using de-stabilizing gender performances to challenge the dominance of a heterosexist regime. But it is not clear what this means in situations where some women are being grossly abused and the legal system seems to be condoning this. Challenging heterosexuality, while I would suggest vital, does not fit with the urgency of rape and sub-sequent abuse by the legal system. Of course, in many respects this is an entirely unfair juxtapositioning. To accuse the sort of politics which might arise out of poststructuralist thought of already failing the rape victim suggests an uncritical attitude to the failures of exist-ing political practices which, in Britain at least, have done little to alter her circumstances (Lees, 1993). Such antagonism is hardly helpful in any case.

The wrath against poststructuralism, which is often couched in terms of its presumed politically reactionary consequences[2] is, I sus-pect, more to do with an anger over the fact that feminists who write in this tradition have not had a great deal to say explicitly about sub-jects like rape, violence or child sexual abuse. The concern is, there-fore, that such feminists do not *really* care about the important things which have vexed other feminists. In other words the conflict over politics and philosophy may implicitly be a conflict over values. This too contains a potential irony in as much as the question of diversity and the abandonment of a search for truth which is central to so much poststructuralist feminist work, has precisely reintro-duced the question of values. In other words poststructuralist poli-tics is about values and is not an implicit rejection or abandonment of the sort of values espoused – although rarely publicly debated – in feminism.

A recent example of this shift towards an open discussion of values in the field of sexuality is the work of Jeffrey Weeks (1991) with his concept of radical pluralism. There has also been a bur-geoning of questions on feminist ethics and values in the last five years. I shall come back to this later, but we should not lose sight of the fact that feminists and other radicals are now debating nor-mative issues openly and are seeking new formulations which can define and redefine harms while allowing diversity. As Kathy Fergu-son has argued,

> The attraction of mobile subjectivities is at heart political and ethical, not simply epistemological. Thematizing ourselves as mobile subjectivi-ties eschews the search for an essential reality to which our representa-tions correspond, while claiming an historical residence in the contentious fields of late modernity and seeking strategies by which to

stay honest about our affirmations while we keep moving toward them. (1993: 154)

My point in this argument is that poststructuralist feminism has not abandoned politics, but is recasting the meaning of politics and is actively encouraging debates over values and difference. Certainly it does not offer solutions and panaceas and to some who seek faith this is a problem. But, in the field of law at least, there remains one problem posed by a shift towards poststructuralism which remains unanswered. This concerns the problem of working in a context in which the judiciary and/or legal jurisprudence retains a view of women as a homogeneous category and then attributes to this category stereotypical behaviours and emotions which it then reifies in its judicial utterances. I have written at length (Smart, 1989) on the law's inability to hear feminist discourse – virtually no matter what form it takes. I have, however, suggested that those forms which conform most to, or deploy for tactical purposes, accepted notions of individual rights, ideologies of motherhood or sexual morality may prove more successful within the confines of the trial and in pressing for legal reforms (Smart, 1990a, 1992b). Thus the more 'reasonable'[3] the feminist argument or the more it deploys certain conventional tenets, the more it may become influential.

Thus work like Butler's, should it be used in the legal forum, would almost certainly be treated as incomprehensible. On the other hand Radical Feminist or Cultural Feminist work may have more of a purchase because it does not challenge common-sense notions of sexual and gender difference, it merely wishes to rearrange them. Equally, lobby politics requires immediately comprehensible demands. It hardly seems appropriate therefore to challenge too extensively the doxic experience of judges and policy makers. The field of law therefore poses substantial problems for a feminist intervention which is influenced by poststructuralist thinking on matters of sex, gender and sexuality. As I have 'confessed' above I do not have a solution to this, instead I wish to explore these issues in relation to two areas of concern. The first is rape which has long been a focus of feminist work. The second is S/M sexuality which has more recently figured in feminist writing and practice but which, in Britain, recently became a *cause célèbre* arising from the criminal prosecution of a group of S/M gays.

Specific instances: rape and S/M sex

Rape, violence and masculine sexuality

Feminist accounts of rape have broadly combined an element of biological explanation (men have the genitals and the physical power) with a critique of how boys/men are socialized into an aggressive heterosexuality which is a means of expressing masculine power (McIntosh, 1992). These accounts have developed in response to the predominant and conventional denial that rape constitutes a form of harm. When rape was seen as merely enthusiastic sex, the harms it generated were belittled and the activity itself treated by the courts as almost an acceptable pastime. In conceptually transforming rape from 'normal' heterosex into an act of violence, feminist work has reclaimed the harm it generates. Moreover, in linking rape with masculinity in general, feminism has captured the ubiquity of rape and challenged the assumption that only a few perverts 'really' rape.

This move to call rape violence has, however, had its critics. Mac-Kinnon (1987), for example, has eloquently argued that this move merely disguises the problem. She argues that the judiciary and the courts cannot distinguish between rape (violence) and consensual sex for the simple reason that under patriarchy consensual sex is a myth for women who do not have freedom of choice. For MacKinnon therefore all heterosex is rape and there can be no distinction. It is therefore entirely problematic to make this distinction because it denies the coercive nature of all heterosex.

At a more pragmatic level the equation of rape with violence is quite problematic in the British legal system. If there is violence done to a person the law presumes there will be some visible damage. Thus grievous bodily harm and actual bodily harm are linked to perceived physical injury. If there is no injury, as might occur with a slap or a push, this is treated as common assault. However, consent is a defence against the accusation of common assault just as it is in rape. So, for example, if one boarded a crowded bus and another passenger stood painfully on your foot, he/she would have the defence that in entering such a situation you knowingly took the risk of some harm. In many rape cases the fear of greater injury is enough to make many women submit and, as is well documented, she may have little in the way of bruises or cuts. Thus to call rape a simple assault, or even actual or grievous bodily harm, would do little for women who are already particularly vulnerable in rape trials because they do not have visible physical injuries.

The device of calling rape violence is therefore useful in symbolic argument. Indeed it is part of the discursive redefinition of sexual abuse. However, transporting it into the legal forum may be far more problematic. If we want to deal with more 'subtle' coercions we need to think of ways in which these can be made visible rather than calling all rape assault. Moreover, as Howe (1987) has argued, while feminism may wish to identify and name certain harms this is a far cry from saying that there should be a (criminal) law against it or that legal reform can/should meet the problem.

It may also be the case that the simple association of rape and sexual abuse with a masculinity which is acquired through a process of socialization is problematic in a number of ways. First, masculinity is not a unitary thing although feminist writings on rape often assume that it is homogeneous, transcultural and transhistorical. Second, the concept of socialization seems an inadequate one when dealing with sexual desire, orientation and identity. Any analysis of sexuality which ignores the unconscious and which fails to recognize the complex interplay between psychic, bodily and social elements in the production of sexuality (even sexuality which manifests itself as violence) is at risk of supposing that all men are 'naturally' heterosexual and all women likewise. Studies on lesbian and gay sexuality and re-evaluations of psychoanalysis have at least pointed out that the process of acquisition of identity and orientation is complex and possibly never 'finished'. Only if we assert that rape is nothing whatever to do with sexuality can we really ignore these issues. Acknowledging that rape is power manifested through sexual behaviour still requires some understanding of this avenue of articulation. We still need to explain how men's and women's bodies are heterosexualized in order to have some insight into this particular manifestation. Moreover, laying rape at the door of early masculine socialization ignores completely questions of 'choice' of erotic subject, and also fails to distinguish between sexual fantasy and enactment. 'Choice' is, of course, an inadequate term, but it does allow for agency. In so doing we can also think in terms of men's responsibilities for the sexual behaviour in question – a responsibility which socialization models tend to overlook. The issue of fantasy also poses certain problems and in feminist work has been explored mostly in relation to the question of pornography. But, put simply, feminists have had to confront the knowledge that many women have rape fantasies, but in doing so have pointed out that this work of the imagination is quite different from inviting a real rape or making false accusations of rape. Yet if men have rape fantasies these are usually taken as an empirical proof of the incipient sexual violence embedded in masculinity. Ironically this is perhaps what judges and juries also do. They see the sexual behaviour of men as a reflection of what men 'are' – and thus excuse it. Some feminists have seen it as a reflection of what men 'are' too – and have condemned it. But perhaps what we need is to deconstruct what men are and to look more enquiringly into the many forms of masculine heterosexuality.

Such enquiries do not abandon the anger that many rightly feel about the abuse of both rape and the rape trial. But perhaps this anger should be directed less at masculinity as if it were some un-differentiated blanket problem and more towards questions of values and responsibilities. This, of course, is precisely what is happening in the area of feminist ethics (see Code, 1988; Tronto, 1989; Sevenhuij-sen, 1991). Building critically on the work of Gilligan (1982) more feminists are exploring a positional and situated ethics which allows for the diversity of experience without abandoning moral principles. Thus in the field of sexuality we might wish to think in terms of a responsibility not to harm which could take into account the struc-tural location of different subjects. Contained within such a formu-lation could be the idea that in cases of rape the accused must show that the woman actively consented, not simply that she submitted. Such formulation also allows for the incidence of female sexual abuse, typically against children, but also against men at times. The problem with formulating sexual abuse as an outcome of masculine sexuality has been the denial of sexual abuse by women. The location of 'bad' sexuality with the homogeneous masculine has meant that women have been denied any responsibility for their own harmful behaviour. Women's (sexual) violence has perhaps been feminism's 'best kept secret' and we need to develop further the means of analysing it rather than denying it.

I do not think that in order to make the case that rape is a bad thing, or to argue that the rape trial is a sick parody of justice from the varying perspectives of women who endure it, we need to construct a monolithic masculinity, especially where this entity is so immune to differences of class and race. It is perhaps time, therefore, to allow some of the understandings on issues of sex, gender and sexuality that have developed elsewhere to filter into our discussions on rape. If we begin to incorporate discussions of feminist ethics we need not fear that this would mean we excuse rapists, nor need we fear that the specific abuses of women's bodies/sexualities need be submerged into a general morass of violence. The idea that the category of woman is constructed does not mean that 'real' women (as historically consti-tuted) do not walk the social landscape. As Butler argues, 'To claim that gender is constructed is not to assert its illusoriness or arti-ficiality, where those terms are understood to reside within a binary that counterposes the "real" and the "authentic" as oppositional' (1990: 32). Thus *we* are not natural, but *we* are real. *We* are also constituted as more than just women; *we* have more than our gender. While there is still a need to avoid falling back into what Butler calls the totalizing gesture of feminism, it does still mean that in struggle with powerful discursive mechanisms such as the law on rape, we can continue to operate with the category of woman – but in the recog-nition that certain political situations require the articulation of apparently naïve categories which have greater significance/depth when subjected to a feminist reading or which should not be presented so naïvely outside the confines of legal 'engagement'.

S/M sexuality

S/M sexuality has, as Ardill and O'Sullivan (1986) have put it, upset the applecart of many feminist assumptions about female/lesbian sexuality. Coming to visibility at about the same time as the 're-emergence' of butch-femme lesbianism these forms of sexuality were greeted by many feminists as virtually atavistic instances of patriarchy's grip on women's sexuality and sexual fantasies. S/M and butch-femme were seen as appalling imitations of heterosexuality in which women who assumed they were expressing some kind of sexual freedom were actually enacting patriarchal indoctrination and undermining the advances made by the Women's Movement. Sado-masochists were seen as appropriating the symbolic dress and paraphernalia of male power and giving credibility to male violence. Femmes were not seen as 'real' lesbians, but women who wanted to sit on the fence and still benefit from the privileges of heterosexual identity (see Morgan, 1993). Joan Nestle (1981) did much to challenge these readings of butch-femme, while S/M lesbianism has been defended against 'literal' readings of theatrical enactments of sexual fantasies by feminists who have argued that lesbianism is actually about sexual desire and lust as opposed to so-called vanilla sex or the virtual celibacy of women-orientated lesbianism.[4]

I do not want to rehearse these arguments here but I do want to pick up on the question of theatrical or stylized enactments of sexual fantasies. As Segal (1992) has argued, much feminist work on sexual fantasies (which is usually a sub-theme to a broader discussion of pornography, rape or S/M) assumes that sexual fantasies are ideologies which are, in turn, controlled or somehow directed by the Patriarchy. Moreover, fantasies are seen as ideas (on the conscious level) which precede action (at least in men) or which establish the extensiveness of patriarchal codes of heterosexuality. In disputing this, and in giving examples of fantasies which are clearly not simply reflections of a political consciousness, Segal argues:

> Such fantasies do not express ideological wobbles in political outlook, but rather have an authentic, autonomous psychic existence of some considerable complexity. . . . For pornography has no straightforward connection with what would be presumed to be its 'real-life' enactment. (1992: 71)

Segal goes on to argue that it is necessary to use psychoanalytic insights into the nature of the psychic, but is, at the same time, wary of abandoning the social context in which the psychic develops. She does not really address the problem of the idea of the autonomy of the psyche and its presumed relation to the social, since if it is truly autonomous the wider social context can hardly be relevant. But she is at least struggling with the complexity of sexual fantasy rather than simply seeing it as a quasi-conscious manifestation of patriarchal ideology.

Feminist work writing on S/M has been concerned mainly with lesbian S/M where it has latterly been hailed as a potentially gender bending, political and subversive behaviour. Less has been written on heterosexual S/M (commercial or otherwise) or on gay male S/M. However Anne McClintock (1993) has recently written on heterosexual S/M and Loretta Loach (1992) on heterosexual women's use of pornography including some S/M. Their research disturbs feminist orthodoxies about sexual practices. Loach for example found 'ordinary' women who used S/M porn and played both submissive and dominant roles in their sexual behaviour. What does not fit with the feminist orthodoxy is that these women controlled the sexual activities they were involved in. They were apparently aware of the issue of power, especially the power of men when women were submissive, but they argued that they could swap roles, or they controlled the enactment of the fantasies. This is a point that McClintock makes as well. She argues that in S/M sexual activity the submissive partner is in control. She points to the elaborate setting up of scenarios and the careful limits placed on activities. Moreover, she focuses on commercial heterosexual S/M which is overwhelmingly a 'service' provided by women for men who wish to be submissive. Without wishing to read too much political meaning into such acts, the idea that men pay money to be submissive, to be beaten, to be treated as a domestic or sexual slave or even to be ignored, does pose a problem for orthodox thinking about male sexual orientation. In being submissive such men do not give up control since they can stop the action at any time, so clearly S/M does not mean that men give themselves up to the power of women. Moreover, the S/M convention that submissiveness is associated with women's dress, underwear or domestic and household cleaning activities hardly seems to signify the hidden social power of women. But that men do desire to be dominated, no matter how safely, does pose a conundrum for conventional ideas that male power leads to the simple and straight-forward sexual domination of women.

This brings me to the specifics of an important show trial which went through the crown court, the Court of Appeal and finally the House of Lords between 1990 and 1993 in England.[5] The case involved a number of gay men who were into S/M. These men would meet at various times for S/M sessions over a period of at least 10 years. At some stage they began to video some of the sessions and, although these were never meant for commercial sale, one fell into the hands of the police who decided to prosecute the men. For various technical legal reasons the police could not charge the men with the most obvious offence which would have been under the 1967 Sexual Offences (Amendment) Act. This legislation legalized consensual homosexuality between men over the age of 21 years, where it occurred in private and where no more than two persons were present. As this was not open to the Crown Prosecution Service and, as it was clear that the videos were only for personal use, there remained only minor offences with which to charge the men, for example running a brothel (disorderly house). The Crown Prosecution Service therefore reached for sections 20 and 40 of the 1861 Offences Against the Person Act. These sections concerned, respectively unlawful wounding and assault/assault occasioning actual bodily harm.

Before discussing this case and its significance I wish to pause to speculate on how some versions of feminist thought on sexuality and law might deal with this situation. I also want to revisit some of the ethical issues I raised in the previous section on rape. If the dominant feminist response to S/M has been a certain repugnance and an argument that it merely enacts male power in a sexual situation then, notwithstanding that the 'submissive' partner was a man, presumably this behaviour would be condemned and use of the criminal law sanctioned. If the sexuality enacted in the scenarios was really only a ruse for power (torture), or even a way of excusing the violence, then the prison sentences handed down to the men would seem appropriate.

The men claimed, however, that the submissive partner consented and indeed that he/they gave very fulsome consent. For many feminists this does pose a problem because it has been argued (rightly in my view) that consent is important in cases of sexual abuse, but that consent should be active consent and not just submission. In this case there was active consent so presumably the men should be acquitted unless we ignore the sexual element altogether and redesignate S/M as serious violence not sex, in which case consent would be immaterial.

The MacKinnon approach might be different. We could imagine that just as she has extended her concerns over the harm of pornography caused to men when they are depicted in submissive ways, she might argue that this consent was no real consent because, by extension from the patriarchal model, men put in the position of women cannot be said to consent. Through such logic the consent issue could be dismissed and the men found guilty.

If, however, we were to allow that S/M is a manifestation of diverse sexualities which, according to an ethical feminism we *might* recognize as legitimate, how then should we respond? We could hardly say that lesbian S/M or heterosexual S/M is permissible, but not gay S/M. On the other hand it is clear that even the recognition of diversity would not mean that feminism would have to proclaim child sexual abuse, paederasty or any form of sexuality to be legitimate. Clearly issues of responsibility, harm (including social harm), privacy and consent would be crucial. Privacy and consent are, of course, particularly problematic concepts for laws on sexuality. We know that privacy has been very narrowly drawn in legal precedent in England and Wales. It has been used against gay men by, for example, insisting that only two men can be in an apartment when 'sex' occurs. So having a friend to sleep over if you are a gay couple could be a criminal offence. Equally it has been used against prostitutes because windows and doorways are deemed to be public space thus restricting women's access to an actual private sphere where the criminal law may not reach. Conversely feminists have argued that the notion of privacy is precisely what has prevented the criminal law from entering the domestic sphere to deal with male violence or child sexual abuse. It is therefore a flawed concept. But I would argue that in the current climate of repression against gay and lesbian sexuality and given the reassertion of the dominance of heterosexuality, we still need to define a private space which, if not absolutely inviolate, does prevent the criminal law exercising its remit overzealously.

Consent is equally problematic for the reasons I have already outlined. It might also seem uncomfortable in the context of poststructuralist thought where the individual has been banished and with him/her presumably the ability to consent also. However, as I also argued above, banishing the concept of the individual does not banish agency. Choices can be made, even if they are not under conditions of our own making (and they never are). Unless we are to deny women any agency we need to acknowledge that they (we) make decisions. We can then consider how coercive the specific circumstances might have been. It would be a mistake, for example, to ignore the powerful assertions made by women in the sex industry on precisely this issue (see Roberts, 1986; Roberts and Roberts, 1986). Some feminisms, I would suggest, have lost credibility by assuming that such women are cultural dupes just waiting to be saved or to see the light.

The concepts of responsibility and harm are perhaps no less contentious. Under the heading of social harm no doubt many of our existing judiciary would like to claim that homosexuality should be recriminalized, especially in the climate of homophobic concerns about AIDS. But it is of course impossible to produce moral codes like laundry lists which will meet every foreseen and unforeseen eventuality before it occurs. And in any case all discursive struggle takes places within an already existing set of assumptions, we never start with a blank sheet on which to write our codes and launch our practice. The point about a feminist ethics is not that it always knows what the outcome should be, nor that it has an exhaustive list of prohibitions, but that it should be able to introduce arguments which have been ignored or trivialized heretofore. What then would this mean for R v Brown?

In R v Brown (see note 5) all the defendants who were charged with offences against the person were found guilty and sentenced to imprisonment for up to four and a half years. On appeal these sentences were reduced but their convictions under the 1861 Act were not quashed. (The House of Lords' decision was not unanimous though and two of the five Law Lords dissented.) Lord Templeman, who gave the leading decision did not hide his sense of repulsion against homosexuality and S/M. His judgement mingled themes of cruelty, perversions, drugs, AIDS, corruption of youth, and the naming of 'forbidden' parts of the body. Such loathing is, perhaps, to be expected, but more surprising was his assertion that the case was really not about sex but about violence. It was almost as if a feminist were speaking about rape – although no judge has, to my knowledge, uttered these sentiments in cases of non-consensual sexual abuse of women.

> There was no evidence to support the assertion that sado-masochist activities are essential to the happiness of the appellants or any other participants but the argument would be acceptable if sado-masochism were only concerned with sex, as the appellants contend. In my opinion sado-masochism is not only concerned with sex. Sado-masochism is also concerned with violence. The evidence discloses that the practices of the appellants were unpredictably dangerous and degrading to body and mind and were developed with increasing barbarity and taught to persons whose *consents were dubious or worthless*.[6]

Treating the activities as violence meant that Templeman could dismiss the relevance of consent (he obviously thought that the people involved were not capable of consenting anyway) since consent is broadly no defence to physical injury of a certain degree. Of course there are many exceptions to this rule. These include male contact sports, professional boxing, surgery and so on. For Templeman and two other Law Lords these other activities were either 'manly' (and hence uplifting) or socially desirable.

Templeman also used a social harm argument. He claimed that

such activities could cause the spread of AIDS and that they could get 'out of hand' and cause even more serious injury. The fact that neither of these things happened was, he argued, irrelevant since potential harm was just as important. Finally he argued that it would be against the public interest for the House of Lords to declare homosexual sadomasochistic activities lawful. In the tradition of judge-made law he, with two others, therefore pronounced gay S/M unlawful and subject to the criminal provisions of the 1861 Act.

Without doubt this decision, unless overruled by the European Court or by Act of Parliament, can now be extended to heterosexual S/M and lesbian S/M. Consent will be no defence. This judgement occurred within weeks of a case where the Director of Public Prosecution was contemplating the prosecution of two gay men who, in their struggle to lower the age of consent for gay men from 21 to 16 years in line with the rest of Europe, admitted that they had had sex together when they were under the legal age limit. It also occurred in the context of the infamous Clause 28, which actually became S2(a) of the Local Government Act 1986 which asserts that,

A local authority shall not –
  (a) intentionally promote homosexuality or publish material with the intention of promoting homosexuality;
  (b) promote the teaching in any maintained school of the acceptability of homosexuality as a pretended family relationship.

Finally it was followed in August 1993 by the latest Papal encyclical Veritatis Splendor which reasserts that only reproductive sexual activity is morally acceptable (*The Guardian*, 16 August 1993).

Under such social conditions the dismissal of consent and the translation of a form of gay sexuality from sex into violence in R v Brown takes on particularly significant meanings for anyone not solely committed to heterosexual activities.

I raised the question earlier of how a feminist ethics might respond to R v Brown. In the first instance I think it would be necessary to consider the nature of the harm involved and whether it merited the intervention of either the civil law or the criminal law. In this specific case Lord Mustill who dissented made it plain that he thought the Crown Prosecution Service simply wanted to find some way of prosecuting the men and so stretched an existing piece of legislation to try to cover a situation with which it was never meant to deal (that is, sexuality as opposed to violence). He argued that if there was a need for a law to cover gay S/M sexual activity then Parliament should so decide (that is, through the democratic process). While being sceptical of this as an example of democracy at work, the idea of opening the issue up to wider debate was clearly significant.

Moreover, in his judgement one learns more about the harms done to the defendants, all of whom had lost their jobs and one of whom had become seriously ill. Moreover, he pointed out that although some of their activities might have been criminal (such as, the disorderly house element) it was not at all clear that consensual S/M was in fact criminal behaviour at the time they engaged in it.

In this case none of the men suffered any lasting injury and the harm that was caused was entered into willingly. So the harm element does not seem great. In terms of social harm it would be difficult to argue against S/M sex unless one knew it was more likely to cause serious injury or to generate violence in general than, for example, football matches or boxing contests. Arguably corporal punishment in private schools which is non-consensual could be said to be more socially harmful. The point is that although one might find arguments against S/M, once the consent point is allowed to stand, it is always possible to find far more problematic behaviours which are entirely lawful and where a feminist ethics might prefer to start.

A feminist ethic would, in any case, need to be alert to the issue of diversity and to the social harm produced by a judgement which would feed into an existing harmful homophobia. Finally the question of responsibility would be met in terms of ensuring there was no coercion and that the participants took care of each other. This was manifestly the case in R v Brown as the participants went to extreme measures to ensure a hygienic environment and that no infections could be passed on.

The Brown decision has left Britain with a law on sexuality which states – symbolically at least – that when women say No to rape they mean Yes, but when men say Yes to homosexual sex they mean No. It is ironic that feminist arguments directed at the problem of rape and intended to help women who are victims, seem to have been taken up to be used against a group of homosexual men (and potentially in future against lesbians too). This could not have been predicted but it should alert us to the problems inherent in imagining that law is a tool we can simply refashion or from attempting to bring into law (whether civil or criminal law) matters we regard as social harms but which might be better dealt with by other strategies.

Conclusion

In Britain there is a sense that there is a closure of options for subversive sexualities. Some of this perceived closure relates to feminist campaigns such as those on pornography in which it is feared that legal censorship will become an acceptable mode of regulating the issue (Segal and McIntosh, 1992; Gibson and Gibson, 1993).

Other elements relate to government legislation, judge-made law or media hysteria over AIDS. All of these developments have had particularly problematic consequences for gay men and lesbians. More recently the issue of the gay gene has led to discussions of eugenic solutions to the 'problem' of male homosexuality (lesbians are excluded still). Meanwhile areas such as rape or child sexual abuse seem impervious to legal reform. Sue Lees's recent study of rape cases in London suggests that the way in which the courts deal with rape can hardly be said to have improved since Adler carried out and published her important study of the Old Bailey in 1987 (Adler, 1987; Lees, 1993).

At the same time, however, sexuality has become a site of political resistance and diversity has been productive of many different accounts of the meaning of sexuality. The idea that heterosexuality is simply patriarchy in the bedroom is no longer so easily asserted and shifting definitions of power have meant that feminist writing has acknowledged that women are more than sexual doormats.

These issues remain highly contentious and we should not lose sight of the ways in which sexuality can operate as a conduit of power, through which power accumulated in other spheres (such as, economic, physical) can be exercised. In the field of law feminist work has to be especially careful in that in identifying problematic practices or even harmful practices, invoking the law may merely introduce a new set of problems rather than solutions. The struggle between anti-pornography feminists and anti-censorship feminists articulates these difficulties well. Other areas such as rape are obviously not focused on whether we should introduce criminal sanctions, since we already have these. The discussions are therefore less hypothetical, but also more constrained by the fear of saying anything which will confirm existing prejudices against raped women or which could contribute in any way to facilitating the already high rate of failure in convictions for rape.

The opportunity to compare the legal response to rape and to consensual gay S/M is instructive. In rape even the bruises and physical injuries sustained are typically subordinated to an understanding of the event as one of sexual passion, notwithstanding that neither aspects were consensual. In S/M the sexual gratification is subordinated to the physical harm, not withstanding that the latter was consensual.[7] It is hard to avoid concluding that the court's response to such cases embodies a tolerance of non-consensual heterosex and a continuing desire to sanction consensual homosexual sex. But these instances also draw our attention to the kind of analysis we have been using in the field of rape which focus almost exclusively on the question of gender rather than sexuality. The focus on gender has – rightly – put both masculinity and power in the frame of analysis. It also imported the crucial idea that masculinity is constructed and thus not immutable. But this focus has sidestepped the problem of sexuality, especially common-sense views that sexuality arises out of biological sex, and that both are immutable and unchanging. Thus judges continue to utter appalling statements about women or children who are raped while excusing men's heterosexual urges. On the other hand homosexuality and lesbianism are still regarded as unnatural.

Deconstructing such beliefs could never be easy, but it is my view that feminist work has not really focused on this anyway because of the lurking similarity between the judicial view and some feminist views, namely that men have basic urges. Although it is held that these can be restrained by the gloss of either civilization (if you are a judge) or socialization (if you are a feminist) these urges will leak through because men are men. Of course in being critical of this lurking essentialism I am not suggesting that feminism gives up its aspirations. As Ferguson states, 'In a world made by and for solid subjects (more accurately, by and for those who believe themselves to be solid subjects), the pull of competing fragments and partial affiliations can be uncomfortable' (1993: 163). It can be more than uncomfortable if it seems that feminism is giving up trying to change the social order to improve the position of women. But this is where feminist ethics or values are so vital. Again to quote Ferguson, 'Mobile subjectivities need not be cavalier about responsibilities to themselves, other persons, or the earth' (1993: 166). Indeed her point is that such subjectivities may care a great deal about such things. Feminist ethics will not be a panacea but they provide a forum for debating what is important to feminism, particularly in the field of sexuality, when our old solid and stable identities of sexuality and gender are increasingly challenged and where even the sexed body may not provide a refuge for the uncertainties that are currently being expressed.

Notes

This chapter was originally published in the *Canadian Journal of Law and Society*, 1994, 9(1): 1–23.

1   We must, of course, be aware that little is secured permanently and that even splendid achievements are not necessarily totally good nor do they benefit everyone for whom they were originally designed.

2   These presumed consequences are, of course, as yet unknown whilst, ironically, the failings of traditional politics are well documented.

3   By 'reasonable' I mean here an argument which fits with legal reasoning – which may not be reasonable at all by any other standards!

4 See Merck (1993) and Ardill and O'Sullivan (1986) for examples of this argument. But also see Linden et al. (1982) for the opposing view.
5 R v Brown and Others (1992) 94 Cr.App.R. C.A. 302; R v Brown and other appeals [1993] 2 All E R H.L. 75. The original criminal trial was held in December 1990 at the Central Criminal Court and was unreported.
6 Lord Templeman in R v Brown [1993] 2 All E R H.L. 75 at 82.
7 Heterosexual S/M has rarely been a matter for the courts and even where it has been an obvious component of commercial sex in the form of torture instruments or descriptions of services offered, such elements have tended to produce mirth rather than specific criminal proceedings on assault.

PART III

FEMINIST THEORY AND LAW

Introduction

The papers in this part span 10 years of theorizing the relationship between law, feminism and women. There is no attempt to offer a single theory, however, and the papers can hardly be said to constitute a progression towards a perfected or well refined position on law. Instead each chapter presents a moment of grappling with ideas or with critical comment from other feminists as I have sought to understand the issues in the light of newly formulated concepts within the broader scope of feminist thought. There is development here – or at least change. However, the most profound issue seems to be the recurrence of one particular theme, namely the puzzle over the relationship between feminist theory and questions of practice, policy and/or politics. This is an issue which undoubtedly defeats resolution, but it is indicative of a core to much feminist work which is committed to social change and reflects a dissatisfaction with how the social world is gendered.

The first chapter in this part, Chapter 8, was originally the first chapter of *The Ties That Bind* published in 1984. This introductory chapter was a very clear statement of the need for feminist work in this field to go beyond both conspiracy theories of law and those which seek to construct grand theories of patriarchy and law. It argues against seeing law as a unitary category which serves the interest of men and in favour of theories which are grounded in the detail of everyday experience rather than in the metatheories of capitalism and patriarchy. In rereading this chapter, I can see that a number of issues that have come to preoccupy me in the 1990s are prefigured. However, the chapter still hints at a fairly straightforward relationship between feminist theory and practice, even though I seem to see no need to spell this out. These issues were perhaps far too readily taken for granted at that time and there was still the hint of a belief in the efficacy of programmes of reform which could be implemented by a benevolent welfare state.

Chapter 9 refines some of the ideas sketched out in the preceding chapter by using the conceptual vehicle of the 'uneven development of law' which suggests that legal reforms do not always produce the changes most desired and that reforms in certain areas may hamper developments elsewhere because of unpredictable changes in the economic base, employment levels, and so on. In some ways this chapter aims to sustain a commitment to engagement with law at a time of considerable disillusionment. It argues that law, or the social context in which law operates, may transform feminist policies into very inadequate interventions on behalf of women. But it also points to achievements, opportunities and possible developments. In this chapter there is a suggestion that the shift away from a simple focus on the content of legislation, or even away from the wider but abstract question of law's relationship to patriarchy, towards a new concentration on feminist jurisprudence, might open new avenues of engagement. In any event, there is no questioning the commitment to treating law as a site of struggle.

Chapter 10 on feminist jurisprudence provides an intellectual map or chronology as seen through my own, latterly somewhat critical, perspective on a form of theorizing which I thought might hold some promise at the end of Chapter 9. This chapter outlines in detail the growth of this alternative jurisprudence, organized under four headings or categorizations which I deploy in order to em-phasize the main concerns and epistemological groundings of each strand. I argue that this mode of theorizing develops largely from feminist academic lawyers and largely from the USA. Undoubtedly part of my dissatisfactions with the route that this theorizing has taken derives precisely from its lack of sociological insight and its tendency to reify law – or at least to presume it should have a central place in the proper ordering of civil society. While being critical, much feminist jurisprudence none the less seems to depict law as an eventual solution for women and it is this that I find ultimately so problematic.

By the time I published 'The Woman of Legal Discourse' in1992, it was clear that the work of feminist theory in law could not be simply to interrogate law, legal practice and legal thought, but also to interrogate itself. Feminist legal thought had a history which could be commented upon and built upon. This chapter attempts to do both of these things, and self-consciously argues that each stage of feminist legal thinking stands on the shoulders of work that has gone before. This chapter is not intended to jettison earlier modes of theorizing law, but to see how new ways of conceptualizing have become possible. To do this I create a typology of theoretical explanations moving from accounts that emphasize the idea that law is sexist, to the idea that law is male, to the idea that law is gendered. Finally I propose that we see law as a technology of gender. By this I mean that law is a discourse which brings the gendered subject into being. I suggest that such a theoretical approach allows us to start asking very different questions about law and also allows us to develop a rather different kind of politics around law. This is asserted rather than developed, however, because the chapter concludes with a case study in the legal discursive construction of Woman, namely, the lone mother. This case study aims to map the construction of the unmarried mother as destabilizer of the conjugal family, and to show how this lone mother does not exist 'in' society waiting for law to inflict policies on her. Rather she is actually brought into being by law (among other discourses, of course, although I think that law is one of the most powerful in this case). The aim of this case study is therefore to do a poststructuralist analysis rather than to comment on such an analysis. I have stressed in Chapter 1 that the attraction of poststructuralism for me is that it does not only comment on epistemologies and ontologies – but that it reads the documents, talks to the subjects, analyses discourses, views representations, denaturalizes concrete bodies and so on (see pp. 8–9). In this section of Chapter 11 I begin this process in one small area.

The final chapter in this part takes up again – this time quite directly – the question of theory and practice. This was written very much as an answer to my many critics who announced that I had abandoned my commitment to feminist politics and that I seemingly refused to engage with law any longer. I attempt to argue that a shift towards postmodern/poststructuralist feminism (see Chapter 1 for a note on the problems with these terms) need not mean the abandonment of either politics or ethics. It is, however, perhaps inevitable that my defence should have materialized more as an attack on alternative feminist positions, in particular standpoint feminism. But if the chapter betrays an irritation, this is possibly not such a bad thing. I am irritated now by certainties and also by the belief in progress. It is perhaps impossible to live in the North of Europe and be unaware of regress and of the undoing of things once thought of as immutable. Just as my work in the mid-1980s was undoubtedly influenced by the consequences of there being a reactionary, dogmatic Conservative Government in power, so my work in the 1990s is influenced by arguments from postmodernist thinking and the actual dismemberment of welfare states and the very political foundations of second wave feminism. Chapter 12 is an attempt to hold on to a politics linked to a feminist ethics, without having to depict politics solely in terms of programmes of reform or in terms of legal rights. While acknowledging that there is still some mileage in these forms of politics (because politics are still *articulated* in these terms) I am convinced that we need to be less punitive towards forms of engagement which do not conform to this style. This chapter ultimately suggests that we need to be prepared to be committed to a feminism without certainties and without guarantees, and that on that basis we can still engage.

8

Legal Regulation or Male Control?

It is part of the feminist intellectual and political tradition to address itself to the nature, form and content of legislation and legal structures. The history of the nineteenth-century feminist movement from Frances Power Cobbe, Josephine Butler, Caroline Norton and Harriet Taylor reveals the extent to which women and feminist groups have identified the law as a major source of women's oppression and have tried to use the law to improve the material and social position of women both in the family and wider society. While it is clear that the law at the end of the twentieth century is far from identical to the law at the turn of the nineteenth century when so many well-known feminists were most active, it is a central proposition in this book [Smart, 1984] that law is and should remain a major focus of feminist concerns.

It may now seem 'self-evident' why early feminists were concerned about the law. After all during the nineteenth century women were denied the franchise and were denied access to the professions and other well-paid occupations; in addition married women were not generally entitled to own their own property and they had no rights of custody over their own children. It is unnecessary to list all the legal ills that faced women at this time (Reiss, 1934; Sachs and Wilson, 1978) but we should recognize how extensive they were and how hard women had to struggle against them to achieve a modicum of reform. Certain reforms were achieved, however, and so it is perhaps less 'self-evident' now why law should still be argued to constitute a major feature of women's oppression. It may seem quite misguided after the efforts of Lord Denning in the 1950s (who was then referred to as a champion of married women's rights) and after the creation of legislation like the Equal Pay Act 1970, the Sex Discrimination Act 1975 or the Abortion Act 1967. Although it may be conceded that none of these recent reforms are perfect it undoubtedly appears to many that the law is 'trying' to improve the position of women; it is much better than it was in the nineteenth century and even appears to be trying to right past wrongs. In this ideological climate it is quite difficult to sustain a critique of law which has wide support when contemporary criticism is not just concerned with the fact that recent reforms are not working adequately – although they clearly are not – but goes beyond this to argue that the law itself reproduces and perpetuates the most secure foundations of patriarchal relations, namely the family and gender divisions. The critique of law that has developed in the last decade has been more far-reaching and more radical than the vast majority of early feminist critiques, and this in spite of the enactment of legal reforms that once would have delighted nineteenth-century feminists.

This recognition of the changing form of feminist critiques of law is not intended as a criticism of early feminists but rather as an indication of how experience has taught that many hard-won legal reforms have actually achieved little in transforming the social order. The Abortion Act of 1967 was a massive improvement on the law prior to that date but it did not give women the right to determine their own reproductive capacity. Such powers are retained by the medical profession; the law simply allows that profession to act benevolently. We have also learned that introducing more women into the legal profession (although there are still very few in proportion to men) or into the ranks of the legislature has not in itself produced any major shifts in public and legal policies. Necessarily, therefore, it has been essential to look more critically at the law to establish how radical demands are transformed into occasions for niggardly benevolence and to raise questions of whether criticisms of the content of law or the constitution of the judiciary and legal profession are really enough. Clearly it would be foolhardy to ask or expect of the law that it should transform itself and the rest of the social order into an epitome of a feminist or socialist state; not only does the law not stand in that sort of relationship with the economic and social order but it is unlikely to be willing to divest itself of its powers. This is of course to depict the issues in very vulgar and simplified terms because the law is not reducible to an object in the world which *has* power. It is a form of the exercise of power and women themselves can use this power. However, before moving on to discuss the nature of law it is important to make the point here that we must have limited expectations of legal reforms and that while formulating radical demands it is vital to know how the law can resist and transform these. It is equally important to envisage ways in which the formal structure of law can be modified so that radical demands are not always deflected or absorbed. Short of some sudden and dramatic transformation of the social order this must be regarded as a long-term process whose outcome is by no means certain.

The purpose of this book is therefore to examine the relationship between law and women's oppression. This oppression takes many forms; it is evident in the education system, in waged labour, in the media, in politics, in the welfare state, in fact it is endemic to society (Mitchell and Oakley, 1976; Wilson, 1977; Barrett, 1980; Roberts, 1981; Coote and Campbell, 1982; Randall, 1982). However it is beyond the scope of this work to deal with every aspect of this oppression and instead I will concentrate on the private or domestic sphere and the relations of reproduction inside the household. My main focus is therefore the 'family' and my reason for giving priority to this ideological cultural and economic domain is outlined in the subsequent section on patriarchy. It is only necessary to clarify here that I recognize that the concept 'family' is not a neutral or purely descriptive term. It is not a description of households, it is far more ideologically constituted than that. As Barrett and McIntosh (1982) have argued,

> It should be remembered that the currently dominant model of the family is not timeless and culture-free. ... This hegemonic family form is a powerful ideological force that mirrors in an idealized way the characteristics attributed to contemporary family life. *It has only a tenuous relation to co-residence and the organization of households as economic units.* (33–4, emphasis added)

But it is precisely because the family is this collection of ideological, cultural and economic factors, imbued with certain power relationships between family members and constantly idealized as the goal to which we should all aspire, that the term family is retained here. It is precisely this conglomeration that I wish to address. It will only be in the final chapter [in Smart, 1984] on policy that I shall introduce a deliberative shift towards the concept of the household.

Patriarchy and patriarchal relations

The concept of patriarchy has become controversial within feminist theory. Its meaning is frequently unclear and its relationship to capitalism has posed apparently intractable theoretical problems (Barrett, 1980; Randall, 1982). For these reasons I avoid the term patriarchy here, although terms such as 'patriarchal relations' or 'patriarchal structures' which I do use are obviously derived in some way from the concept of patriarchy. However such terms do not necessarily invoke a system with a concrete base, a particular mode of production or a rigid system of male domination. They imply a more fluid system, containing numerous contradictions and employing varying and various mechanisms and strategies in the exercise of power. Yet they still take patriarchy as a referent and so it is important, in the current climate, to justify their use through a brief discussion of the debate on patriarchy.

Central to this debate on patriarchy is the problem of definition. As

Beechey (1979) has shown, the meaning of patriarchy varies considerably according to the particular discourse within which it is located (that is, psychoanalysis, materialist feminism, revolutionary feminism). Consequently the debate is not a purely semantic one but one involving fundamental differences in approach to, and analysis of, sexual oppression. The concept of patriarchy poses the most severe problems for socialist or Marxist feminists precisely because the use of such a term is taken as involving the integration of Marxian theories with concepts derived from opposing, or simply different, discourses. There are two facets to this problem. One is that for socialist feminists patriarchy implies a concept that is usually constructed as transhistorical rather than as historically specific. Moreover, it is a term that usually implies the prioritizing of sexual oppression over class oppression while at the same time containing elements of a biological determinism or essentialism. All of these features are rejected or at least problematized by socialist feminists and in consequence there is a tendency to reject the term patriarchy altogether. Sheila Rowbotham's critique is one example of this rejection. She maintains:

> the word 'patriarchy' presents problems of its own. It implies a universal and historical form of oppression which returns us to biology. . . . By focusing upon the bearing and rearing of children . . . it suggests there is a single determining cause of women's subordination. (1979: 970)

The second facet of the problem is of a different order. Patriarchy is not rejected just because it has 'become associated' with particular analyses but because it is constituted *within* specific discourses and cannot be isolated and used in conjunction with concepts derived from elsewhere. The most critical attack on feminists who attempt this marriage of concepts comes from Cousins who argues:

> it is frequently the case that there is an impossible recourse to two 'materialisms'; on the one hand, the concept of patriarchy with its corresponding causality of cause as origin and on the other hand, a Marxist concept of social totality with its corresponding causality of determination in the last instance by the economic. In so far as they locate a different 'material basis' and do so through a different concept of determination, they cannot be coherently sustained as being complementary. (1978: 65)

Michèle Barrett has similarly been critical of such an enterprise, pointing out that although the concept of patriarchy is consistent within certain discourses it becomes problematic within an analysis of sexual oppression under capitalism. She states:

> It seems admissible in some contexts to refer to patriarchal ideology, describing specific aspects of male–female relations in capitalism, but as a noun the term 'patriarchy' presents insuperable difficulties to an analysis

that attempts to relate women's oppression to the relations of production
of capitalism. (1980: 19)

It may be that this formulation is not without problems inasmuch as it
seems to posit patriarchal ideology as something that can cross
discursive divides while the concrete version is so differently
constituted that it necessarily must remain within the discourse in
which it was originally formulated. This criticism aside, however,
both Cousins and Barrett have identified a problem inherent within
the rules of formal theory. I shall return to this point later, but firstly I
wish to look at one of the 'insuperable' difficulties referred to by
Barrett which is encountered in attempting to integrate feminist
concepts into Marxian discourse.

The most common theoretical problem encountered by socialist
feminism is the relationship between class and sexual oppression, or,
to put it differently, the relationship between the mode of production
and relations of reproduction. Having rejected the primacy of gender
relations the problem has become one of how to formulate an
analysis that either gives equal weighting to both, or more usually, to
theorize the way in which patriarchal relations are ultimately
subordinate to the mode of production, or determination by the
economic in the last instance. An example of the latter approach is
McDonough and Harrison's paper 'Patriarchy and relations of
production' (1978). In this paper they posit two separate structures of
oppression in which sexual oppression is subordinated to class
oppression. They argue, 'Though women are placed simultaneously
in two separate but linked structures, those of class and patriarchy, it
is their class position which limits the conditions of the forms of
patriarchy they will be objectively subjected to' (1978: 36). Moreover, they further subordinate relations of reproduction to the
relations of capitalist production by arguing that the former operates
to sustain the latter. For example, they state, 'Thus the natural and
material function of women to procreate for social use is transformed
into two economic functions necessary to perpetuate the social
relations of capitalist production' (1978: 34). This element of a
functionalist argument in which relations of reproduction are seen to
react to the needs of capital is evident elsewhere in the work of
socialist feminists. For example, Mary McIntosh, while rejecting the
concept of patriarchy as such, reproduces the same problem inherent
in understanding the relationship between gender relations and
capitalist relations in her analysis of the state. She argues, 'the state
can initiate or guide changes in the family household system in
relation to capital's need for the labour power of married women as
well as in relation to the reproduction of the class in general'

(1978: 279). Patriarchal relations are thereby understood to change according to modifications in the requirements of a separate or determining economic formation while women's experience of patriarchal relations are mediated by their position in this alternative material structure. This adherence to a determination by the economic in the last instance has meant that patriarchy or gender relations are always depicted as somehow contingent upon another essentially economic structure, and that relations of reproduction are afforded virtually no autonomy other than those characteristics which are derived historically from a period prior to capitalist development.

Having raised these problems and pointed to the difficulties of referring to a concept of patriarchy, however, I do not wish to suggest that these feminists are incorrect to subsume patriarchal relations to the mode of production. Neither is it my intention to try to develop an alternative theoretical model; rather I wish to shift the debate altogether away from the extremely formal terms in which it tends to be expressed. It is the way that correctness and incorrectness are at issue that is part of the problem that socialist feminists face. It might be useful to take an analogy to clarify this point. During the 1970s the domestic labour debate traversed similar ground. Feminists became preoccupied with the correct definitions of productive and unproductive labour, and of use and exchange value. Undoubtedly, as Kaluzynska (1980) argues, part of this process was an attempt to make feminist theory respectable by showing that it could be integrated into Marxist theory. It is also probable that the debate was entirely necessary in order that feminist theory could progress. But in retrospect it was a sterile debate which could not be resolved. The fact that housework was a valuable but unwaged activity was not ultimately affected by whether that value was synonymous with the concept of value as employed in Marxist analyses. Similarly with concepts like patriarchy or patriarchal relations, there seems little point in attempting to justify their use by 'fitting' them into alternative theoretical positions. But neither is the rejection of such concepts justified because they simply fail to 'fit'.

The evaluation of these terms must be judged on criteria other than whether or not they can be encompassed by Marxist theory. Moreover, if the criteria by which we evaluate the existence of, the relative influence or autonomy of, or the ideological versus material content of patriarchy are founded upon rigid rules of formal theory rather than on concrete analysis, then feminist analysis will become increasingly academic and removed from feminist politics. The theoretical problems that the concept patriarchy has posed for so many feminists might be more revealing of the inadequacy and inflexibility of dominant schools of thought rather than an inherent incorrectness in the range of ideas and experiences embraced by the concept. If the concept were to be abandoned, as some feminists would argue it should be, then feminist theory could be deprived of its major instrument of criticism against social, political and economic theories which exclude the category of women and ignore the special nature of their oppression. It would also remove a symbolic concept which has provoked major developments in theorizing and understanding women's oppression and which reflects the necessary autonomy of the women's movement in the political sphere. As Alexander and Taylor have argued, '[Patriarchy] has helped us to think about sexual division – which cannot be understood simply as a by-product of economic class relations or of biology, but which has an independent dynamic that will only be overcome by an independent feminist politics' (1980: 161). However, if patriarchy does come to constitute an obstacle to understanding the oppression of women then it should be modified, but its inadequacy as an explanatory concept should not be judged in terms of its failure to reside within a Marxist discourse nor because it has most usually been constructed in terms of a biological essentialist or a universalism.

To understand more adequately the specificity of women's oppression it might be useful to turn away from trying to integrate the monolithic structures of *capitalism* and *patriarchy* and instead to concentrate on concrete instances of gender domination and its interrelation with factors of race and class in specific instances. Although this approach may raise the problem of losing sight of the totality this is by no means inevitable and it avoids the overwhelming problem of striving to produce a general theory grounded in the epistemological foundations of entirely separate discourses (for example, Marxism and Psychoanalysis). Moreover, it is more likely to produce analysis of direct relevance to political action and strategy by the women's movement. In consequence the way in which patriarchal relations in the concrete are mediated or determined by, or are even determining of, features of a given mode of production can be analysed in their historical specificity rather than in terms of a generality that has no room for what Rowbotham has referred to as subtleties nor for contradictions.

I shall argue here that the 'family' constitutes one instance of the operation of patriarchal relations in the concrete. Indeed the 'family' can be identified as a focal point at which a range of oppressive practices meet. It is both an ideological and economic site of oppression which is protected from scrutiny by the very privacy that 'family life' celebrates. But the family has not been selected simply because it provides one such instance of sexual oppression but because the concept of patriarchy (with all its failings) has alerted us to the analytical and political centrality of the family for feminism. A major site of women's oppression has thus already been identified as centring on male domination over female sexuality and women's reproductive capacity (Rowbotham, 1973; McDonough and Harrison, 1978; Dally, 1982) as well as the organization of unwaged domestic labour in the family (Delphy, 1977; Bland et al., 1978; Mackintosh, 1979). Moreover, it has been shown to be necessary to comprehend these relations before attempting to understand women's position in the waged-labour market or elsewhere precisely because women are never independent of the domestic sphere, or as McDonough and Harrison term it, the relations of reproduction. In other words as waged workers women are still wives and mothers and even as single women they are potential wives and mothers. Women, as Mitchell (1975) has argued, are still primarily defined in terms of the kinship structure and not as individual workers who can 'freely' sell their labour power. Women do not negotiate on the labour market on the same terms as do men and to understand this difference their position within the kinship or family structure needs to be examined first. As McDonough and Harrison maintain,

> A wife's relation to capital is always a mediated one because of her primary responsibility to service the family: her relation to production is always mediated through her relation to her husband, precisely through the relation of human reproduction. (1978: 31)

This necessarily poses problems for orthodox materialist analysis of women's class position because it is not only the domestic labourer whose class position is allocated via her husband rather than by her direct relation to the means of production, but also the female wage-labourer who cannot operate 'freely' on the labour market. The undervaluation of female labour (waged and domestic), which is justified in terms of women's wages being merely 'pin-money' or the assumption that housework is not *real* work, is precisely a consequence of patriarchal relations within the family. Hence patriarchal relations are not confined to the domestic sphere, they spill over into all the other structures and institutions in society. For example the justification for treating girls differently from boys in the education system also points back to the domestic expectations attaching to girls. It is for this reason I shall argue that the relations of reproduction should be seen as central to any attempt to understand women's oppression in the present.

A woman's indirect relationship to the means of production does not only affect her class position and weaken her ability to negotiate for a wage on the same terms as men, it also makes her extremely vulnerable to the man she is married to or living with as he is, for the vast majority of women, her only access to a relatively decent living wage. Certainly it is increasingly difficult for a household with children to manage on one wage, but men are still generally paid a 'family wage' and women are still paid an average of only two-thirds of men's earnings (Snell et al., 1981; Coote and Campbell, 1982). Consequently women's inability to secure a decent wage in their own right combined with a domestic household organization which usually requires her for some period of her life, particularly when she is caring for young children, to limit her access to an income through the man she is living with, produces not only financial dependency but also extreme vulnerability. This vulnerability is hidden much of the time by the structure of the domestic economy, particularly the institution of housekeeping which can masquerade as a wage, or simply by the privacy of domestic life which obscures the extensiveness and special nature of the poverty suffered by women. The work of Jan Pahl (1980, 1982) has indicated quite clearly the relationship between male power in the family and the unequal distribution of the 'breadwinner's' wage among his dependants. The extent of the poverty of women and children is often not revealed until the family unit breaks down. It is at that point that men most often reveal their reluctance to support their dependants and when some women even begin to experience a higher standard of living on supplementary benefits than they ever did on their housekeeping (Marsden, 1969; Binney et al., 1981). But although family breakdown can raise the standard of living of some women because of their lack of access to the breadwinner's wage during the marriage, it can mean the converse for other women who have been able to live at a reasonable standard as long as they were married but who, on divorce, find themselves powerless to command a similar wage or salary level in their own right. It is at that point that the reality of their economic vulnerability becomes apparent. It is because the 'reality' of women's relationship with men inside the family is revealed at the stage of divorce or breakdown that research at this point provides so many insights into the nature of marriage and the family. At that point all privacy is denied to the family as the legal and welfare investigations begin. It is in fact astounding how quickly the private troubles of the family can become the public property of the legal profession and the welfare agencies. For the purposes of looking critically at the family this stage of transition from private to public is therefore a useful and revealing one. In particular the way in which law permits of and then processes divorce and legal separation provides a fascinating instance of law's relationship to the family and hence patriarchal relations.

Law and patriarchal relations

The nature of law and its relation to a given social formation is currently an issue of debate and enquiry, particularly within Marxist schools of thought (Hall et al., 1978; Hirst, 1979; Picciotto, 1979). However, such debates have consistently given priority to issues of social class and related economic and political forms of domination. Such analyses have not conceded the equal significance of sexual oppression to their general thesis.[1] The work of Bankowski and Mungham (1976) is one example of this problem. I do not wish to undervalue the usefulness of their forceful critique of the legal profession nor to query their argument about the growing extensiveness and domination of law over the lives of 'ordinary people'. However, it is clear that the authors only conceptualize ordinary people as men. This is not simply evidenced by their continual reference to men rather than men and women,[2] although this is an important indicator of their priorities, for example:

> We want a society where men can freely come together and decide how to run their lives. (p. xii)

> But one thing we know is this: law is an imperial code, it emasculates man by offering the solution of his problems to 'experts'; it reflects the professionalised society. The only way out is for men to seize their lives and transform themselves and the world. (p. xiii)

> We suggest . . . that many of the consequences of good intentions . . . have the effect not of widening the area of men's freedom but of compounding their domination. In other words, those who press forward claiming a solution to men's problems are, themselves, part of those problems. (p. 81)

However it is not just that their reference to men excludes women but the way in which their whole conceptualization of the issues at stake excludes the possibility of introducing sexual divisions as a relevant matter. Even their empirical study is constructed in such a way that matters particularly pertaining to women cannot appear. They concentrate on the duty solicitor scheme and law centres. The former is a scheme designed to assist people on criminal charges who arrive in court with no legal representation. As most people facing criminal charges are men it is not especially pertinent to women as a whole although it would have been possible for Bankowski and Mungham to consider this issue (for example, in relation to shoplifting or prostitution). The selection of law centres also tends to exclude women because although women as a group undoubtedly have problems that would take them to law centres, these community agencies do not deal with family law or divorce matters. It is therefore extremely difficult on both a conceptual and an empirical level to identify a space in their work for the existence of sexual as opposed to class oppressions.

This is not an attempt to argue that every study of law should be a study of women and law or patriarchal relations and law. But it is to argue that analyses which attempt to make general statements about the nature of law and the relationship of law to the social order cannot justifiably exclude gender oppression while pertaining to account for class oppression. Social class is contaminated by gender divisions; it cannot simply be separated out and treated discretely. Moreover it has to be recognized that radical changes which may allow for the actual creation of an idealist concept of society where 'men can freely come together' may do very little to allow women to 'freely' come together. It is therefore necessary to be critical of such work not only on the analytical level but also on the political level inasmuch as conclusions drawn from such analyses may do little to alter the specific nature of women's oppression.

I now wish to turn to an examination of the relationship between patriarchal relations and law. As I have already indicated this relationship has traditionally been a focus of feminist interest although it has usually been expressed differently, for example in terms of law and sexual inequality or discrimination. But in spite of these differences, the role of law in reproducing, creating or obscuring sexual inequality, and the potential of law to relieve women's oppression, has occupied feminists and social reformers for decades. For example in *The Subjugation of Women*, which was published in 1869, J. S. Mill and Harriet Taylor placed considerable emphasis on the need for full legal equality for women. They argued that women should have the same formal legal rights as men in order to remove artificial obstacles to social equality. They also maintained that the legal subordination of women to men in marriage helped to create a situation in which 'each individual of the subject-class is in a chronic state of bribery and intimidation combined' (quoted in Gardiner, 1976: 41). For Mill and Harriet Taylor, women's legal disabilities regarding property ownership and divorce led to conditions of virtual slavery which could only be relieved by granting women equal legal rights. Engels (1972), however, who has provided a more radical resource for feminists, argued that legal inequalities were a reflection of social inequalities and that consequently the law could not constitute a solution to oppression. He maintained that formal legal equality could not bring an end to patriarchal (or class) relations, and that paper equality could do little to eradicate inequalities that were embedded in social and economic conditions. Nevertheless, he still treated the achievement of legal equality as a valid political strategy. He argued that:

the peculiar character of man's domination over woman in the modern family, and the necessity, as well as the manner, of establishing real social equality between the two, will be brought out into full relief only when both are completely equal before the law. (1972: 82)

In other words, for Engels it was necessary to demonstrate that legal reform would not eliminate the structures of dominance that exist outside or beyond the law, but it was none the less important to lay bare both the error of the liberal position and the real basis of sexual domination by showing the ineffectiveness of legal reforms in transforming the social order.

Engels however did not go on to substantially develop his ideas on women's oppression and the law, and, as I have argued, most of the Marxist or radical analyses of the law that have been produced over the last few decades have been more concerned with the law and the state debate in connection with crime, wage-labour or class relations than with patriarchal relations. Feminists however have maintained a parallel interest in law, although most of the feminist literature in this area has concentrated on the social implications of legislation (for example, Land, 1976) or on the roles that law traditionally allocates to women (for example, O'Donovan, 1979). As yet there is little material available on the relationship between law, the state and the specific reproduction of patriarchal relations in ideological and material terms. What work there is that addresses itself to the nature of law as such has tended to depict it and its enforcement as *sexist*. The recognition that the judiciary tends to be a predominantly male group, the identification of laws (such as those on rape and prostitution) which are particularly oppressive to women and the observation of statutes that exclude women or concede to them fewer rights than to men, have led many feminists to perceive the law as biased or prejudiced against women. For example Karen DeCrow argues that 'then as now, the rights of women were interpreted in the courts by men, and usually by men who had been raised in the male supremacist tradition' (1975: 187). The problem with this type of analysis is that it appears to presume that the courts operate 'fairly' and in an unbiased way towards other litigants (that is, men). It also seems to presume the possibility of a juridical structure which could be uncontaminated by other social institutions and values. Moreover, the bias that operates is seen to operate through the agency of individuals who implement the law or who draft it. This is not to argue that individuals are insignificant to the process of law, nor to exclude the influence of the political and social views of individual judges and other legal personnel. But it is to argue that this level of analysis is insufficient on its own. In Marxist theories of law this position (for example, Griffith, 1977) which tends to explain the class nature of the law in terms of the class background of the judiciary, has been consistently criticized (for example, Hall et al., 1978). As Picciotto argues,

> While obviously factors such as the cultural and ideological background of judges are very relevant, it is inadequate to attribute the class character of a social institution simply to the social origins of those who control it. Most Marxists would agree that revolutionary change entails the transformation of the very character of social institutions such as the state and the legal system, and not simply the replacement of the personnel which operates them. (1979: 166)

Unfortunately there has been a tendency for the work of feminists and their sympathizers to analyse the law in this way. For example Sachs and Wilson (1978) treat the all-male character of the judiciary, in combination with their class background, as a sufficient explanation for the operations of the law in relation to women. In particular they concentrate on the refusal of the judiciary at the turn of the century to allow women to be defined as 'persons', which in turn denied women access to the professions. This they argue was due to the judiciary's desire to protect the material interests of men against the threat of women leaving the home and securing well-paid employment. For example they maintain,

> In the case of beliefs related to male domination, the argument would be that upper-middle-class men in diverse occupations shared an interest in keeping women as head servants at home and keeping them out of the ranks of competitors at work. In other words, men had and still have a material stake in resisting the emancipation of women. (1978: 11)

The judiciary as men are therefore understood as subscribing to sexist attitudes to protect their material interests. These views, which are specific to their gender and class are not biologically determined, are reflected in their adjudications which in turn, according to Sachs and Wilson, renders the law as a whole sexist.

It is not that Sachs and Wilson are necessarily wrong to attribute these economic interests to male judges. The problem with that analysis is the failure to distinguish between the judges and the law. To put it a different way, they fail to distinguish between legal *regulation* and *male control*. This is not a problem that is peculiar to Sachs and Wilson[3] and it is one that consistently recurs in feminist (as well as other forms of radical) analyses. The work of Susan Edwards (1981) provides another example of the elision of these concepts, or perhaps it would be more accurate to suggest that it provides an example of how difficult it is to talk of structures of power and mechanisms of regulation without attributing these to biological agents who then become the personifications of power and control. For example Edwards argues, following Foucault, that:

> This process of linkage is decisive, since it is through a specific location of prohibition and regulation of sexuality within discursive practices of law and medicine, for instance, that control over female sexual behaviour is secured. (1981: 13)

However later she suggests that:

> Throughout the nineteenth and twentieth centuries, the sexual behaviour of all women was the object of control, both direct and indirect, and not of protection. *Male control* extended throughout all patriarchal institutions, though the degree and form of control varied according to the social class of women concerned. (1981: 55; emphasis added)

Not only do we have the concepts of control and regulation treated as if they are synonymous when in fact control is a much more rigid and direct manifestation of power, but also a shift away from 'practices of law' to 'male control'. This is not simply a matter of semantics because although it may be that it is men as biological entities who exercise most legally constituted forms of power and indeed men as individuals who benefit most from the oppression of women, the law is not simply a conglomeration of individual, biological men. Neither is it a collection of individuals in this way, even though individuals have a responsibility for how they interpret or enforce the law. The problem therefore which faces many feminists in trying to analyse the law and its relationship to patriarchal structures is how to appreciate the full complexity of the law while at the same time locating a political responsibility on actors in the present and yet without reducing the law to a simple exercise of male power. This is not an easy task because the various levels of analysis can become confused. It is all too easy to move from an instance of the exercise of sexism, for example a chauvinistic utterance and a discriminatory decision by one or even a number of judges, to a statement that the law is sexist, or that it is an instance of male power exercised in the interests of men. It is this failure to keep separate these levels of analysis that has produced feminist versions of the conspiracy thesis in the field of law.

Perhaps this development is not altogether surprising, after all the failure of law to improve the social and economic position of women, even where it is expressly designed to do so (for example, Equal Pay Act 1970 and Sex Discrimination Act 1975), and the outrage that many feminists feel over the outcome of rape trials or the 'unwillingness' of the police to protect women against domestic violence, has led to a situation in which law as a whole can easily be taken to be an instrument of patriarchal oppression. Indeed it may seem hard to avoid this conclusion particularly when working in the areas of rape, prostitution and domestic violence. Moreover, there are similarities between this approach and certain Marxist analyses of class oppression in which the law is depicted, historically and in the present, as a means of controlling the working classes through restrictions on unions and strikes and through the biased interpretation of law by the judiciary. This conspiracy thesis is not only made to rest on evidence of overt forms of oppression, such as legislation that permits a man to rape his wife, but also on legislation or legal practice which on the 'surface' is non-sexist but in 'reality' discriminates against women. For example DeCrow argues:

> Women have fared miserably under the law, not only in the decisions which went against us, but even in the cases that went 'for' us; and we are deluding ourselves if we think that women can get justice in the courts. The record of court decisions, statutes, state constitutions, and legislative interpretations – all of these were written by men. And until they begin to be written by feminist women and feminist men, women will never achieve equity in our legal system. (1975: 3)

But the idea that law simply serves the interests of men against those of women and that legislation and legal practice is constantly guided by these principles does not stand up to closer examination. There are in fact three main problems with this approach which need to be examined in turn.

First, this approach treats law as an entity unto itself. It suggests that having identified male interests it operates conservatively to protect them in all circumstances. Yet clearly there have been 'victories' over the forces of reaction, yet how are these to be explained if the law always protects the interests of men? It is, of course, possible to resurrect the concept of repressive tolerance but this reifies the law to an absurd degree and also ignores the fact that many reforms were the consequence of hard struggle engaged in by women. It is also the case that legislation, while remaining unchanged, can have different consequences at different moments in history. For example the Married Women's Property Act of 1882 brought in the principle of separate property and thereby allowed married women to own their own property separately from their husbands. This was hailed as a victory for feminist principles at the time. However, with a changing economic climate and the increase in married women working this principle became the basis in the 1950s for excluding women from any share in the matrimonial home if they could not establish strict legal ownership. The principle of pure separate property was then largely abandoned after pressure from women's groups and women MPs. It is arguably difficult to analyse all these historical changes simply in terms of one overriding concept, namely male interest. Ultimately of course everything *can* be reduced to serving male interests, but in that instance the concept would come to have no explanatory powers at all.

A second problem with the conspiracy thesis is that it presumes a readily identifiable set of male interests which can be unambiguously served. Yet the issue of the custody of children on separation or divorce is one indication of how inaccurate this is. On one hand the courts appear to favour the mother over the father in principle because although the primary consideration must be the 'best interests of the child', those best interests are usually identified with having a mother to look after the child's daily needs. In this way the courts reinforce the mothering role, although in the majority of cases they simply give judicial sanction to a de facto custody, as most children stay with their mothers when there is a breakdown. The reinforcement of this role needs to be considered in the context of the considerable power it can give women within the politics of personal relationships. Prior to the 1886 Guardianship of Infants Act women did not even have the same formal rights to custody as men, and until after the Second World War it was common for adulterous mothers to be punished by being deprived of their children entirely. The courts now in fact distinguish between the 'bad wife' and the 'bad mother' and it is unusual for them to give custody to a father unless the mother is a lesbian or she neglects or abuses her children. In consequence, while the law is in one instance reinforcing the ideology of motherhood, it has also increased the power of mothers within the family, which can hardly be said to simply serve the interests of men.

Finally, to assert that the law serves the interests of men ignores the impact of the class structure which mediates the consequences of legislation. For example, in awarding maintenance the courts can reduce a husband's income below subsistence level even in the knowledge that the Supplementary Benefits Commission will not raise his income because benefits cannot be used to pay a court order. The interests of poor or low-income men are therefore not served at all by the enforcement of maintenance (albeit it is not enforced very effectively). Moreover, although the proportionate financial burden of maintenance payments may be less for middle- and upper-class men due to tax relief and wider margins of disposable income, they do not interpret the duty to maintain ex-wives as in their interests either. Indeed pressure groups like Justice on Divorce argue that maintenance payments for ex-spouses are entirely unjust to men. It would seem, therefore, that in this area at least the law, if it serves any one entity's interests, is serving the interests of the state in protecting the public purse, rather than operating to protect the interests of men as a category.

Besides these three main points it is perhaps worth considering the problem of overemphasizing the significance of law as an agency of regulation. Stuart Hall and his colleagues (1978) for example have argued that there has been a shift in the position of law, and not just its content, since the last war. Basically they suggest that the law itself has become more 'liberal' while other agencies have appropriated some of the former regulatory function of the law. The development of social work is an example of this tradition, and it is not only encroaching on the criminal law – particularly in relation to juveniles – but also on family law where a number of judicial functions are gradually being taken over by welfare agencies, especially in relation to the custody of children. It may therefore be increasingly inadequate to discuss the law in isolation from other social institutions which operate in a quasi-legal manner and can command the backing of law where necessary.

So far the law has been depicted as a purely coercive agency or force (Foucault, 1981) but it is possible to argue that the legal system is also part of the 'production of consent' and that it has a positive and educative function which orchestrates 'public opinion' (Hall et al., 1978). The law therefore does not simply reflect 'public opinion' (itself a controversial concept), it is part of the production of consensus around such issues as the importance of law and order, the sanctity of private property and the sacred nature of the family. Again the law may no longer be a primary agency in this respect; for example the media, the structure of language, and the education system may now be held to be of greater salience. Yet the law, through its refusal to recognize such phenomena as rape in marriage, by its treatment of wives' earnings as husbands' property, by its reluctance in practice to recognize domestic violence, and by its criminalization of women prostitutes sustains, perpetuates and justifies a consensual view on sex roles and the relative rights and duties of men and women.

The law can therefore be understood as a mode of reproduction of the existing patriarchal order, minimizing social change but avoiding the problems of overt conflict. In agreement with Harrison and Mort (1980) I would argue that legislation does not create patriarchal relations but it does in a complex and often contradictory fashion reproduce the material and ideological conditions under which these relations may survive. They argue that,

> The State can be seen to draw on, transform and modify particular sets of patriarchal relations, through legislation governing the transmission of property, marriage and sexuality, but it cannot be seen to *create* those relations. (1980: 81)

Moreover, Harrison and Mort similarly identify marriage, divorce and sexuality as sites of particular fruitfulness when analysing patriarchal aspects of state formation. They suggest that sexuality stands in a less direct relationship to the capitalist state than marriage with its emphasis on property divisions and transmission and the sexual division of labour; however, they argue that legislation governing these areas secures the continuation of 'specific forms of patriarchal relation involving the subordination of women' (1980: 79). This is broadly the position that I adopt with two provisos. The first is that I do not regard the law as a homogeneous entity but as a collection of practices and discourses which do not all operate together with one purpose. The second is that legal practices cannot simply be read off from the stage of economic development of capitalism. By this I mean that I do not perceive the law simply as a superstructural reflection of the economic base but recognize that it contains within itself its own constraints and motivations as well as being influenced by political and ideological factors which are independent of economic developments. It is for this reason that I give detailed attention to the operation of law in specific historical periods as well as focusing a close concentration on legal practice in the present. I shall tend to reject general theories on law and patriarchy in favour of less deterministic accounts of specific legislative changes in relation to family structures and dominant sexual practices. The purpose of the following chapters is therefore to document in some detail the complexities and contradictions of the practice of law as it relates to the ongoing oppression of women. This is not to suggest naïvely that what follows is a theory-free account of legal practice through the ages, but it is an attempt to construct a feminist account which avoids oversimplification and conspiracy and allows fully for the 'contradictions' and 'subtleties' that Sheila Rowbotham has identified as essential to any analysis of women's oppression.

Notes

This chapter was originally published in C. Smart (1984) *The Ties That Bind*, Routledge.

1 One possible exception to this is the work of Ian Taylor (1982) which does address the family and sexuality and attempts to introduce feminist ideas into a socialist framework.

2 It is not adequate to answer this criticism by reference to the linguistic device of using men as a term that includes women. Language is also a reflection of patriarchal relations. See Spender (1980).

3 Mark Cousins (1980) for example has criticized *Women, Crime and Criminology* (Smart, 1976) for precisely this reason.

9

Feminism and Law: Some Problems of Analysis and Strategy

In the UK there has been a long tradition of feminist involvement with law. This historical involvement has been orientated towards developing legal strategies to create progressive social change which would lead to an improvement in the position of women in marriage (Holcombe, 1983), in education (Sachs and Wilson, 1978), in politics (Strachey, 1978) and in many other areas. Feminist engagement with theories of law and the state is a more recent development. Analyses of law have tended to be treated as a secondary concern in the face of the more immediate demand for active campaigns. There are, however, signs that this situation is changing and that a body of theoretical analysis is developing from feminist work on law.

There are, in my view, two main reasons for this development. First, the history of feminist struggle in the site of law is increasingly well documented and this now informs contemporary feminism. An important aspect of the influence of this history is a growing awareness of the paucity of gains for women arising out of the pursuit of law reform. In addition to which, contemporary feminists who have themselves been involved in campaigns for law reform which have appeared in the first instance to bring 'success', are now increasingly 'disappointed' as they witness the erosion of the beneficial effects of these reforms. These 'disappointments' have led to a re-evaluation of the usefulness of promoting legal change as a method of resisting the oppression of women. It is this reconsideration of strategy which has inevitably encouraged the development of analyses of the role of law in creating, reproducing or mitigating forms of oppression.

The second reason for the development of feminist analyses of law is related to wider developments in feminism. Arguably the early feminists did not develop a body of theory on the oppression of women. Women's oppression may have been accounted for in terms of the physical or social or economic power of men; even biological determinist theories may have been relied upon to justify extending more favourable treatment to women, but there was no equivalent to contemporary theories of patriarchy. Feminism fell largely into a tradition of 'liberal' politics, reacting to inequalities and injustices in a relatively ad hoc way. Feminists not in this mould (for example, Sylvia Pankhurst) relied on including feminism in existing theoretical frameworks such as socialism and Marxism. But contemporary feminism has attempted to avoid both of these options and has, to a large extent, developed its own, more independent theoretical tradition. The injustices and inequalities now experienced by women are theorized as part of a system of oppression, and the state (and within that the law) is recognized as fully implicated in the oppression of women.

The problems facing feminism at the end of the twentieth century are, therefore, considerable. On the one hand, tradition demands a continuing practical engagement with law reform, although experience reveals the limits of this strategy. On the other hand, the development of analyses of law and the state reveal the central role of law in reproducing aspects of women's oppression, but give few indications of how to put such insights into operation short of the traditional demands made of law (for example, for equal treatment, more extensive rights, etc.).

Obviously, it is possible at this stage to point to the development of Marxist theories of law in order to draw parallels between the history of feminist struggles and socialist struggles. There are many examples in this literature of the problems of liberal analyses of the state, the inevitable failure of utopianism, and the reactionary nature of bourgeois reformism (for example, Schöttler, 1986). These examples could be drawn upon by feminists in order to identify the pitfalls of engaging with law in the hopes of transforming society. But this of course, presumes a congruence between feminism and Marxism which does not exist. There is as yet no certainty that law is in the same relation to patriarchy as it is to capitalism; nor indeed that socialist strategies per se will assist the aims of feminism. As MacKinnon has argued: 'Interpreting further areas of law, a feminist theory of the state will reveal that the idealism of liberalism and the materialism of the left have come to much the same for women' (1983: 658). This suggests a number of significant differences between Marxist analyses of law and developing feminist analyses. Obviously, on one level feminist struggles are not reducible to class struggles – in which case the position of law in feminist theory may be theorized differently from theorizations within Marxism. In addition, however, the body of knowledge that has developed within the confines of the law and the state debate in Marxism, has not included gender within its conceptualization of forms of oppression. We cannot therefore assume that gender can be 'slotted in' with the expectation that feminists should simply learn from the history of another struggle. It is a fundamental misconception to believe that feminism will 'catch up' by walking in the footsteps of the Marxist legal theorists.

In this chapter I shall begin to explore some of the contradictions and problems facing feminists who continue to engage with law as part of a political struggle. This should be seen as an attempt to draw together the insights of feminist work in the UK in recent years which has contributed to the development of a feminist analysis of law. It is hoped that other feminists will respond to this so that it will be possible to develop collectively, and in an international framework, a more adequate theory of law and programme of strategy.

Some lessons of history

There is no simple relationship between law and the economic structure of society. Certainly the development of law cannot simply be 'read off' from economic changes in a determinist fashion. As Hirst (1980, 1985) has argued, law has an autonomy from the state, and law itself is not a unified entity, indivisible in terms of structure and effects. Neither can legal changes be regarded as 'causing' economic or social change, although legislation may, in some instances, provide the means to achieve change. For example, Dahl has argued that:

> By reflecting women's lives and living conditions in legal decisions, the law offers an important source of understanding of women's social situation. The effect of legal provision goes beyond this however, by contributing towards the maintenance and strengthening of women's economic situation. In some instances legal provisions can even transform the economic situation of women, so the law should not be perceived simply as a passive reflection of economic inequality. (1984: 137)

This 'strengthening of women's economic situation' has had important ramifications in the field of employment but has also had important consequences for the position of women in the family. I shall map out some of these developments in an attempt to draw some lessons from history and to point to specific instances where law has maintained, strengthened and at times reduced women's economic situation. I shall also consider instances where economic changes appear to have produced legal change before considering briefly the more fundamental critique of law arising from the work of Kingdom, of Gilligan and of MacKinnon.

Law, economy and family: an instance of change
Women's participation in the labour market in the UK began to change significantly in the postwar era, and it is possible to show that

this had both a direct and an indirect influence on the development of matrimonial law in the 1960s. Basically, as I shall outline, the involvement of married women in waged work altered considerably their position in law *vis-à-vis* their husbands. By 1971 over 60 per cent of all women in paid work were married and although their earning power was generally limited, this ultimately led to the introduction of legislation on married women's property, the matrimonial home and the whole range of matrimonial proceedings.

During the 1950s and much of the 1960s the woman who gave up work to get married or to rear children was severely disadvantaged by the strict application of the doctrine of legal ownership in divorce proceedings. Under this doctrine, the ownership of the matrimonial home, furniture, savings and other matrimonial assets was determined by the name on the title deeds or proof of purchase. Homes were almost always conveyanced into the sole name of the husband, and most items of furniture, especially if bought on credit, would be in the husband's name.

But married women's participation in the labour market began to alter this strict interpretation of legal ownership in marriage. This occurred for two reasons. First, as married women began to earn wages, they could establish that they also had contributed in cash to the purchase of matrimonial assets. The courts could recognize the value of capital (money) and this came to override the technical definition of 'legal' ownership. Hence women could prove that although the 'matrimonial assets' were in their husband's name (and therefore technically their husband's property) they had contributed financially and should therefore share in ownership. Second, women were able to argue gradually that even where they did not contribute to the accumulation of property in the form of money, they did contribute in money's worth or in kind. The power of this argument arose from changes in patterns of women's work which revealed that women were in the labour market until the birth of their first child (rather than until they were married as formerly). The work they carried out in rearing children gradually became regarded as an economic asset to the family.

The process by which this occurred is complex. Basically the courts had begun to improve the economic position of wives in paid employment, but the position of the wife at home caring for children and who could not accumulate wages was left unprotected. This became intolerable in a climate in which the dominant ideology celebrated the non-wage-earning mother, but offered her no protection from economic harm. But for the courts to 'recognize' her position it was essential for married women to have the 'option' of entering the labour market (that is, to abandon the idealized role of wife and mother). It was therefore the growing economic power of women in the labour market which indirectly improved the position of women outside the labour market. Through this process women's domestic labour was slightly redefined. It became less a form of unpaid leisure and more a form of economic contribution to the husband's accumulation of capital. Of course this redefinition was not extensive, it applied only in divorce settlements and in practice it did not mitigate against the economic impoverishment of women through marriage and child care. But it did extend some protection.

This interpretation of the influence of women's economic activity on matrimonial law is, however, subject to certain qualifications. The economic position of women is always mediated through the dominant ideology of motherhood. Women are never simply economic actors as men may be; they are mothers, or potential mothers, as well. This alters their relationship to the labour force. It also alters their relationship to law. Hence the change in women's economic position in the family resultant upon their increased participation in the workforce 'improved' their position as spouses but weakened their position as mothers (because mothers are not workers in the dominant ideological construct of motherhood – this is more fully discussed below). Hence it is possible to observe that the development of case law in the 1960s was an attempt to preserve the position of the mother by extending to her the same 'rights' as those earned in wages by working wives.

This development, is, however, only one 'instance' of a legal change which is related in a complex manner to economic and social change. It is not possible to read off from this a simple improvement in the position of women in general nor a relaxation of the influence of law in maintaining women as dependants of men in marriage. Although women's 'bargaining power' increased and the subsequent legal changes operated to render marriage less blatantly disadvantageous to women, they did not alter the fundamental division of labour in marriage, nor fully equalize the power relations therein. Hence there were some gains for women in the reform of divorce legislation, but they were in themselves limited and, moreover, subsequent social and economic changes throughout the 1970s quickly transformed many gains that were made.

While these are examples of the ambiguous way in which legislative change develops, it is equally important to consider the way in which legislative change, introduced to meet changing social and economic conditions, is rapidly overtaken by further changes in these same conditions. The cases of equal pay legislation and matrimonial law provide clear examples of this process.

Equal pay
Equal pay legislation in the UK was interpreted in a very restrictive way by the judiciary on its implementation in 1975 (see Snell et al., 1981; Hepple, 1984). Moreover, the legislation itself was so complex and so difficult to pursue that the early gains achieved by women in certain industries were not sustained in following years. As Hepple has shown, the number of completed applications to industrial tribunals fell from 1742 in 1976 to a mere 39 in 1982. Moreover, the success rate of those going to a hearing during this period ranged from 12.2 per cent in 1976 to 4.4 per cent in 1980. What is more, there is clear evidence that cases are being deterred, at the early stages of a complaint, from going as far as industrial tribunals (Gregory, 1982) and that trade unions in the UK do not always actively pursue women's claims and interests (Hoskyns, 1985).

A more serious problem to the 'success' of the legislation was the rise of mass unemployment in the UK after 1979. As far as women's employment is concerned, this drop in demand for labour has led to a growth in part-time work, as well as the loss of employment altogether. This part-time work has carried with it far fewer 'rights' and benefits (for example, no holiday pay, sick pay and reduced employment protection). In addition, part-time work has not been covered in practice by the equal pay legislation until recently. This has been because part-time women workers have rarely been able to compare themselves with part-time men workers doing the same job in the same firm, as the Act required until 1984.

Mass unemployment has also made the boundaries of the gender-segregated labour market more rigid, making it more difficult for women to move into 'men's' work and hence to fight for equal pay. Moreover, there is the tendency, during periods of high unemployment, for arguments that married women should leave the labour market to gain support. This has made it all the more difficult to gather support to demand effective equal pay legislation. In addition there has been a clear Government policy in the UK since 1979, to reduce legislative constraints (frequently described as burdens) on employers. This trend has not applied to equal pay legislation, however, because of the legislative influence of the European Court.

In fact EEC membership has proved to be important as a means of protecting the small legal gains made by women in the face of a reactionary government. For example, it is entirely due to UK membership that the Equal Pay Act has been moderately improved by the introduction of the Equal Pay (Amendment) Regulations 1983. Without the ruling of the European Court in July 1982 (Commission of the European Communities v. UK, case 61/82 (1982) ICR 578) that the existing UK legislation did not comply with Article

119 of the Treaty of Rome, it is exceedingly unlikely that the legislation would have been modified.

The political aim of reducing legislative protections for the workforce has, however, been applied to employment protection legislation. Under regulations revised in 1985 (Unfair Dismissal (Variation of Qualifying Period) Order), full-time women workers who are dismissed because of pregnancy will no longer be able to claim unfair dismissal under the 1975 Employment Protection Act unless they have worked for the same employer for two years. This also means that pregnant women may be sacked before they can qualify for maternity leave and maternity pay. Hence the effects of this amendment will be much wider than those relating to cases of unfair dismissal. Under such deteriorated employment conditions, the issue of equal pay becomes less significant in political terms, and, arguably less important to women than maternity rights. Hence the situation facing women in waged work comprises an increase in part-time rather than full-time work, a decrease in maternity rights or protections, combined with a limited incremental improvement in equal pay legislation.

Matrimonial law

In the field of matrimonial proceedings, there has been a similar process where economic changes have overtaken the potential benefits of law reform. The 1973 Matrimonial Causes Act in the UK was regarded as a major advance for the status of women on divorce. On the face of it the legislation gave wives the right to share in the matrimonial home, the right to receive maintenance (even if they sued for divorce or were responsible for the breakdown), and the right to a share of the matrimonial assets and even their husband's business assets. However, the reality of the situation is far more complex than this.

First, many of the rights that wives were granted, were based on the traditional role of wives as mothers caring for children. Hence women did not accrue rights, but they were entitled to certain benefits while they had the care of children. The law's first obligation was to the children of the marriage, and women benefited largely in relation to their role as carers. Second, in making divorce more easily attainable, it was presumed that the majority would remarry (see Smart, 1984). It was not envisaged (except by a handful of older feminists in the House of Commons) that men would remarry and start second families, while women left with the care of children would be much slower to remarry. Under such conditions the legal requirement on a man to support his first wife and children rapidly became untenable in practice. In 1984 the law was changed to reduce his liability to reflect the de facto situation, namely that few men paid maintenance to their wives on divorce.

Third, the failure of the private system of maintenance to support the growing numbers of female-headed one-parent families, created a situation in which women were increasingly dependent upon state benefits for economic survival. At the same time, however, the value of such benefits was declining. For example the Equal Treatment Directive of the EEC required that married women should not be disadvantaged as far as their entitlement to replacement of earnings benefits was concerned. Hence married women became entitled to the same National Insurance Benefits as men and single women. Yet at the same time the value of these benefits declined and the earnings-related element was abolished. Married women were admitted to the scheme on equal terms at the moment at which it became virtually insignificant as a source of income maintenance.

In conclusion, the reform of matrimonial legislation improved the formal legal position of women in the early 1970s. However, the escalating rate of divorce and the failure of governments to provide an adequate replacement income (or the opportunity to earn a living wage) to lone mothers in the decade since the reforms, has culminated in the increasing impoverishment of women outside marriage.

There is one further development which should be noted. This is in relation to the custody of children on divorce. It has been the practice of the courts to award custody to mothers in most cases. This is almost always uncontested by the father, and mothers almost always have de facto custody prior to a judicial hearing. However, this practice is now subject to scrutiny and there is pressure on courts to award custody jointly to both parents in future. This development arises from the influence of the fathers' rights movement which has taken the traditional feminist demand for equal treatment by the law, to apply to custody disputes. Hence they have argued that equal treatment demands that mother and father have joint custody (although routine care of the child usually remains with the mother). This development is supported by the growth of the 'ideology of fatherhood' which argues for the essential presence of men to ensure the 'normal' development of children. This trend in the area of custody is a major disadvantage to women. Not only does it enable the authority of the father to extend itself into the woman's household after divorce, it does nothing to reduce the adverse economic consequence of the care of children for women. Yet it does threaten to remove the children after the economic sacrifices have been made.

In the fields of matrimonial law, employment law and social

security law it is possible to speak of a process of uneven development. It is inaccurate to assert that nothing has changed to improve the position of women. Equally there has been no linear development of progressive legislation. Advances in one area (for example, equal pay) are mitigated by reactionary measures elsewhere (for example, employment protection legislation). Similarly, the extension of equal treatment under social security legislation has occurred at a time when the value of National Insurance Benefits has been seriously eroded. Finally, women's property rights have improved on condition that they are the primary carers of children, and yet at the same time there is a growing challenge to women's right to sole custody of children on divorce.

This 'ebb' and 'flow' or, to put it more figuratively, the experience of running hard to stand still, has been accounted for in a number of ways. For example the struggle for formal equality has been criticized (rightly) as a political palliative. Yet equally persuasively, Hoskyns has argued that 'even crude legal instruments can be important to weak and disadvantaged groups in society and can give them at least some purchase on the political process' (1985: 73). The experience of feminists working in this field is therefore rarely an absolute one. This is almost certainly linked to a recognition of the range of political gains that are achieved by feminist campaigns. Such gains may, for example, arise out of the political activity itself and not the objective goal of the particular campaign. This experience, and the feminist perspective on law that arises from it can best be articulated by the concept of uneven development.

The uneven development of law

The idea of the uneven development of law is an important one. It allows for an analysis of the law that recognizes the distinctions between law-as-legislation and the effects of law, or law-in-practice. It rejects completely any concept of law as a unity which simply progresses, regresses or reappears as a cycle of history to repeat itself. It perceives law as operating on a number of dimensions at the same time. Law is not identified as a simple tool of patriarchy or capitalism. To analyse law in this way creates the possibility of seeing law both as a means of 'liberation' and, at the same time, as a means of the reproduction of an oppressive social order. Law both facilitates change and is an obstacle to change. This is clearly related to the dilemma facing feminist politics in the UK. There is an ambivalence about resorting to legal reform to promote change, yet any attempts to dismantle previously hard-won reforms are resisted strongly.

Legal reform is both valued and undervalued as a means of achieving social change.

Legislation in the areas of pornography and reproductive rights provides an illuminating example of this uneven development. The decade of the 1960s is commonly regarded as an era of permissive legislation in the UK (Hall, 1980). Hence legislation introducing legalized abortion for non-medical reasons, and legislation reducing censorship on theatrical displays (and ultimately books and magazines) are linked together under the permissive banner. For some, this legislation represents the triumph of liberalism over Victorian hypocrisy and repression. For others it symbolizes the moral decline of the nation (Whitehouse, 1977). Both schools of thought can be seen as treating legislation as indivisible, a unity that represents either progress or regress.

From the position of a feminist analysis of law, neither position is correct. The lack of control over pornographic material is analysed as an instance of the exercise of power by others over women's bodies. The availability of abortion on the other hand, represents a limited extension of power over reproduction, and hence women's bodies, to women themselves. This is an oversimplification of the feminist position, but it serves to identify an instance of one dimension of what is meant by the uneven development of law.

To follow the example one stage further, the legislation on abortion is not itself an unambiguously positive development. While extending self-determination to some women, it also gives to the medical profession the power to withhold or to extend the surgical procedure. Although the technology of abortion is becoming increasingly simple, its control rests with doctors as opposed to nurses or women themselves. To this extent doctors can decide who should, and who should not, have an abortion. In the exercise of their discretion, the ethnic origin, the class background, or the marital status of a woman may become exceedingly important. The law-in-practice does not therefore operate simply to give women greater self-determination over biological reproduction.

Notwithstanding this and the development in the USA and, to a lesser extent, in the UK of do-it-yourself abortion kits, there is no widespread demand to deregulate abortion as such. Legislation covering the professional qualifications and training of people administering abortions, or legislation ensuring high standards of care in hospitals or clinics, is not rejected. As Kingdom (1985a) has argued, it is no part of the feminist demand for greater control over reproduction to insist on a return to a system of unrestricted *laissez-faire* with no safeguards to protect women's health.

As the law is a complex formation, it cannot be relied upon to meet fully the goals of any one system of politics. This also applies to governments inasmuch as there are unforeseen and unregulated outcomes to legislation for the state as well as for individuals or political groupings. Hence the law is not the mere instrument of an omnipotent state. Its effects are uneven in all dimensions, and the aims of legislators and even governments may be thwarted by the relative 'independence' of law and the judiciary.

The recent history of domestic violence legislation is an important example of this. In 1976 and 1978 the Government introduced two legislative measures to deal with domestic violence. These were respectively the Domestic Violence and Matrimonial Proceedings Act and the Domestic Proceedings and Magistrates' Courts Act. The introduction of this legislation arose directly from the political lobbying of groups such as Women's Aid and the Women's Liberation Movement. Arguably the social and political pressure for this legislative reform had its foundations in the changes in the economic position of women described above. Yet its force lay in an argument which was based on establishing women's helplessness and vulnerability in the family and in marriage. It was not an argument based on the growth of women's independence in the public sphere, but an argument which relied on revealing women's powerlessness and their need for external intervention and help (before they could help themselves).

In this context, battered women were provided with an array of remedies in law (see McCann, 1985). These remedies, which included exclusion injunctions, powers of arrest and non-molestation orders, were not as extensive as the campaigners would have wished. None the less, on the introduction of the legislation in the second half of the 1970s, women clearly resorted to its use in considerable numbers. This use of the legislation led quite quickly to a hostile police and judicial reaction. The police, who had not supported the legislation in the first instance (Select Committee, 1975) systematically failed to exercise the powers given to them under the Acts (Faragher, 1985). The judiciary, on the other hand, gradually imposed more and more restrictive interpretations on the legislation, to the point of effectively returning women to the same position as prevailed prior to the introduction of the new Acts. In other words, law-in-practice severely undermined law-as-legislation.

The failure of the domestic violence legislation, which has since been compounded by changes in housing legislation and the crisis in housing generally, can be attributed to a 'refusal' of legal agents to implement the legislation as intended. The express purpose of the reform was unacceptable to those required to implement it, and the change of political administration in 1979 meant that there was no response from the legislature to challenge this development. Equally there was little response from the campaigning groups who had worked so hard to introduce the legislation.

This is in part due to the despondency created by the 'failure' of legislation to achieve change, but it is also linked to wider economic and social trends. For example, the crisis in housing has led to a situation in which women, fleeing from violent men, cannot be adequately rehoused. It is widely acknowledged, therefore, that improvements to the legislation would be pointless without a change in housing policy. Domestic violence legislation has therefore fallen prey to the effects of the uneven development of law. Law-as-legislation has been undermined by law-in-practice while changing social conditions in housing have undermined the purpose of regulating the way in which the law is implemented.

This concept of uneven development is not new. In feminist literature it was developed by Juliet Mitchell (1971) as a means of explaining the shifts and changes in women's position throughout history. Mitchell states:

> Past socialist theory has failed to differentiate woman's condition into its separate structures, which together form a complex – not a simple – unity. . . . [Women's condition] must be seen as a specific structure, which is a unity of different elements. The variations of woman's condition throughout history will be the result of different combinations of these elements – we will thus have not a linear narrative of economic development . . . for the elements will be combined in different ways at different times. . . . This complex totality means that no contradiction in society is ever simple. As each sector can move at a different pace, the synthesis of the different time-scales in the total structure means that sometimes contradictions cancel each other out, and sometimes they reinforce one another. (1971: 100–1)

These concepts of 'complex unity' and 'uneven development' not only help to explain the broad issues of women's oppression – in Mitchell's terms Production, Reproduction, Sexuality and the Socialization of Children – but also narrower segments within this theoretical formulation. Hence the development of law may be treated as part of the complex unity and, within this the uneven development of law can be mapped onto changes in the main structures of production, reproduction, sexuality and socialization. At times law may facilitate developments in one of these key structures, at other times it may provide an obstacle to some strand of development.

This concept of uneven development has a particular importance in relation to a feminist analysis of law and social change because of the position occupied by law in popular consciousness and hence in political movements like the Women's Liberation Movement. History is widely regarded as a linear process of improvement and positive development. In this framework, law reforms are usually identified as the milestones at which progressive change was introduced. There are such milestones in feminist history. For example, the 1882 Married Women's Property Act which allowed married women to own their own property, or the 1918 Representation of the People Act, which first gave women the vote in general elections. These are celebrated as victories. Given such a framework of history it is difficult not to aspire to similar 'victories' in future. Indeed a history of struggle with milestones of victories is a vital element in sustaining the motivation for future political, economic and social change. Through this mechanism it appears to be politically possible to act against oppression, poverty and injustice. But law reform contains within it definite limitations. As Polan has argued:

> it is not so much that laws must be changed; it is patriarchy that must be changed. Actions taken within the legal system cannot by themselves eliminate patriarchy, which is a pervasive social phenomenon. Because law is one, but only one, locus of male supremacy, legal efforts to end women's subordinate status cannot effectively challenge or cripple patriarchy unless they are undertaken in the context of broader economic, social, and cultural changes. (Polan, 1982: 301–2)

None the less, as Dahl (1984: 137) has argued, legislation may at times help to introduce the conditions under which more profound changes may occur.

Some problems of practice

This analysis of the development of law as an uneven process cannot be said to represent an adequate feminist theory of law, however. For example, it gives few indicators as to which conditions are most likely to facilitate change and it provides little promise as to the success of strategies to change the law. It might appear that law reform becomes little more than a lottery (a state of affairs which does perhaps quite accurately reflect the experience of feminist campaigners!).

In the face of this difficulty, feminist lawyers and others have begun to shift their focus away from the traditional concern with the content of law, or even its method of implementation. Instead there has been a growth in the analysis of the *form* of law. This shift is based on the recognition that the limits of the law are not only constituted by structural factors such as economic conditions, but also by the structure of law itself and that which is held to constitute legal knowledge and jurisprudence.

One strand of this development is associated with the work of Elizabeth Kingdom (1985a, 1985b). In examining the relationship between law and feminist campaigns for law reform, Kingdom has argued against the deployment of the term 'rights' so frequently associated with feminist claims. While recognizing the political purchase of the demand for more rights or equal rights, she points to a number of practical problems. First the rhetoric of rights can be appropriated by any political group, including anti-feminist groups. Hence there is nothing inherently progressive about the concept. Moreover, in campaigning on that terrain, she argues that feminists provoke counterclaims to rights which the law may be more structurally inclined to uphold. For example, in the case of sterilization she argues that the law is more likely to uphold a husband's rights over his wife's body than the less clearly defined demand for women to have control over their own reproductive capacity.

Second, Kingdom argues that the concept of rights derives from liberal individualism which has no place in the development of a socialist feminism. In this argument, she is asserting the priority of the collective over the individual. This strict position is more closely associated with Marxism than with feminism and it is interesting to note that some Marxists are retreating from this orthodox position to accept the need for legal protection for the individual even under socialism (Hirst, 1985). None the less, this critique remains important in that it relates to the problem in the present of trying to operationalize the claim to rights within a legal system that has no constitutional or historical base to recognize *general* rights. While specific rights exist under legislation, there is no constitutional bill of rights in English law to facilitate the development of new concepts or general concepts of rights. Hence there is no right to health and no right to work, even though both of these may form the basis of political demands that promote legal reforms of some sort.

Kingdom recommends abandoning the concept of rights as a means of pressing feminist claims in law. Similar conclusions have been reached by feminists approaching these issues through a very different avenue. These are feminists who are working on the concept of a feminist legality or jurisprudence. Their argument is not that the concept of rights should be rejected, but that the concept of rights contained in law at present is a 'distinct male vehicle for resolution of moral problems and dilemmas' (Schneider, 1984). These feminists argue that rights, as they are presently constituted, reflect the experience or power of men, and a moral or philosophical base which derives from men's experience of the world, or men's ability to define the world. Under such conditions, legal rights cannot meet the needs of women.

The two feminist authors who have presented this argument most clearly are Catharine MacKinnon (1982, 1983) and Carol Gilligan

(1982). MacKinnon adopts the view that the form of law is the reflection of male power. She focuses on the supposed neutrality of law and the power of men to objectify the world. In so doing she points out they also objectify women. Hence she argues that it is part of the feminist project to reject the 'objective' and the 'neutral' as these are the very projections of male power that objectify women. She states:

> If objectivity is the epistemological stance of which women's sexual objectification is the social process, its imposition the paradigm of power in the male form, then the state will appear most relentless in imposing the male point of view when it comes closest to achieving its highest formal criterion of distanced aperspectivity. When it is most ruthlessly neutral, it will be most male; when it is most sex blind, it will be most blind to the sex of the standard being applied. . . . Abstract rights will authoritize the male experience of the world. (MacKinnon, 1983: 658)

Within such a framework there can be few gains for women through the mechanism of law as currently constituted. Women cannot expect help from a legal system that 'sees and treats women the way men see and treat women'.

There is not space here to outline fully the development of work in this field, nor to discuss adequately the work of Gilligan (1982) which is also fundamental to this school of thought. Gilligan's work, however, differs from MacKinnon's in its focus on psychology and the idea of the differential moral development of boys and girls. It is her view that male and female children develop different moral codes with boys favouring logic and neutrality, and girls being more orientated towards a relational morality. From this she argues that a legal system based on a male moral code, emphasizing objective rights and neutrality, will never reflect the interests of women.

It should be recognized though, that this conceptualization of law presumes a legal system arising from the structure of men's psychology rather than from, or in relation to, social or economic structures. In the formation of the patriarchal state it gives priority to the psyche rather than the material. In this respect it poses other problems for the process of change; to change the legal system presumably we must change men's experience of the world and there are no clear indications of how to do this.

Notwithstanding these criticisms, the work on feminist jurisprudence posits a profound challenge to the assumption that while the content of legislation and its implementation may be oppressive of women, the form of law is gender-neutral. The problem remains, however, of how to develop a feminist theory of law which will avoid the apparent psychological determinism implicit in the work of Gilligan, or will avoid locating men as biological agents as *the problem*, rather than structures of patriarchy, as is the tendency with MacKinnon's work. It is essential that the basis for this development remains the interrelationship between theory (or analysis) and practice (or action). A theory which denies women's experience, or posits an omnipotent male state, renders such action impossible. On the other hand an analysis which allows for a concept of uneven development recognizes that each shift in law indicates the importance of a political engagement which is intrinsic to feminism. The goal of engaging with law as part of the process of transforming the conditions under which women live, is a strategy which integrates the theory and practice of feminism.

Note

This chapter was originally published in *International Journal of the Sociology of Law*, 1986, 14(2): 109–23.

10
Feminist Jurisprudence

Until quite recently the subject of jurisprudence in law schools has failed to address itself to, or defend itself against, the growing feminist challenge to its orthodoxy. Feminist jurisprudence has not been taken seriously although, as I hope to show here, it poses a very real threat to the complacency of traditional jurisprudential thinking. One small indication that this neglect might be changing can be found in the criticism that Freeman (1987) has directed at the major text on jurisprudence that he co-edits (Lloyd and Freeman, 1985). In his auto-critique he points out that only three of the papers in the extensive collection (over 100 extracts) are by women, and that probably only one could be called a feminist. He rightly admits that this is a failing. However, we should not assume from this that jurisprudence is about to undergo radical transformations. The addition of one or two feminist articles to a major teaching text might indicate that there is such a thing as feminist legal scholarship but it would not transform the subject. Yet this is precisely what feminist jurisprudence wishes to achieve.

I shall argue in this paper that traditional jurisprudence can neither assimilate nor continue to avoid feminist legal scholarship. Feminism has gradually and painstakingly created a fundamental critique of orthodox jurisprudence which insists that all the taken-for-granted assumptions about universality, objectivity and neutrality are swept aside to make room for a completely different conception of law and its underpinnings. Feminist legal scholarship is no longer assuming the stance of a supplicant requesting that the orthodoxy hears the case for women's rights or extends the benefits of objectivity and neutrality to the female legal subject. Rather, feminist work has shown that the foundations on which jurisprudence rest are deeply imbued with a masculine perspective and privilege. Moreover, it has become clear that what is required is either a radical transformation or an abandonment of jurisprudence altogether.

This chapter will therefore briefly map the development of feminist jurisprudence from its early conception in the first feminist movement of the nineteenth century. It should then be possible to see how different interpretations of jurisprudence have been favoured at different times, or how certain developments seem to coincide with other developments in specific geopolitical spaces (that is, the USA as compared with Europe). To do this I shall construct certain categories in which the different schools of thought can be located. However, the reader should recognize that this is a device to untangle what might otherwise appear to be a complex web of interconnections with no beginnings or ends. I shall construct a story of feminist jurisprudence, but there will be other stories that remain to be told and the categorizations I use should not become fixed and rigid.

Tentative beginnings

Mitchell (1987) has argued that the history of feminist thought and the history of the idea of equality are virtually synonymous. From the seventeenth century onwards, she argues, the notion of equality informed individual feminist demands or, perhaps more accurately, the concept of equality provided the political and conceptual context in which a feminist voice could be constructed. The work of Mary Wollstonecraft (1975, but first published in 1792) is an example of how the growth of liberalism as a philosophy allowed women to make demands for freedom, equality and personhood in the way that disenfranchised men had been able to. As Mitchell argues:

> feminism as a conscious, that is self-conscious, protest movement, arose as part of a revolutionary bourgeois tradition that had equality of mankind as its highest goal. The first expressions of feminism were endowed with the strengths of the concept of equality and circumscribed by its limitations. (1987: 31)

Perhaps the most significant 'limitation' to which Mitchell refers is the way in which the individual in liberal thought is constructed as a fully autonomous being and as capable of competing on equal terms with others within the parameters of a capitalist economic system. The liberal concept of equality therefore demanded democracy *within* capitalism (and patriarchy) rather than a transformation of the economic and cultural system itself. The broad notion of equality did not become condensed into the narrower and more practically applicable notion of 'equal rights' until the last half of the nineteenth century. Mitchell argues that it was at the point that feminism became an organized political force (a movement rather than a scattering of individuals) that demands were coalesced into demands for equal legal rights. There is a world of difference between the work of early feminists like Mary Wollstonecraft who discussed the subjugation of women in terms of the stunting of women's personalities and talents, the limitations of women's educational horizons, the power of social mores to restrict women's activities and the overwhelmingly stifling effects of sexual morality, and the later work of J. S. Mill and Harriet Taylor (1869) or Caroline Norton (1982, originally published in 1854), Frances Power Cobbe (1878) or Barbara Leigh Bodichon (1869) who were more interested in specific legal rights. From the middle to the turn of the nineteenth century feminist demands increasingly took the form of narrowly conceived reforms to law or equal rights claims. So while law did not feature in Wollstonecraft's exegesis in the eighteenth century, it became a central focus for later feminists.

We can therefore argue that the nineteenth century marks the beginnings of a feminist jurisprudence, even though such a conceptualization would have been quite foreign to feminists then. The principles of this jurisprudence were synonymous with the liberal philosophy of equal rights. However, feminist campaigns around law were always grounded in the material restrictions that women encountered, for example bars to entering universities and professions, marriage laws which deprived them of almost all legal rights, or absolute restrictions on political participation. It should also be appreciated that this focus on law was not simply a reflection of the narrow horizons of bourgeois women in the nineteenth century. Law had begun to play a very specific role in the oppression of women in the eighteenth and nineteenth centuries. This period marked a major growth in legislative activity when women's 'disabilities' became codified rather than simply being a matter of common law or practice.

The law could, therefore, be identified as a very real obstacle to women. It formalized their social and economic disabilities and, in many ways, extended and legitimized them. Moreover, as law became the vehicle for extending rights to categories of men, it expressly excluded women. This gave law the appearance of being the source of the 'problem', or at least the potential solution to the problem. Hence feminist campaigns focused on the injustice of law and its denial of basic rights and freedoms to women. It would, however, be erroneous to imagine that all feminist demands of law took the form of equality claims. In fact from the middle of the nineteenth century we can see the emergence of the alternative strategy of making claims based on difference. What we now refer to as the equality/difference debate in feminist analysis of law has a very early precedent in the work of Caroline Norton in the 1860s and later on can be seen in the work of Eleanor Rathbone in the 1920s. Both of these early feminists eschewed equality in favour of demands based on the special position or qualities of women as mothers. Rathbone, who was required to justify her stance by equal rights feminists, argued that the law should reflect the situation in which women find themselves and that women's greatest needs were in the sphere of motherhood, which had nothing to do with questions of equality and equal pay.

A fundamental difference of view was therefore apparent in the first wave of the feminist movement. These two opposing strategies of equality and difference in legal campaigns reflected competing concepts of justice and fairness. One model saw justice epitomized in the desserts law meted out to men and required the same standard for women. The other model took the 'reality' of women's lives as its starting point and argued that law should be moulded to meet existing needs. It is important to recognize, however, that these early feminists were not in the business of constructing models of justice in an abstract way. Few women were to be found in the universities and none in the legal profession. Early feminist thoughts on jurisprudence therefore stemmed directly from campaigning and the largely middle-class background of the women involved. Thus, while later feminist work in this area retains these elements of conflict between equality and difference, the corpus has been significantly altered by the entrance of women into the academy and law schools, and also into politics and law-making. In particular we see the growth of a self-conscious theoretical orientation rather than a reliance on appeals to apparently self-evident notions of justice and fairness. From the 1960s onwards we therefore witness rapid changes to what we can call feminist jurisprudence and it is to these developments I shall now turn.

Feminist jurisprudence and the second wave of the women's movement

The second wave of the women's movement began at the end of the 1960s and beginning of the 1970s. Although it has been argued that there has always been a women's movement (Spender, 1983) there is no doubt that this period marked a revival of feminist politics on a wide scale in North America and Europe. The 1960s and 1970s were a period of economic and cultural optimism and, in western 'developed' countries, these decades marked a time of legislative activity which focused on pressing social problems such as divorce, abortion, child benefit, equal pay and sex discrimination, racial discrimination, capital punishment, housing and many other issues (Hall, 1980; Smart, 1984). There developed a strong commitment to radical lawyering in which lawyers were seen as crucial to the battle against injustice and inadequate civil rights and provisions. The identification of social problems met with a variety of legislative responses aimed at relieving the problem, or at least some of its symptoms.

By the end of the 1970s the political climate had changed. Not only were progressive social reforms to become a thing of the past but certain gains were to be challenged. In any case feminists had begun to have renewed doubts about the usefulness of law reform. But by this time they were themselves practising and academic lawyers. It was this combination of factors, most especially in the USA, that provided the foundations for feminist jurisprudence. On the one hand feminists wanted explanations about why law reforms had achieved so little when they seemed to promise so much, and on the other hand feminists had moved into the very heartland of law and legal practice. They had come to know its operations inside and out and were able to identify that it was not only legislation which was the problem, but such accepted elements as legal reasoning, ethics and concepts of justice, objectivity and what MacKinnon (1983) has called the maleness of law. Feminist legal scholarship found itself in a position to challenge fundamentally the traditional premises of law and legal knowledge. This discovery of the limitations of law was not a naïve rediscovery of what social scientists claimed already to know, but an insider's discovery which was able to locate with much more subtlety the kind of resistance law could produce in response to threatened changes. So for feminists closely involved in law the emphasis shifted from being one of optimism and campaigning to taking law more seriously as the emphasis of analytical study.

What we might call a self-conscious feminist jurisprudence arose out of this specific historical moment and has really been framed to address questions like 'What is wrong with law?', 'Why do rights framed to overcome discrimination against women serve to benefit men?', or 'Why do law and legal practice work against the interests of women?' It has very different antecedents to more traditional forms of jurisprudence and, in the main, it is not interested in creating abstract or philosophical models to explain the origins or legitimacy of law. Feminist jurisprudence to date has therefore taken the form of a critique although some feminists are beginning to suggest moral or ethical principles which might replace existing legal principles in an attempt radically to transform the form and content of law.[1]

The development of feminist jurisprudence has not taken the form of a linear and chronological ordering of ideas, but rather a scattered and somewhat tangential set of thoughts, some developing in the USA and others in Europe and Australia, some within the field of civil law and others with a more specific concern with criminal law. There are key writers who shall be examined in some detail, for instance Tove Stang Dahl (1987), Catharine MacKinnon (1982, 1983,

1987) and Carol Gilligan (1982). However, the movement towards feminist jurisprudence goes much wider than these contributions. For this reason it is perhaps useful to try to group together the feminist work in this field into different categories. Instead of relying on traditional categorizations of radical, socialist, cultural feminism and so on, I propose to use loose groupings based on the focus of the work. The categories I have identified are: the master theory approach; the experiential/epistemological approach; the psychological/modes of reasoning approach, and the social justice/harm approach. Some authors fit into more than one category and the boundaries between all four inevitably blur under close scrutiny.

The master theory approach
By the master theory approach (or metanarrative) I mean the attempt to account for everything in relation to one mode of explanation. Thus in the 1970s many scholars insisted that Marxist theories of capital could account for 'everything' worth accounting for. This meant that they argued that racial and sexual oppression either could be explained by reference to class oppression or that these forms of oppression were so insignificant that they did not require explanation. Feminism includes a variant of this approach in the tendency to assume that every significant phenomenon can be accounted for by reference to the operations of patriarchy or the needs of men.

The urge to produce the one theory which would account for the oppression of (all) women became evident in feminist work in the 1970s. It is therefore unsurprising to find that it is a strand in some of the early work on feminist jurisprudence. There are two prime examples of this genre which I shall examine. The first is by Rifkin (1980) which seeks to sketch out for us the whole story of the origins of law and patriarchy, and the second is by MacKinnon (1982, 1983) who has constructed the most precise version of a metanarrative in feminist legal scholarship and who has set the parameters for later work in the USA and, more recently, elsewhere.

Janet Rifkin's article entitled 'Toward a theory of law and patriarchy' was published in 1980. It marked an important shift away from the established 'sexism and law' paradigm in which feminists would expose exactly how sexist were the legislation, the legal and criminal process, and the judges. Rifkin stood on the threshold of the concept of feminist jurisprudence but did not in fact use the term. Her aim was to provide a framework in which the fundamental connections between culture, patriarchy and law could be revealed. She speaks of law in terms of a paradigm of maleness and this marks a major shift away from the empirically correct, although analytically

limited, observation that men make and operate the law. Consequently she achieves a shift of emphasis away from men as biological
beings towards the problem of masculinity and masculine values
which are cultural constructs rather than biological facts.

Her argument is that patriarchal culture originates at the moment
of the exchange of women, at which point women become property.
This is a complex argument which requires some knowledge of
structural anthropology. But Rifkin is really using this framework as
a device to persuade us that two major developments occurred at the
same moment. These developments are first, the beginnings of
culture which is founded upon patriarchal values (that is, the
exchange of women) and second, the creation of property whereby
women (along with cattle, tools and so on) become a form of
commodity or property. Onto this she grafts the familiar idea that law
has two main functions, namely the protection of (men's) property
and the mystification of the real nature of this patriarchal arrangement (or culture). So while setting law into a cultural context derived
from a structuralist school of anthropology, she engages the idea of
law as ideology, using ideology as meaning mystification derived
from a version of Marxist thought. Law is therefore a distortion of the
reality while justifying the subordination and oppression of women
and celebrating masculine values. The point that is so interesting
about the article is not this rather crude conspiracy thesis as much as
her assertion that law is grounded in the oppression of women
because it is grounded in culture. Whether or not we accept this
account as it stands, Rifkin provides a coherent argument against the
prevailing notion that when sexism occurs it is an epiphenomenon
which can be dealt with fairly superficially by the introduction of
more or different legislation. Here we have an insightful hint as to
how difficult the feminist project in law and jurisprudence is going to
be. Her assertion that the paradigm of law is a symbol of male
authority marks the beginnings of a new mode of conceptualization.

Catharine MacKinnon's major contribution to this field came in
two linked articles published in the US feminist journal *Signs* in 1982
and 1983. Although her work has developed since, these two papers
provide the theoretical coherence for her later work (1987). The first
article was entitled 'Feminism, Marxism, method and the state: an
agenda for theory'. In this MacKinnon develops a theory of women's
oppression which closely parallels Marx's early theory of exploitation
and alienation. She argues that 'Sexuality is to feminism what work is
to Marxism: that which is most one's own, yet most taken away'
(1982: 515). So, modifying Marxism, she embarks on her own version
of the metanarrative by substituting sex for work (or labour) to
produce a compelling framework which takes sexual exploitation as

the basis of women's oppression. She is also able to argue that all women have this one thing in common, and that what they have in common is more significant than their differences. She argues that she is constructing a theory of power and, implicitly, it is one which will explain the oppression of all women at all times. So for example she states:

> Feminists do not argue that it means the same to women to be on the bottom in a feudal regime, a capitalist regime, and a socialist regime; the commonality argued is that, despite real changes, bottom is bottom. (1982: 523)

Having identified sex as the core of women's oppression and men's power, MacKinnon goes on to argue that men also have the power to define the world (and hence make it real) from their own perspective. This male point of view is taken to be objectivity. In turn this is taken to be the only possible reality: the real truth of things. This male gaze is turned on women to produce them as men wish to define them. This process MacKinnon describes as objectification; women are objectified. This is the defining characteristic of women's sexuality, that is it is objectified by and for men. In constructing this complex argument MacKinnon is making important links between power and knowledge and the power to define. In her theory women are the victims of this process, but feminism can construct its own method of resistance. This method is consciousness raising by which women can collectively and critically reconstitute 'the meaning of women's social experience, as women live through it' (1982: 543). So, while standing inside the reality constructed by the male perspective, women can collectively redefine their experiences and produce an alternative critical and reflexive form of knowledge. MacKinnon does not pursue this in detail but in outline we are provided with the basis of a feminist theory of knowledge to counter what she regards as 'male' epistemology (which passes itself off as objectivity). She constructs feminism in opposition to male power. In her work feminism is what reveals the workings of male power and the extent to which women's experience has been devalued.

In the second article, 'Feminism, Marxism, method and the state: toward feminist jurisprudence', MacKinnon turns her focus on law which is for her a straightforward extension of the state. She writes, 'As a beginning, I propose that the state is male in the feminist sense. The law sees and treats women the way men see and treat women' (1983: 644). She argues that jurisprudence as currently constituted is the institutionalization of objectivity (that is, a male perspective which is also male power). She explores this argument through the example of rape and the parallel between men's inability to differentiate between rape and intercourse and the law's inability to do so as well. From this starting point MacKinnon is able to elaborate a complex argument which shows that only from a woman's point of view is rape an injury. Because the legal system insists that rape only occurs when a man has a guilty intent, if he does not perceive what he does as being anything other than sex, then neither will the law. Hence as far as the law is concerned she is not violated; there was no injury; she simply had sex. As men have no glimmer of an insight into what women want, MacKinnon goes on to argue, accusations of rape are truly mystifying to them. The point is, however, that the law reflects the male understanding rather than the experience of the woman who has been violated.

What is so important about this analysis is that it reveals the depth of the problem of law. It is clear here that the problem is not going to be successfully tackled without challenging fundamental principles of neutrality, objectivity and meaning (knowledge). The jurisprudence that MacKinnon is moving towards is therefore not concerned with concepts of equality or fairness; instead she is concerned with how male power is exercised in the guise of the neutral and objective standards of law. She does not provide a blueprint for a feminist jurisprudence, rather, in this early article, she aims to expose the maleness of law.

The question that must be asked, however, is how much of an advance is her conclusion that law (including legal reasoning and values) is male on the earlier (vulgar) Marxist analysis that law is bourgeois? Here again we encounter the problem of the master theory. Having identified sexuality as the mainspring of women's oppression, MacKinnon quite logically focuses on rape to make her points about law and jurisprudence. The logic is seamless and the argument extremely powerful. But the same could be said for Marxist analyses which identify the exploitation of labour as the mainspring of class oppression and then point to labour/trade union legislation as proof that law merely reflects (or is synonymous with) the interests of the capitalist class. These arguments assume the unity of the state and the unity of law. They also assume that law is merely an arm of the state and that there exists a coherent set of interests which are always smoothly met. MacKinnon gives us a partial story and attempts to convince us that it is all that needs to be said about law and jurisprudence. She argues that her analysis which identifies the basis of women's oppression (sex), the process by which oppression is achieved (objectification) and the methodology for challenging oppression as well as providing the basis of a new form of knowledge (consciousness raising) supercedes Marxism as a satisfactory version of events. Yet the claim is too sweeping, not because Marxism cannot be superceded but because the theory deals with race and class only by collapsing them into gender oppression. Just as Marxism has collapsed gender and race into class so MacKinnon's approach gives no room for other oppressions. She falls into the seductive trap of the master theory in attempting to explain everything and the value of her critique of jurisprudence risks becoming lost in the attempt to beat Marxism at a game that it is probably no longer playing (Fryer et al., 1981).

The experiential/epistemological approach

This loose category embraces work which gives priority to women's experience as a basis for jurisprudence and for a new way of knowing. It is committed to the production of a new epistemology which can form a concrete base from which to reject or criticize orthodox or male forms of knowledge, and hence jurisprudence. These ideas are prefigured in MacKinnon's work but are developed differently by other feminists. The two main orientations to be found in this work also coincide with geopolitical variations. Hence the MacKinnon approach is developed in the work of North American legal feminists, while a more social scientific approach has been developed by feminists in Scandinavia. What they have in common is the claim that women's experience must be revealed and communicated in order to transform the form and content of law and prevailing concepts of justice and fairness. While the North Americans rely on the method of consciousness raising to achieve this, the work of the Institute of Women's Law in Oslo depends on the methods of social scientific research informed by feminism.

Experience, consciousness raising and epistemology   Lahey (1985) provides an excellent example of the first (North American) approach to feminist jurisprudence. Avoiding any hint of liberalism she argues that 'The struggle for feminist representation in the production of knowledge is . . . a political struggle' (1985: 522). Her paper does not aim for a feminist certainty to replace patriarchal knowledge, nor does it claim that consciousness raising produces a truth to replace the patriarchal lie. Rather she develops an argument in which consciousness raising can be seen as a method to produce moments of knowing. She argues against hierarchies of knowledge and is undisturbed that this method produces different knowledges and different subjectivities. For Lahey feminist method is a voyage into ambiguities and uncertainties. Certainty is part of objectivity, which she insists is merely male subjectivity elevated to a realm of universality and neutrality as a consequence of the workings of male power. For her there is no neutral space, knowledge cannot reside outside of politics and one's own point of view.

Lahey does not claim that consciousness raising is a perfect method either; she sees it as a continuing, imperfect struggle. Her main tenet, however, is that consciousness raising produces feminist theory, but it is only feminist as long as it remains grounded in women's experience. Theory that is not so grounded but which derives from abstractions, she argues, is dangerous to feminist thinking. Her sphere is therefore small-scale and interpersonal with the requirement for constant reference back to women's experience. This is quite a different approach to the one demonstrated by MacKinnon even though the language deployed is similar. There is no tendency to construct the metanarrative, the overarching explanation which accounts for everything. Instead Lahey provides uncertainty. She does not try to beat the male theorists at their own game, but alters the parameters of doing theory.

The modest and intentional uncertainty of Lahey's argument is not, however, a defining feature of all feminist work in this field. By the time Wishik's article is published in 1986 certainties are being formed. She states:

> feminist jurisprudential inquiry focuses particularly on the law's role in perpetuating patriarchal hegemony. Such inquiry is feminist in that it is grounded in women's concrete experiences. These experiences are the source of feminism's validity and its method of analysis. Feminist inquiry involves the understanding and application of the personal as political. Feminism's method is consciousness-raising. (1986: 69)

Gone are the doubts about consciousness raising as a method, and the problems which might arise in assuming that the concrete experience of all women can be communicated and pressed into a feminist policy are glossed over. That different women may want very different things, indeed things which may be in conflict, does not occur to the author. Here we see a determined zeal overtaking the political sensitivity of earlier writers like Lahey. Why should Wishik assume that all women want to engage in consciousness raising? What power is exercised in the consciousness raising process? How can *all* women's experience be represented unless it is, a priori, assumed to be fairly homogeneous?

Wishik continues, 'In addition, feminist jurisprudence can help us envision the world we wish to create – that is, a world without patriarchy. It can also assist us in focusing our deliberations about the nature of that world' (1986: 72). This becomes a version of feminist idealism. It is not that the thinking of alternatives is so problematic, rather it is the naïvety of the idealist thinking about the nature and significance of law. Here feminist jurisprudence becomes almost a messianic movement and notions of the limits of the ability of law (whether feminist or not) to transform social reality are forgotten.

Scales (1986) takes up and furthers the debate on legal objectivity and its part played in denying the reality of women's experience. In a long article (to which I cannot do justice here) she attempts to substantiate the idea that objectification – and hence objectivity – is the source of women's oppression. She relies on the work of Dinnerstein (1978) and Gilligan (1982) to point out that objectification is part of gender differentiation (the process that boys and girls go through in becoming masculine or feminine) and hence is part of masculine consciousness. So objectivity is not just a stance that law adopted after prolonged consideration, it reflects something much deeper and much more powerful, namely the celebration of masculine existence and consciousness. From this we can see, according to Scales, that objectivity is more than masculine in the cultural sense, it is also masculine in the psychological sense. We can also understand (assuming that we share her faith in the object relations school of psychoanalysis to be found in Dinnerstein's work) why it is a symbolic standard which inspires such a deep commitment.

In arguing that none the less we must abandon objectivity, Scales does not mean to advocate the abandonment of standards. What in fact she argues is that our standards must emerge from an evaluation of results and not from an a priori abstract concept which prevails regardless of its results. (For instance equality is a useless standard if it merely treats the unequal as equal; what is needed is equality of outcome.) She goes on to argue that feminism is ideally suited to this approach because it has always been results-orientated and has a methodology which reveals the experience against which legal procedures must be tested. This method is, once again, consciousness raising. Before discussing Scales's version of this it is perhaps important to note at least one problem in her approach. Being results-orientated is not such a panacea as it might appear. We cannot, even among feminists, assume a consensus over what a good result is. Moreover, results orientation may not be that far removed from what judges do already. The idea that a pure principle is applied regardless of outcome is part of the myth of legal method perpetuated by law. Critics of the legal system have long pointed out that judges come to the decisions which they prefer and then, post hoc, read the principles which support their decisions into their interpretation of case law (see Sumner, 1979). Therefore, pressing for a results orientation alone may achieve very little.

On consciousness raising Scales states that the experiences which it reveals do not need validation by traditional methods – indeed she suggests they cannot be validated by these criteria. Relying on

MacKinnon (1983) she argues that feminism does not need an abstract concept of truth, rather she insists that the expression of experience is all there is. Feminism therefore provides law with what Scales calls 'dramatic eye-witness testimony'. It has the capacity to place what law has regarded as irrelevant or subjective onto the agenda and to use this alternative knowledge as the basis for new standards and principles in law.

Scales therefore provides an argument for the validity of what might be called 'subjugated knowledges' (Gordon, 1980). What is missing, however, is any critical evaluation of the practice of consciousness raising. It is given the accolade of a method rather than a practice, and in this respect it is claiming a place on the very hierarchy of knowledge it shuns. 'Method' is a term used in scientific or social scientific activity and it therefore seems odd to find it appropriated so unproblematically here. There is also a more fundamental problem than this misappropriation and that is that the denial of truth is insincere. In challenging the idea that only the knowledge that has been produced by so-called objective methods is the truth, this version of feminist jurisprudence claims to abandon truth altogether. Yet implicit in this work is the idea that feminist accounts are more valid than masculinist accounts. Scales argues:

> Heretofore, the tried and true scientific strategy of treating non-conforming evidence as mistaken worked in the legal system. But when that evidence keeps turning up, when the experience of women becomes recalcitrant, it will be time to treat that evidence as true. (1986: 1402)

Consciousness raising is therefore seen to produce a more powerful truth, not a variety of truths. In this form feminist jurisprudence, which sets out to deconstruct method and truth, creates its own version of the same problem. It does not challenge the central place of epistemology in social science, it merely asserts that it has a more reliable access to unassailable knowledge.

Experience, social science and law   While North American feminist legal scholars have turned to consciousness raising as a way of challenging legal orthodoxy and the problem of method, the approach taken by the Institute of Women's Law at Oslo, exemplified in the work of Tove Stang Dahl (1987), adopts a very different approach. Before highlighting the differences, however, it is important to be aware of certain similar premises. Both approaches presume that the basis for restructuring law must be women's experience. Hence both move away from abstract concepts and from law itself to start with women. But there is a basic presumption here, namely that 'women' is not an abstract concept but a concrete and automatically knowable category. Obviously there is something in this; just as we know a tree when we see one, we know a woman. This, however, is merely an act of recognition based on a constructed typology of physiological difference. It ignores the fact that the definition of gendered existence may vary considerably; furthermore it presumes that experience of a gendered existence is natural. In so doing, this form of feminism mistakes the product of its politics for a pre-cultural reality. By this I mean that it is the gaze of feminism which has produced Woman as a specific and significant category; women (as identified by feminism) do not exist outside this process of recognition. In a similar way other discourses (opposed to feminism) have produced Woman as an insignificant, malign, ignorant, invisible (etc.) category. The problem is that feminism ignores its role in constituting Woman in a particular form at a particular moment in history, and assumes that it discovers a reality which is merely waiting to be emancipated. As Riley argues:

> There is a wish among several versions of Anglo-American feminism to assert the real underlying unities among women, and of the touchstone of 'women's experience'. It is as if this powerful base could guarantee both the integrity and the survival of militant feminism. . . .
> Because of its drive towards a political massing together of women, feminism can never wholeheartedly dismantle 'women's experience', however much this category conflates the attributed, the imposed, and the lived, and then sanctifies the resulting melange. (1988: 99–100)

The concepts of Woman and of experience are therefore not unproblematic but they form the taken-for-granted basis of this approach to jurisprudence. This would not be an issue if it were admitted that this was a political device or a value position, but the concepts invoked often seem to hold the promise of an unassailable truth with which feminism can defeat not only other politics but also inferior (less truthful) knowledges.

The claim to truth is not a trap that Dahl falls into, however, in spite of her unproblematic use of the terms 'women' and 'experience'. She argues:

> Women-centred policy considerations are the *values* that are accorded special weight in women's law. These values – ideals of the 'good society' – are essential, both in the evaluation of existing law, and as criteria for the structure and methodology of women's law, and even as indicators of reform ideals. The values are thus used analytically to give substance to the expression women's law, born of the intention to describe, explain and understand women's legal position. (1987: 83)

Dahl deploys the concept of justice in her approach. This is not an abstract notion, however, but one which, she argues, is based on what women want. Like Scales she appears to reject the idea of the application of principle from on high and her aim is to start with beliefs which are widely held (by women) and from these to construct moral principles. Dahl therefore suggests that we start with the needs and wants of women in general and their opinions about what is fair and just.

This approach differs considerably from the consciousness-raising method. The latter presumes that the basis for law will be a feminist consciousness, while the former is content with women's consciousnesses. Dahl starts where women are, not where feminists are. From this starting point she argues that there are new legal categories which must be constructed, for example money law, birth law, housewives' law and paid-work law. This reorganization breaks down the traditional categories of law and arranges them on the basis of women's needs. It would, however, be incorrect to assume that Dahl does not herself have an ethical starting point which seems to pre-date her enquiries into what women want. For her the principles of freedom, equality, dignity, integrity, self-determination and self-realization are paramount. She treats these as unproblematic in the sense that she presumes that there is already a consensus of opinion behind her. She is not wrong in this respect, for these are exactly the concepts implicit in much feminist work which never strays into such philosophical territory. Concepts of integrity and self-determination form the very cornerstone of much feminist work on rape, for example. But the problem is that these are precisely the abstract ideas which she argues women's law eschews. There would therefore seem to be a contradiction between the aspiration to start with women's definitions of morality, justice and so on, and the imposition of a predetermined set of values which are assumed to provide the correct framework for women's law.

There is also another difference between Dahl's approach and the North American (and British) approach, even though on the level of values there may be similarities. Dahl does not locate her analysis within a theory of the state or law. The question of power which is so central to MacKinnon, for example, is missing here. It is implicit in Dahl's work that eventually the state and law will come round to accept that its conceptualizations of justice have been too limited. It would therefore be easy to criticize Dahl's position as a form of liberal feminism but this would be to ignore certain historical and political developments which have occurred in Norway. The state has become much more welfarist and progressively interventionist in Norway than is apparent in the UK or USA in the late 1980s. There appears to be an optimism about law and welfare reforms which has diminished elsewhere. Notwithstanding this fact there is a major disparity between this formulation of feminist jurisprudence, which ignores the problem of power (whether male, state or legal), and most of the other forms discussed in this chapter.

The effects of this difference can be remarked elsewhere. Dahl argues that the way to transform existing law and produce women's law is to bring to bear the methods of social science to the formulation and modification of legislation and legal practice. In other words it is depicted as a process of education. Yet, surprisingly, she is unconcerned with questions of the application by judges of legal logic to decision making because she maintains that the vast majority of women are not affected by the sort of law that goes on in court or which exercises the minds of judges. Women's lives are affected by administrative law and more mundane regulations which she treats as outside (or beneath) the application of formalistic legal thinking. Her strategy therefore is to leave the 'higher reaches' of law alone. Indeed she does not wish to challenge or interfere with legal method at all. She argues, 'Legal doctrine, i.e., the interpretation of law according to prescribed methodology, should remain the core area of legal science because it is there that lawyers have their own tools and a distinct craft' (1987: 32). This would be heresy to MacKinnon and others (myself included) who have precisely argued that it is this 'craft' which is so fundamentally oppressive to women. But Dahl is content to leave it alone as if it occupies a separate sphere and is indeed a neutral tool which is applied when necessary. Yet she is not prepared to ignore the development of legal theory which she identifies as the formulation of statements about the relationship between legal rules and reality. It is here that she sees social science methodology beginning to play a major role, and where empirical studies on the lives of women will provide a corrective to existing theories of law. Hence women's experience will be communicated through the process of research. This will, in turn, produce a 'consequence-orientated' and 'realistic' legal theory. Again these are almost the same terms used by North American feminists (such as results-orientated) but within a very different theoretical context.

There is one further important difference between Dahl's work and that of other feminists in the field (at least outside Norway). This is her adoption of scientific methodology as unproblematical. She argues, 'While politics first and foremost deals with power . . . it is the primary duty of science to seek knowledge and understanding, and by means of this to promote action' (1987: 23). In saying this she does not exclude the importance of an exchange between the women's movement (politics) and women's studies (science) but while she sees the insights gained from political activity as providing vital directions for feminist research, she regards the fruits of research as providing the best solutions to the problems thus identified. Dahl's work would therefore, in my view, fall directly into that category of work called feminist Fabianism. By Fabianism here I mean the idea of promoting science as a value-free and superior form of knowledge whose results can be applied to improve society and eradicate social problems. Although this has been social science's main claim to relevance and authenticity during the development of the postwar welfare state, it is now a position which is increasingly regarded as inadequate (not just by the right; see Bauman, 1988). Not only is the clear-cut distinction between politics and knowledge now questioned (not least by feminist scholars) but the idea that retrospective empirical studies provide answers to future problems is also subject to scrutiny (see Smart, 1986, 1990b).

Dahl's feminist jurisprudence, therefore, may have the appearance of similarity with other forms but it does espouse a very different political stance. She does, however, reintroduce ideas of justice which have remained untouched in other feminist works on law (if not philosophy) until quite recently. Yet questions of justice and ethics have become increasingly important to discussions on jurisprudence and we shall return to this theme below.

The psychological/modes of reasoning approach
The main contribution to this approach is the work of Carol Gilligan (1982). Indeed it is probably fair to state that Gilligan's work launched feminist legal theory down the path of psychology and moral reasoning. Her book, *In a Different Voice*, is a critique of Kolberg's theory of moral development in which he outlines these stages in children. Kolberg used boys in his experiments yet claimed a universality for his results. He therefore failed to recognize the part gender might play in the development of moral reasoning. He elevated the boys' development to a model of development for all children. If girls were to develop differently his study would have failed to notice it. Indeed, as Gilligan points out, traditionally moral philosophers and psychologists have in any case tended to assume that it is only men who develop the highest standards of moral reasoning. Women were rejected, a priori, as having less moral sense and as having less ability to be objective. Hence the way men reason has become *the* way in which reasoning is done.

Gilligan's thesis does not dispute this difference, rather she seeks to re-evaluate what has been rejected in the feminine mode. So she stresses the way that the masculine mode, which she calls the ethic of justice, has been both celebrated and used as the basis of our legal system. This ethic of justice relies on objectivity, rationality and emotional distance. The feminine mode, which she calls the ethic of caring, is based on connectedness, subjective emotion and responsibility for maintaining relationships. The ethic of justice is founded on the idea that everyone should be treated the same, while the ethic of caring means that no one should be hurt.

This work has generated a complete re-evaluation of the concept of justice and objectivity in much feminist work. Gilligan has provided a new 'angle' to the argument that law is male, which is based on psychology rather than philosophy or sociology. Her work also complements the influential work of feminists like Chodorow (1978) and Dinnerstein (1978) who have studied the psycho-social development of girls and boys and have argued that a basic element of masculinity is separateness and individuation, while a fundamental element of femininity is connectedness. These works therefore argue that the problem of maleness and masculine values is located in the psychic development of children.

Because Gilligan's starting point is developmental psychology rather than law or culture, she begins with the way in which boys and girls reason (in the present) and works from there, rather than asking why they reason so differently. In this respect she is close to Dahl, who also starts from the position of where women are. This stance has led to considerable criticism. Scales for example has stated that 'Just as Gilligan's work has the potential to inspire us in historic ways, it could also become the Uncle Tom's Cabin of our century' (1986: 1381). MacKinnon (1987) is even more scathing in her criticism, arguing that Gilligan merely attempts to give value to the form of femininity that patriarchy has imposed on women. The problem with Gilligan's approach, therefore, is that it may merely affirm the feminine rather than promoting the feminist. In using terms like the ethic of caring Gilligan inevitably reaffirms that women are naturally caring – even though this may not be her intention. Moreover her analysis can be used to keep women excluded from the corridors of justice since her version of the way that women reason would seem to be an unacceptable mode.

However, these criticisms are in many ways misguided. All 'knowledge' can be put to reactionary use and Gilligan's work does not carry a special responsibility in this respect. What is useful about her work is the way in which she identifies a hierarchy of moral reasoning and her recognition that there are subjugated modes which could be used to challenge an existing orthodoxy. This is not an entirely new approach. It can be found in work on customary law which, when compared with western law, is construed as quite inadequate. What Gilligan identifies as male has, therefore, also been identified as western, imperialist or 'white' thinking (Harding, 1986). Such work locates modes of thinking in their cultural and historical specificity and challenges the orthodoxy of claims to universality and naturalness.

In terms of a specific contribution to feminist jurisprudence, Gilligan suggests that what is needed is a more generative view of human life in which the ethic of justice and the ethic of caring can both be deployed. This is perhaps the weakest part of her thesis, since she assumes that law really does operate by an ethic of justice rather than by making claims to objectivity and neutrality as part of the exercise of power. She also fails to appreciate that what she calls the ethic of caring does already operate in the legal system (Daly, 1989a). These weaknesses perhaps stem from the fact she is a psychologist with little knowledge of law's operations and how (or whether) moral values become transposed into law. Despite this her work has been extremely influential in generating ideas about legal and moral reasoning and in raising debates about what form feminist values might take. It is to this issue I shall now turn.

The social justice/harm approach
This approach to feminist jurisprudence marks a shift towards the attempt to construct feminist values which could actually be deployed in the practice of law. As noted above, Dahl's work in Norway has also adopted this strategy, but here I want to focus on different contributions from the USA and Australia.

One crucial development in this approach was the attempt to redefine certain social practices as 'harms'. Hence behaviour now labelled sexual harassment has been construed as a harm. Although there is considerable resistance to labelling certain sexualized exchanges as sexual harassment, once so labelled there follows an automatic assumption that some harm has been caused. Another equally important area has been the redefinition of the harm that pornography causes. This has attempted to shift the understanding of the harm away from one of moral harm – in the traditional Christian sense – to one of harm to women – in the feminist sense (MacKinnon, 1987).

Wishik (1986) has called for a global use of the term harm, that is she argues that feminist jurisprudence can identify the harms of patriarchal law and can begin to describe an existence unharmed by patriarchy. This is a very unfocused use of the concept of harm which has little strategic value. West (1988) is more specific in her use of harm in the attempt to build what she calls a reconstructive feminist jurisprudence. She argues that feminists have succeeded in having harms recognized by law only when the harm is made analogous to the deprivation of a right which masculine liberal jurisprudence can comprehend. She is therefore critical of the strategy on sexual harassment which turned it into the infringement of a civil right in order that law could recognize it as an offence. Although there was some 'success' in this strategy it left the problematic rights-based jurisprudence untouched.

Consequently West argues that it is vital to reassess what harms are done to women and what harms the legal system fails or refuses to acknowledge. Here she relies on the work of feminist psychologists (such as Dinnerstein, 1978) to argue that what matters to women is intimacy and connectedness and protection against invasion. However, law protects or values autonomy and individuation and protects against annihilation. Hence law responds to the harm of rape when it entails a good deal of violence (that is, the threat of annihilation). It cannot respond to a rape which is an unwanted invasion. Equally the law cannot recognize the harm of foetal invasion (as West describes unwanted pregnancy) even though it threatens a woman's bodily integrity. This is because it does not threaten her life, only her 'self'. So West concludes that feminist jurisprudence must re-articulate women's rights 'in such a way as to reveal, rather than conceal their origin in women's distinctive existential and material state of being' (1988: 61). Hence the right to abort should no longer be a right to privacy (as it is currently construed in the USA) but a right to defend against a particular bodily invasion.

These attempts to redefine harm are useful in the way they reveal the acceptedness of the harms which law maintains deserve protection. But they also raise a number of problems. First, we can see in West's work a return to the old problem of equality and difference. In a way which is more sophisticated than Gilligan she is rehabilitating the difference approach.

Second, in more specific terms, her examples of reframing the basis of current jurisprudence pose a number of difficulties. It would, for example, seem necessary to define all pregnancies as bodily invasions in order for some women to exercise the right to abort. Yet not all women experience their pregnancies in this way. Moreover, defining pregnancy in this way may simply encourage greater medical intervention in and control over the pregnant mother. Defining the foetus as separate from the mother may seem helpful in terms of abortion but it has reactionary consequences in terms of the development of foetal rights and the possibilities of prosecuting mothers for harm done to the foetus in utero (Smart, 1990c). Equally, sexual intercourse which is welcomed is not necessarily experienced as a bodily invasion. The problem is that the term invasion, which is used to convey harm, assumes there is a harm regardless of the views or consciousness of the woman involved. This may make it easier for women who are raped or unwillingly pregnant to make claims of the law, but it does not necessarily reflect the 'true subjectivity' of women that West wishes to see reflected in jurisprudence. Rather it elevates a particular (radical) feminist version of women's experience into a norm for all women.

Ultimately, and unfortunately, West's work slides into liberal utopianism which seems to be the pitfall of so much North American feminist jurisprudence. She argues that law provides a way to counter profound power imbalances which, in my view, hugely overstates the power of law to achieve structural change within a capitalist and patriarchal state. She goes on:

> In a utopian world, all forms of life will be recognized, respected and honoured. A perfect legal system will protect against harms sustained by all forms of life, and will recognize life affirming values generated by all forms of being. Feminist jurisprudence must aim to bring this about. . . . Masculine jurisprudence must become humanist jurisprudence, and humanist jurisprudence must become a jurisprudence unmodified. (1988: 72)

And, I am tempted to add, pigs must learn to fly.

For a more pragmatic approach it is useful to turn to the work of Adrian Howe on social injury (1987). She borrows the idea from the criminologist Edwin Sutherland who deployed it to extend the use of the concept of crime to include activities like white-collar and company crime which have been regarded as less problematic or damaging than, for example, theft or burglary. Howe uses the term social injury rather than the more typically feminist 'harm' (although the two are related) because she argues that injury is something the law can recognize and which can therefore become actionable. She sees this process as a form of political action rather than idealizing a feminist jurisprudence. She acknowledges the differences between women and argues that the idea of redefining injury on the basis of women's experience can still accommodate these differences. But the most significant difference between Howe's work and that of the 'idealist' feminists is that she makes it clear that redefining certain experiences as injuries should not automatically lead to the assumption that legal action – and most particularly criminalization – is desirable. She holds back from the assumption that there should be an inevitable movement between redefinition and a legal response. In this respect she takes a similar line to Daly (1989b) who is quite categorical that criminalization (of pornography) is misguided (see also Brants and Kok, 1986). The important feature about Howe's approach is that for her it is the redefinition which is important, not the legal action. Although she concedes that legal sanctions can provide legitimate recognition of a social injury, she does not insist that law should be put in the position of validating or invalidating every harm that women identify. What is not clear, however, is which harms should become actionable and which should not. Howe uses the example of pornography, pointing out that women have different and conflicting views on whether or not it causes a gender-specific harm. She suggests that it should become actionable only if it is 'shown to legitimate "the expropriation of our sexuality"' (1987: 433). However, this evades the fundamental problem of whether such a connection could ever be unambiguously shown or universally accepted. It postpones making a decision on the grounds that we may eventually have the full facts which will make the answer obvious. So the problem with Howe's approach is that it does not provide any clear instances of when or how we should use the concept of social injury. Her paper does, however, constitute a major advance over many other forms of feminist jurisprudence in that it does not presume that a recourse to law is necessarily a solution. While exploring the idea of a feminist jurisprudence Howe remains sceptical of law and the power of law to order our existence (even a feminist existence). This brings me to the one question which it has been impossible to pose until now. This is, 'do we really need a feminist jurisprudence?'

A future for feminist jurisprudence?

I have suggested elsewhere that the search for a feminist jurisprudence is like a modern quest for the Holy Grail (Smart, 1989). In the work of authors like West and Wishik, for example, it does seem to take an exaggeratedly idealized form in which feminist jurisprudence becomes the answer to women's oppression. Linked to this is the failure to think critically about what is meant by women's experience which is thought to provide the basis of this feminist vision. Whether it is idealized or not the question that is rarely addressed is whether we really do need a feminist jurisprudence. The strength of the feminist work so far lies in the critique that has been mounted of the foundations of traditional jurisprudence. It challenges all the main assumptions of jurisprudence, except the assumption that we need some form of jurisprudence. This is because the central role of law as an organizing principle of everyday life is rarely challenged in the construction of the new jurisprudence.

Taking the problem of women's experience first, I have argued that the terms 'experience' and 'consciousness raising' have become virtual slogans which are almost meaningless. This is not to argue that feminist policy should divorce itself from the multiplicity of women's different experiences. Instead what is needed is a recognition that knowledge of these experiences will not provide simple answers. This has been well documented, especially by black women who have made it clear that they are critical of the goals and practices of a women's movement which is predominantly white but which proposes to speak for all women. Matsuda (1987) has argued most cogently that radical jurisprudence in the USA does not yet seem to have room for the experiences of ethnic minorities (see also Monture, 1986). The proposal for a feminist jurisprudence therefore already looks suspect in that it is unsure what it might mean for black women (let alone for black men). But the problem is not only to try to find a space for other silenced experiences (although this is difficult enough), rather it lies in what is to be done when different experiences conflict. Muslim women, Afro-Caribbean women, Native women, Jewish women and Irish women may all have very different experiences which cannot easily be collapsed into a single feminist jurisprudence.

The second problem I have identified is perhaps even more serious for feminist legal scholarship. I want to argue that in spite of the value of the critique mounted by feminist jurisprudence, in constructing a new jurisprudence feminists give a renewed legitimacy to the power of law to organize and regulate our lives. For example almost all the feminist work cited above takes issue with law's claim to objectivity and neutrality, claiming that what passes for these qualities is really male subjectivity and interests. But the claim to objectivity and neutrality has always been exactly that – a claim to be refuted, not taken seriously. The law does not operate according to any one set of standards, nor is the law itself a unitary phenomenon which has one direction and purpose. There is no single foundation to jurisprudence and no single outcome to the application of any one principle. In other words it is more complex and less of a conspiracy than the model implied in much of the work on feminist jurisprudence would have us believe. This leads to the question of whether it is sensible to try to impose a unitary standard on law except as an intellectual exercise which reveals the failure of law to be objective and so on. A simplified model of law may be useful in the construction of a critique, but it is a poor basis for a reform strategy. Perhaps even more important is the way in which the search for a feminist jurisprudence retains law as a central focus of feminist strategy. Of course feminists cannot help but respond to the growing influence and intervention by law into new areas of regulation. But maybe the response should be one of resistance rather than calling for more law – even law based on agreed feminist principles. A feminist jurisprudence gives renewed hope that law can be rehabilitated, but the resort to law remains a white middle-class privilege unless there are commensurate fundamental changes elsewhere. And if we could have those fundamental changes we should ask the question why we would still wish to retain such a reliance on law to tackle the oppression of women.

Clearly feminist legal scholarship cannot ignore the way in which traditional jurisprudence is formulated and the way it influences the practice of law. However, it faces formidable problems. The form that it has taken in the 1980s has been defined by the interests largely of white, North American, feminist legal scholars. Although self-critical work is beginning to appear (see Kline, 1989), feminist jurisprudence tends to be limited by the very paradigm it seeks to judge. In criticizing law for being male it cannot escape the related criticism of promoting a (classless, white) female point of view as the solution. Neither can it escape idealizing law as a solution to women's oppression. The question is whether feminist jurisprudence can overcome these conceptual and political problems or whether we need to start from somewhere else fundamentally to challenge the power of law and the heritage of traditional jurisprudence.

Notes

This chapter was originally published in P. Fitzpatrick (ed.) (1991), *Dangerous Supplements: Resistance and Renewal in Jurisprudence*, pp. 133–58, Pluto Press.

1 Feminist legal scholarship and campaigns during the second wave also focused attention on the question of rights and how to reformulate them in order that women's needs could be better addressed. Although this is an important element in the development of feminist jurisprudence space will not allow me to explore this question here. See Smart (1989: Ch. 7) for a detailed discussion.

11

The Woman of Legal Discourse

Feminist socio-legal theory has been developing in exciting and (happily) controversial ways over the last 20 years. The developments that we can see almost certainly parallel developments in feminist thought elsewhere. This should hardly surprise us, yet the field of law poses quite specific intellectual and political problems for feminist theory which may not be found in other fields.[1] These problems are threefold and, surprisingly, cumulative, considering that they originate from quite different constituencies. The first constituency voices a resistance to the idea that theoretical analysis is relevant to law outside the narrow confines of courses on jurisprudence. This could be said to be the 'black letter' constituency. The second voices a resistance to the idea that specifically *feminist* theory is relevant to law because it is argued that law (at least in most developed countries) has transcended 'sexual bias'. This is the liberal constituency. The third voices a form of resistance to all theory and is based on the argument that, because law is a practice which has actual material consequences for women, what is needed in response is counterpractice not theory. This constituency demands 'practical' engagement and continually renders (mere?) theoretical practice inadequate. This argument comes from certain feminist constituencies which may define 'doing' theory as male. These three elements present a major obstacle to proponents of feminist legal theory as they (we) meet with the frustrations of being ignored or seen as outmoded in and by law and are simultaneously moved to renounce theory by the moral imperative of doing something through or in law.

But feminist socio-legal theory faces another difficulty in as much as the tension that has always existed around the issue of whether to try to 'use' law for 'women' has taken on a new shape. This tension traditionally used to take the form of an assertion that law, being an epiphenomenal effect of patriarchy, could hardly be used to dismantle the said patriarchy. Attractive and succinct as this may sound, we now recognize that it is both an oversimplification and a recipe for despair, given that theorizing everything as an effect of a monolithic patriarchy rendered feminism itself little more than a false consciousness at best, or a device for sustaining patriarchy at worst.

Our theories of gender and of law have moved on, but there has been another important development. The entry of feminists into law has turned law into a *site* of struggle rather than being taken only as a *tool* of struggle. Yet the increase in numbers of feminist legal scholars and practising lawyers has (ironically) led to what I regard as contradictory consequences. The first, which I applaud, is a refinement of our theories of law, especially in relation to legal method and logic. The second, which is perhaps more problematic, is a renewed vigour in attempting to deploy law in the cause of women.[2] My concern over the latter move is not an attempt to resurrect the old argument I have just rejected above but rather reflects my concern that this renewed strategy continues to give law a special place in the resolution of social problems. This tendency, which is perhaps most clearly evident in North America, fails to challenge not only law's inflated vision of itself and thus empowers law (Smart, 1989), but it also enhances law's imperialist reach.[3] The move to use law for 'women' also collides with the recent and profound recognition in feminist theory deriving from other disciplines, that to invoke an unproblematic category of Woman, while presuming that this represents all women, is an exclusionary strategy (see, for example, Spelman, 1988). But I now find myself in advance of my argument and so I wish to return to an earlier stage in the mapping of feminist socio-legal theory. In order to do this I shall concentrate on two related arguments. The first will address the question of how law is gendered, the second examines law itself as a gendering strategy.

How law is gendered

There are three phases we can identify in the development of the idea that law is gendered. These are basically stages of reflection in feminist theory which have provided a foundation of understanding and have been largely, but not entirely, superseded (see also Naffine, 1990).[4] The first stage is epitomized by the phrase 'law is sexist', the second by the phrase 'law is male' and finally we reach the point of arguing that 'law is gendered'. These three levels of argument may be found to be deployed simultaneously in some feminist work on law; however, it is useful to differentiate between them in order to see what analytical promise each approach has.

Law is sexist

The starting point of the 'law is sexist'[5] approach was the argument that in differentiating between men and women, law actively disadvantaged women by allocating to them fewer material resources (for example, in marriage and on divorce), or by judging them by different and inappropriate standards (for example as sexually promiscuous), or by denying them equal opportunities (for example, the 'persons' cases, Sachs and Wilson, 1978), or by failing to recognize the harms done to women because these very harms advantaged men (for example, prostitution and rape laws). These were (and remain) important insights, but the attribution 'sexist' really operated more as a strategy of redefinition than as a mode of analysis. Thus the attribution of the label 'sexist' was a means of challenging the normative order in law and reinterpreting such practices as undesirable and unacceptable.

Law is undoubtedly sexist at one level. However, this attribution did not really begin to tap the problem that law poses and does, I would suggest, slightly misrepresent the problem. The argument that law is sexist suggests that a corrective could be made to a biased vision of a given subject who stands before law in reality as competent and rational as a man, but who is *mis*taken for being incompetent and irrational. This corrective suggests that law suffers from a problem of perception which can be put right such that all legal subjects are treated equally. This form of argument is by no means a simplistic one. It is framed with different degrees of sophistication from those who suggest that the introduction of gender neutral language into law rids us of the problem of differentiation and hence discrimination (for example, spouse instead of wife, parent instead of mother) to those who appreciate that discrimination is part of a system of power relations which needs to be addressed before the sexism can be 'extracted'. For the former, sexism is a surface problem to be tackled by re-education programmes and a rigorous policy of hiding visible signs of difference. For the latter, law is embedded in politics and culture and the route to fairer treatment for women lies in changes which will allow women to occupy different positions in society so that differentiation will become redundant.[6]

The problem with these approaches is that the meaning of differentiation tends to become collapsed into the meaning of discrimination and the fulcrum of the argument rests with the idea that women are treated badly in law because they are differentiated from men. It is often remarked that this means that men are retained as the standard by which women must be judged.[7] Irksome and nonsensical as this may seem, pointing it out only leads us to imagine that judging women by the standard of women is the solution. This may not be a great leap forward if those women who set the standard are white and middle class. If they are, we are left with an equally problematic legal system in which sexism is apparently eradicated but other forms of oppression remain. But this fallacy of substitution is not the core problem of a perspective which invokes the concept of sexism rather than gendering. The concept of sexism implies that we can override sexual difference as if it were epiphenomenal rather than embedded in how we comprehend and negotiate the social order. Stating it more boldly, sexual difference – whether we see it as constructed or not (Fuss, 1989) – is part of the binary structure of language and meaning. If eradicating discrimination is dependent on the eradication of differentiation, we have to be able to think of a culture without gender. Thus what seems like a relatively easy solution such as the incorporation of gender-neutral terminology into law, masks a much deeper problem. Moreover, as many feminists have argued, it is not at all certain that the desired outcome of feminism is some form of androgyny.

Law is male

The idea that 'law is male' arises from the empirical observation that most lawmakers and lawyers are indeed male. It transcends this starting point however because of the realization that maleness or masculinity, once embedded in values and practices, need not be exhaustively anchored to the male biological referent, that is, men. Thus MacKinnon (1987) has made the point most eloquently when she argues that ideals of objectivity and neutrality which are celebrated in law are actually masculine values which have come to be taken as universal values. Thus, in comparison to the 'law is sexist' approach, this analysis suggests that when a man and woman stand before the law, it is not that law fails to apply objective criteria when faced with the feminine subject, but precisely that it does apply objective criteria and these criteria are masculine. To insist on equality, neutrality and objectivity is thus, ironically, to insist on being judged by the values of masculinity.

As with the 'law is sexist' approach, the 'law is male' perspective covers a range of more or less sophisticated positions. From the early work of Gilligan (1982) which *seemed* to attach male or masculine values to the biological referent and thus appeared biologically reductionist,[8] to more recent work (Mossman, 1986; Tronto, 1989; Young, 1990) which details the exclusion of values of caring in preference for 'uncaring' (that is, impartiality), or the actual rules and methods for arriving at the legal (and hence impartial) decision by systematic exclusion of other perspectives.

Yet, important as these insights are, they perpetuate a number of specific problems. First, this approach perpetuates the idea of law as a unity rather than problematizing law and dealing with its internal contradictions. Second, and without necessarily being explicit, this approach presumes that any system founded on supposedly universal values and impartial decision making (but which is now revealed to be particular and partial) serves in a systematic way the interests of men as a unitary category.[9] We can see, therefore, that while great care is taken in these arguments to effect a distance from a biological determinism, there lingers an unstated presumption that men as a biological referent either benefit or are somehow celebrated in the rehearsal of values and practices which claim universality while (in reality) reflecting a partial position or world view.[10] Yet we know that law does not serve the interests of *men* as a homogeneous category any more than it serves the interests of *women* as a category. It might, of course, be argued that these authors do not make this connection between male value systems and the interests of men and that I am forcing their argument to the sort of limits where any argument would start to look absurd. But there is a reason for stretching this argument, perhaps unfairly, which does not lie in the rather futile desire to show that no feminist argument transcends biological reductionism.

Any argument that starts with ceding priority to the binary division of male/female or masculine/feminine walks into the trap of demoting other forms of differentiation, particularly differences within these binary opposites. Thus the third problem with this sort of approach is that divisions such as class, age, race, religion tend to become mere additives or afterthoughts. This process of adding 'variables' which appears on the face of it to overcome the criticism of racism and classism levelled against feminist theory, in fact merely compounds the problem by obscuring it. As Spelman has stated:

> according to an additive analysis of sexism and racism, all women are oppressed by sexism; some women are further oppressed by racism. Such an analysis distorts Black women's experiences of oppression by failing to note important differences between the contexts in which Black women and white women experience sexism. The additive analysis also suggests that a woman's racial identity can be 'subtracted' from her combined sexual and racial identity: 'We are all women.' (1988: 125)

Or, as Denise Riley has stated more succinctly, 'Below the newly pluralised surfaces the old problems still linger' (1988: 99).

Law as gendered
The shift between the categories 'law is male' and 'law as gendered' is fairly subtle, and the transition does not entail a total rejection of all the insights of the former. But while the assertion that 'law is male' effects a closure in how we think about law, the idea of it as gendered allows us to think of it in terms of processes which will work in a variety of ways and in which there is no relentless assumption that whatever it does exploits women and serves men. Thus we can argue that '[t]he same practices signify differently for men and women

because they are read through different discourses' (Hollway, 1984: 237). So we do not have to consider that a practice is harmful to women because it is applied differently in relation to men. Rather, we can assess practices like, for example, imprisonment without being forced to say that the problem of women's prisons is that they are not like men's. But further, the idea of 'law as gendered' does not require us to have a fixed category or empirical referent of Man and Woman. We can now allow for the more fluid notion of a gendered subject position which is not fixed by either biological psychological or social determinants to sex.[11] Within this analysis we can turn our focus to those strategies which attempt to do the 'fixing' of gender to rigid systems of meaning rather than falling into this practice ourselves.

This means we can begin to see the way in which law insists on a specific version of gender differentiation, without having to posit our own form of differentiation as some kind of starting or finishing point. We can therefore avoid the pitfall of asserting a pre-cultural Woman against which to measure patriarchal distortions (that is, a starting point), as well as avoiding a Utopianism which envisions what women will be once we overcome patriarchy (that is, the finishing point). Thus we can take on board the sort of argument made by Allen (1987) in relation to the way in which law can only see and think a gendered subject without invoking the same form of differentiation ourselves. Her argument is worth rehearsing here. She examines the use of the concept the 'reasonable man' in criminal law. It has always been taken to be an 'objective test' of *mens rea* (guilty intent) but Allen demonstrates the sheer impossibility of this proposition. She states:

> Legal discourse thus incorporates a sexual division not only into what the law can legitimately 'do', in terms of particular provisions and procedures, but also, more profoundly, into what it can reasonably *argue*. Yet beneath even this we can trace a third and yet deeper level of sexual division in legal discourse – at the level of what the law can intelligibly *think*. What is revealed in these arguments is that ultimately legal discourse simply cannot *conceive* of a subject in whom gender is not a determining attribute: it cannot *think* such a subject. (1987: 30, emphasis in original)

With this approach we can deconstruct law as gendered in its vision and practices, but we can also see how law operates as a technology of gender (de Lauretis, 1987).[12] That is to say we can begin to analyse law as a process of producing fixed gender identities rather than simply as the application of law to previously gendered subjects.

The revised understanding of 'law as gendered' rather than as sexist or male has led to a modified form of enquiry. Instead of asking

'How can law transcend gender?', the more fruitful question has become, 'How does gender work in law and how does law work to produce gender?' What is important about these enquiries is that they have abandoned the goal of gender neutrality.[13] Moreover, law is now redefined away from being that system which can impose gender neutrality towards being one of the systems (discourses) that is productive not only of gender difference, but quite specific forms of polarized difference. Law is seen as bringing into being both gendered subject positions as well as (more controversially?) subjectivities or identities to which the individual becomes tied or associated. It is therefore appropriate, at this stage in the argument, to turn to the concept of law as a gendering strategy which needs to be read in conjunction with the idea of 'law as gendered'.

Law as a gendering strategy

In this section my argument will develop the point that Woman is a gendered subject position which legal discourse brings into being.[14] This is of course a sweeping statement; one that will invoke the cry that women have always existed, they did not have to wait for law to give them entry into the Social, that law is hardly so powerful, that women are the product of natural, biological processes and so on. I can concede some of these points for certainly law alone does not constitute what Woman is, but it is perhaps necessary to consider what is meant by Woman and by 'gendering strategy' before looking in more detail at the parts played by law and legal discourse.

Woman is no longer self-evident (Riley, 1988; Spelman, 1988; Fuss, 1989; Butler, 1990; Hekman, 1990).[15] Such a statement is, of course, an affront to common sense which knows perfectly well what women are and reacts keenly should anyone try to blur the naturally given boundaries between the two (also naturally given) sexes. Yet first we must concede a distinction between Woman and women. This is familiar to feminists who have for some centuries argued that the *idea* of Woman (sometimes the *ideal* of Woman) is far removed from real women. Moreover, feminism has typically claimed an access to real women denied those who perceive the world through patriarchal visions. So the distinction between Woman and women is not new but it has become more complex. For example, we have begun to appreciate that Woman is not simply a patriarchal ideal and that the women that feminism(s) invoke(s) are perhaps the Woman of/ constructed by feminist discourse(s) rather than an unmediated reality simply brought to light. In other words, the claim to an absolute reality located in the body of women against which the excesses of patriarchy can be measured has become less tenable. Feminism does not 'represent' women. Indeed as Butler has argued,

> [T]here is the political problem that feminism encounters in the assumption that the term *women* denotes a common identity. Rather than a stable signifier that commands the assent of those whom it purports to describe and represent, *women*, even in the plural, has become a troublesome term, a site of contest, a cause for anxiety. (1990: 3, emphasis in original)

Some have argued that this form of thinking removes feminism's constituency and thus threatens feminism as a political and social movement. However, this assumes that both intellectual innovation and political work must have an absolute, unmediated object of knowledge on which to ground itself. This requirement seems to be set stringently for any forms of poststructuralist feminism, while many other feminisms are allowed to operate on the basis of 'as if'.[16] Indeed, feminism has long taken issue with common sense and its counterpart the 'unmediated real'; recognizing the cultural and historical elements of knowledge and rejecting the claim to a transcendental authority. So if we accept that Woman and women are not reducible to biological categories or – at the very least – that biological signs are not essences which give rise to a homogeneous category of women, we can begin to acknowledge that there are strategies by which Woman/women are brought into being. These strategies (in which I include law as well as discipline[17]) vary according to history and culture, they are also contradictory and even ambivalent. They may also be strategies without authors in as much as we should not imagine that strategy here implies a plan, masterminded in advance by extra-cultural (Cartesian) actors.

There is, of course, a distinction to be made between the discursive production of a type of Woman and the discursive construction of Woman. I want to invoke both of these meanings because it is my argument that they work symbiotically. Put briefly the (legal) discursive construction of a *type* of Woman might refer to the female criminal, the prostitute, the unmarried mother, the infanticidal mother and so on. The discursive construction of Woman, on the other hand, invokes the idea of Woman in contradistinction to Man. This move always collapses or ignores differences within categories of Woman and Man in order to give weight to a supposedly prior differentiation – that between the sexes. Thus this prior differentiation acts as a foundationalist move on which other differentiations can be grounded. Thus the female criminal is a type who can be differentiated from other women but, at the same time, what she is is abstracted from the prior category of Woman always already opposed to Man. Thus she may be an abnormal woman because of her distance from other women, yet simultaneously she celebrates the natural difference between Woman and Man. Only by under-standing this double move can we comprehend what we might otherwise mistake for inconsistency or oversight. Rather than taking it as a contradiction which can be resolved by the application of a little logic, we should recognize that the very foundation of the discursive construct of modern Woman is mired in this double strategy.

Thus Woman has always been *both* kind and killing, active and aggressive, virtuous and evil, cherishable and abominable, not *either* virtuous *or* evil.[18] Woman therefore represents a dualism, as well as being one side of a prior binary distinction. Thus in legal discourse the prostitute is constructed as the bad woman, but at the same time she epitomizes Woman in contradistinction to Man because she is what any woman could be and because she represents a deviousness and a licentiousness arising from her (supposedly naturally given) bodily form, while the man remains innocuous.[19]

While these strategies which produce gender are many and varied, I want to tell a straightforward story so that I can reach my topic of law without too much further delay. It has been argued that the end of the eighteenth century and the nineteenth century in Britain marked an important moment in the history of gender. What was witnessed was a polarization of genders in which difference became increasingly fixed and rigid, and at the same time was naturalized (Davidoff and Hall, 1987; Jordonova, 1989; Laqueur, 1990). Scien-tific discourses were central to this process, giving new vigour to traditional religious and philosophical beliefs about the inferiority of women. Women became more and more closely associated with their bodies, and their bodies became both overdetermining and patho-logical. It becomes possible to argue that scientific, medical and later psychoanalytic discourses operated to create the very gender differ-ences we have come to take for granted as natural but, more importantly, these discourses have rendered natural the ideal of natural differences. At the same moment, of course, feminism was constructing a very different Woman, one who was not a semi-invalid (if middle class) nor sexually licentious and vicious (if working class). Yet even this feminist discourse fixed difference in the realm of the natural.

For my analysis of law, the nineteenth century is also particularly significant. This century marks both the pinnacle of law's exclusion of women from civil society (for example, the denial of the legal personality of married women) and the moment when written law began to inscribe in finer and finer detail the legal disabilities of Woman. (Put another way, we can say that gender became increas-ingly fixed in terms of its attributes and in terms of being increasingly polarized.) At the most basic of levels we can see that legislation dating from the eighteenth century and before was sketchy in its terms and succinct to a fault (at least to twentieth-century eyes). But the nineteenth century marks a moment in which there grows a greater refinement and a 'pinning down' of relevant categories and legal subjects.

We could therefore claim that nineteenth-century law brought a more tightly defined range of gendered subject positions into place. We can also see how law and discipline 'encouraged' women to assume these identities or subjectivities. This idea is perhaps best pursued with an example and the one I wish to trace concerns motherhood, but not the good mother, or even the 'good enough' mother – I am interested in the bad mother.

An example of law as a gendering strategy: specifying the category of the bad mother

Although I have specified the nineteenth century as a particularly significant moment in the fixing of gendered identities, I shall start my story earlier than this in order to identify how the nineteenth-century engagement of law and discipline, as two different forms of regulation, marks a break with earlier periods.

Thus my story begins in 1623 in England. In that year a new statute was introduced, creating a new crime and criminal. The statute made it a penal offence for a mother to kill her bastard infant on pain of death. The point about this new law was that the mother was to be presumed guilty if her infant died, and it was for her to provide evidence of her innocence. A presumption of guilt was extremely rare in English law and so the unmarried mother was brought into being in law as a culpable murderer. It should be stressed that at this time the state did not regulate marriage or even insist on formal marriage and so the condition of being married or not married was in some ways more fluid, especially as some people did not marry until they had several children together.

Thus we have the problematization of a specific form of mother-hood. Its regulation was to take the form identified by Foucault (1977) as the power of the sovereign to inflict death. This woman is perhaps one of the first to enter into statute specifically as Woman.[20] Her entry marks a number of associations which are implicit yet must be understood for the legislation to make any sense. Not only is she unmarried and hence without protection, she occupies a specific class position (that is, poor), she is deprived of the material conditions to raise a child, yet she is to be put to death for seeking to escape her plight – even if the child died of natural causes (or the effects of poverty on pregnancy and childbirth).

This piece of legislation was so draconian that it was rarely enforced because juries failed to convict. We can, however, map how the strategy of inflicting harsh punishment on the few became translated into modes of discipline and surveillance of the many. The penalties became less harsh, but fewer women could escape the reach of the revised forms of legal categorization.

In 1753, Lord Hardwick's Marriage Act began the process of regulating marriage such that there no longer existed indeterminate states of semi-matrimony – women were either married or unmarried. In 1803, the draconian Infanticide Act of 1623 was transformed into legislation against the concealment of birth. A presumption of innocence was restored and the penalty much reduced. However, its aim was to bring more women into the reach of the law because there was no requirement to establish murder. In the same year (1803), the first criminal statute on abortion was introduced. Abortion at any stage of pregnancy was criminalized and, although there was a distinction made between the pre- and post-quickening stages, this was later removed. English law never criminalized the production and sale of information on birth control (as, for example, Canadian law did), but the spread of such information was effectively controlled by the use of private prosecutions against blasphemous or obscene libel. In 1882 the age of consent was raised to 13 and in 1885 to 16. Thus marriage could not take place before these ages and this exposed young women who became pregnant, but could not marry, to legal and philanthropic scrutiny. In 1913 the Mental Defective Act facilitated the incarceration of unmarried mothers on the grounds of moral imbecility or feeble-mindedness.

My point is not just that these different forms of law constructed a category of dangerous motherhood, but that the net of law widened at precisely the same time as it made it increasingly difficult to avoid unmarried pregnancy and childbirth. The end of the nineteenth and early part of the twentieth century also coincides with the problem of the surplus woman, who had no chance of marrying anyway because of the export of men to the colonies or their slaughter in various wars.

The penalties (especially for infanticide) became less harsh, but more women were caught in the net of inescapable motherhood. If they attempted to escape through the use of contraception or abortion they were condemned as prostitutes or (virtual) murderers, if they failed they were subject to newer forms of discipline in the shape of philanthropy and mental health legislation/provision. We can see, therefore, how motherhood was actually materially constructed as a 'natural', hence unavoidable, consequence of heterosex. Means of avoiding motherhood were denied to women, and the inevitability of the link between sex and reproduction was established through the harsh repression of those deploying traditional means of rupturing this link. We see the rise of compulsory motherhood for any woman who was heterosexually active. But by compulsory motherhood I do not simply mean the imposition of pregnancy and birth, but also entry into the nexus of meanings and behaviours which are deemed to constitute proper mothering. Moreover, as the nineteenth century turned into the twentieth, we witnessed the growth of surveillance and institutionalized intervention into women's lives through the establishment and spread of health visitors and social workers (Davin, 1978; Donzelot, 1980)

The unmarried mother obviously served (and still serves) to reinforce our cultural understanding of what 'proper' motherhood means. In this sense she is a *type* of woman rather than Woman. Yet she simultaneously operates in the discourse as Woman because she always invokes the proper place of Man. She is the problem (supposedly) because she does not have a man. Therefore Man is the solution, he signifies the stability, legitimacy and mastery which is not only absent in her but inverted. The unmarried mother is therefore also quintessential Woman because she represents all those values which invert the desirable characteristics of Man.

At this point it may appear that my concerns are with the symbolic. However, my interests extend beyond this because my purpose in mapping the development of the legal subject 'unmarried mother' is to throw light on the dominant regime of meaning which always already treats this woman as problematic and destabilizing. Just as Foucault has shown that categories such as the criminal or the homosexual are not pre-existing entities to be investigated and understood by science, so we can also see that the unmarried mother comes into being as a consequence of specific strategies and knowledges. While she is not a fixed or unchanging category she enters into an established web of meanings which make instability and dangerousness virtually self-evident and matters of common sense.

The significance of this for the contemporary situation is that more and more women can be fitted into this category. The Act of 1623 that I started with affected relatively few women. Now the category includes the never married and the divorced lone mother. (The widow is rarely included because she is thought to keep the symbolic father alive, and so is hardly a lone mother.) More recently this category has extended further to include the 'surrogate' mother and the woman seeking infertility treatment. I should therefore like to close with a contemporary example. In 1990 the British Parliament passed a piece of legislation entitled the Human Fertilisation and Embryology Act. Section 13(5) reads, 'A woman shall not be provided with treatment services unless account has been taken of the welfare of any child who may be born as a result of the treatment (including the need of that child for a father)'. This legislation also continues the fiction that a woman's husband is the father of her children even if he is not biologically related to them (AID) and creates a new form of illegitimacy by insisting that the husband and biological father of a child will not be treated as the legal father if his sperm was used or if an embryo of his was implanted after his death.

These measures are nonsensical unless you already know that the mother without a husband is a danger. These measures may seem quite different to the measures passed in 1623 or later on in the nineteenth century, but they build upon an understanding of the category Woman of which law is a partial author. It is this Woman of legal discourse that feminism must continue to deconstruct but without creating a normative Woman who reimposes a homogeneity which is all too often cast in our own privileged, white likeness.

Conclusion

It is of course almost impossible to conclude. In any case I do not want to impose a false closure where we are just beginning to ask more and more challenging questions. From where I stand, feminist socio-legal scholarship faces two main tasks at the beginning of the 1990s. The first is to grasp the nettle that law is not simply law, by which I mean it is not a set of tools or rules which we can bend into a more favourable shape. Although we have known this for a long time, I am not sure we have done enough with this knowledge. The desire to be political has been confused with the desire to be practical, and thus law has continued to occupy a conceptual space in our thinking which encourages us to collude with the legalization of everyday life. We must therefore remain critical of this tendency without abandoning law as a *site* of struggle. The second is to recognize the power of law as a technology of gender, but not to be silenced by this realization. Thus we should see the power of law as more than that negative sanction that holds women down. Law is also productive of gender difference and identity, yet this law is not monolithic and unitary.

Moreover, much more work needs to be done in tracing how women have resisted and negotiated constructions of gender, since we should not slip into a new form of determinism which suggests that, because power constructs, it produces women in some predetermined, calculated, powerless form. I am suggesting therefore that law remains a valid focus of feminist theoretical and political scrutiny, but that we need to recast our understanding of the relationship between 'law' and 'gender'. Recognizing that law is a more complex problem than might once have been thought need not, however, lead to despair since we can quite clearly see that feminist scholarship and enquiry are also much more tenacious and insightful than might once have been imagined.

Notes

This chapter was originally published in *Social & Legal Issues: An International Journal*, 1992, 1(1): 29–44.

1 It is important to define what I mean by the field of law. Although the term 'law' implies a singularity or unity, law is many things. At one level it is what is passed into statute as a result of a political process. Statute law is open to interpretation, of course, although not a 'free' interpretation. A range of conventions apply which we can refer to as legal methodology. We cannot understand law without a critical appraisal of this methodology. At another level there is the practice of law. While legal method conforms to conventions which can be (arguably) revealed, legal practice is far less visible. I refer to how solicitors and other legal actors like the police use the law (and interpret it with less scrutiny) in everyday practice. This kind of law is known to be a long way away from law 'in books' or in case law, but it is not unrelated to it of course.

But law is also more than the summation of these elements. It is also what people believe it to be, in as much as they may guide their actions by it. Indeed, we could go further to suggest that law creates subjectivities as well as subject positions. Take, for example, the category of bastardy which became the category of illegitimacy in the twentieth century. This was both a mere legal category, but it also became an economic positioning and a psychological condition. We created disadvantaged children and disinherited adults through this legal category.

2 The work of Catharine MacKinnon is perhaps most instructive in this respect. For while analysing law and legal method as irrefutably male, she pursues a litigation strategy which celebrates law as a solution to the very problems it epitomizes. (This is not to suggest, however, that she is unaware of this contradiction.)

3 In using the term 'imperialist reach' I am referring to the process of legalization of everyday life which has become increasingly visible in the western developed countries in the past century, but which has gathered pace in the last forty years. Hence the idea that every social problem has a legal solution has become more widely held, and when law fails the solution is often posited as more law to cover the inadequacies of existing law. Within this general framework, litigation has come to play a special role either through developing 'test case' strategies (proactive) or through more defensive measures like exploiting the judicial review procedure. My point is not that nothing can be achieved by these strategies, nor that there are self-evidently available alternatives waiting to be deployed, but that this legalization of everyday life transforms (and changes) the problems it encounters, it gives the impression that there are procedures that are emanci-patory rather than disempowering, it gives decision making to legal and quasi-legal tribunals and courts (that is, to judges) and hence empowers law

further. It also requires a growing dependency on a legal elite who are the only persons who can interpret and negotiate the increasingly complex system of law.

4   Ngaire Naffine (1990)has also mapped the development of feminist legal theory in a similar way in her extremely useful book *Law and the Sexes*. She refers to three phases of feminism: the male monopoly, the male culture of law, and legal rhetoric and the patriarchal social order. Her first two phases correspond closely to my 'Law as Sexist' and 'Law as Male', but a different focus emerges with our analysis of the third phase and subsequent ideas for directions of theoretical endeavour.

5   I must acknowledge that sexism is not a term we hear a great deal any more. It was current in the 1970s and early 1980s, but it has been abandoned somewhere along the way except in fairly polemical texts. Yet I have chosen to revive it here because, although the term itself has fallen out of fashion, the form of analysis it represents has not. Moreover, this form of analysis transcends old boundaries between socialist, liberal and radical feminists since all have deployed some version of it with greater or lesser degrees of sophistication. I am therefore using it as a kind of shorthand, not as a straw woman that I can easily knock down. The concept of sexism is the base line of feminism, and I know I have often been reduced to this line when I begin the story of feminism for the 'uninitiated'.

6   Katherine O'Donovan's (1985) work might be said to represent this sophisticated end of the 'law is sexist' argument. Her argument calls for the abolition of the private/public distinction in the ordering of everyday life. It is this distinction which, she argues, is the stumbling block to the usefulness of even a reformed legal system. Thus abolishing the system which differentiates between men and women (that is, the private/public divide) would create the conditions under which law could cease to disadvantage women.

7   The argument that men set the standard by which women are judged (i.e. equality = being treated the same as men; difference = being treated differently from men) should not be taken as the same as the argument that suggests that standards in law are based on a masculine imperative. The former takes as its object an unproblematic empirical referent called men. The latter invokes the concept of gendered values which are not linked to any assumptions of a biologically given category of men (or women). While the former invites us simply to substitute women for men, the latter invokes ideas about how values, standards and principles are never free of their cultural context but how in a phallocentric culture some values come to be taken as universal and gender-free.

8   I would argue that it is incorrect to take Gilligan's work as biologically reductionist. She bases her analysis on a psycho-social process of gender identification which in turn produces different moral standpoints which can be typified as masculine and feminine. If her work is reductionist it is in specifying a psychological process in childhood as being so overdetermining that it produces masculine and feminine ways of reasoning.

9   Kingdom (1991) would also add that any analysis of law which treats it as a 'front' for something else like patriarchy or male values, adopts an essentialist view of law. In such an approach law is always understood by reference to something else and this diverts attention from an analysis of the specific workings of law.

10   I wish to make it clear that I do not absolve myself from this criticism. It is all too easy when criticizing others to give the impression that one would never have made such an obvious 'mistake' oneself. Not only have I done so, I almost certainly continue to do so. In any case an 'error' is usually only apparent after ideas have been worked on for a while. And perhaps it is misleading to speak in

terms of errors when we know that each development of feminist thought depends on the groundwork that has gone on before, even if this groundwork is superseded.

11 Note I am using the term 'fixed' here. I am not sure that I concede to Butler (1990) that gender is mere performance and that there need be no relationship between sex and gender. However, I do accept Fuss's (1989) argument that constructionist arguments are just as over-determining as biological essentialist arguments. As I have no answer to these problems I prefer to leave the issue open.

12 While I am borrowing de Lauretis's concept of technology of gender here I am aware that I may be forcing the category somewhat. Law cannot be analysed in exactly the same way as film or television or other media yet her concept invokes the activity of producing gender differentiation which I wish to capture here.

13 What is perhaps unfortunate is that the perception of feminist legal scholarship held in many quarters is that the idea of gender neutrality and equality remains the pinnacle of feminist aspiration.

14 The term legal discourse is now, of course, quite familiar in writing influenced by Michel Foucault. However, it may be worthwhile for me to clarify my usage of the term. I take discourse to refer to a body of texts, not necessarily drawn from one discipline, which are productive of a given type or subject. The classic examples in Foucault's work are the lunatic, the criminal and the homosexual. These types or subjects, he argues, were brought into being by specific discourses of the late eighteenth and nineteenth centuries. Walkowitz (1982) makes a similar argument on how laws on Contagious Diseases in the second half of the nineteenth century were productive of the category or subject prostitute.

This approach turns materialism on its head, although it does allow for consideration of what is referred to as non-discursive elements. Thus there is no denial of the material but the conceptual dominance of materialism and 'realism' is revoked.

15 Indeed there are those who would argue that Woman has always been problematic to feminism, for example de Lauretis (1987). I am not sure that I agree with this as a general statement because feminism as a political movement seemed to be untroubled by the question of 'What is a woman?', even if these philosophical discussions were then ongoing.

16 By 'as if' I am using the shorthand terminology which acknowledges that, for example, pure communication is impossible but we act in the everyday world 'as if' it were. Thus, while we doubt the foundations of knowledge we none the less act. My point about poststructuralism is that it is more open about acting 'as if' than forms of epistemology which invoke the 'real'.

17 I make this point because I differ from Foucault in seeing law as part of the ancient regime which operates in different ways from the mechanisms of discipline. While acknowledging that there are differences, I would argue that law has come to deploy many of discipline's mechanisms. See Smart (1989) for a fuller discussion of this.

18 Unlike the concept Woman, the term femininity has never allowed these multiple meanings. The concept of femininity has always been contingently related to Woman, introducing both class and race dimensions rather than being a final or closing statement on the nature of womanhood. When I suggest that femininity invokes class and race, rather than being a quintessential statement on gender difference, I mean that only white, middle-class women were allowed entry into the feminine. Women of African descent 'were' never feminine,

Asian women 'were' always passive and obsequious, Jewish women 'were' aggressive, white, working-class women 'were' uncouth, and so on.

19 There is only one exception to this that I can think of and that is the situation in which divorce law came to recognize the undesirability of men 'consorting' with prostitutes, by giving the wife a right to a separation where her husband had knowingly communicated a venereal disease to her. It should also be noted that in the UK we have legislation against 'kerb crawling'. However, this does not create a category of licentious men in the way that legislation on soliciting creates the category of prostitute.

20 Of course the Common Law tradition of English law means we cannot identify a moment in which other categories of woman (e.g. the wife) entered into legal discourse. Ecclesiastical law also has origins which are not easily traceable, yet Woman is clearly to be found there in the regulation of divorce *a mensa et thoro* and in relation to abortion. She also entered as a specific category of offender for whom certain sorts of punishment were deemed inappropriate.

12

Proscription, Prescription and the Desire for Certainty?: Feminist Theory in the Field of Law

There was a time, or so the story goes, when feminist thought arose from the forge of political activism; when this thought did not have a mind of its own – so to speak – and we (for we knew who we were then) had a Utopian vision towards which all effort, both intellectual and strategic, was expended. The image of this period, located perhaps some 10 or 15 years ago, now mesmerizes us as we struggle with the new enemy within. This enemy is called 'uncertainty' and it is rumoured to be born of that male conspiracy to undo feminism, namely postmodernism.

What is required, or so it seems, is a return to orthodoxy and a clear naming of allies and adversaries. We need to recreate a Utopian vision (to generate enthusiasm among the sisters), we need theory that generates strategies and programmes, and we need to do all this in a way which does not exclude minorities within minorities. Thus we know that, 'Should postmodernism's seductive text gain ascendancy, it will not be an accident that power remains in the hands of the white males who currently possess it' (Hawkesworth, 1989: 557). Or that 'Postmodernism, with its "deep scepticism" and "radical doubts" is not the medicine required to cure intellectual and social life of the affliction of various orthodoxies . . . What is sorely needed . . . is theory that permits us to achieve appropriate and intelligent trust in the self and in its various abilities to come to know what is real' (McGowan Tress, 1988: 200). I do not mean to isolate Hawkesworth or McGowan Tress specifically from the range of voices of concern. Nor do I intend to imply that they have expressed unambiguously the sentiments outlined above – which are obviously something of a caricature. But their work, along with many other feminist authors in the realist or standpoint tradition, suggests to me a certain *yearning* for a Golden Age within feminism which never really existed.

To put it quite simply, feminism has always been fragmented, even if the fragments were organized differently. The *unity* that existed was based on class and colour blindness (at least in the United

Kingdom). The certainty that existed resided in righteous indignation (not unjustified of course) and a faith in the power of the (welfare) state to change conditions of existence if *it* so chose.

I am unhappy with the idea of a unitary feminism which acts as if it were an evangelical faith which must either condemn or assimilate difference. An example of this approach is, of course, MacKinnon's work (1987). Cornell has said of MacKinnon, 'Under her analysis, feminism becomes a series of normative injunctions, hidden behind a supposedly materialist analysis. Those who do not abide by the analysis do not obey and by definition are not feminists' (1992: 6). Nor am I comfortable with feminism as a super-science which can confound those Enlightenment boys with a new strong objectivism (Harding, 1991). These aims are antithetical to feminism if only because feminism has always been so many contradictory things. It follows, therefore, that I am uncertain why we should *now* strive to construct a unifying epistemology to give direction to, or perhaps merely justify, diverse political action. The question then is 'Why are we trying to pin feminism down, especially in the form of standpoint feminism, at this particular moment?' And 'What form are these wider concerns taking in the field of feminist legal thought?'

Standpoint epistemology

Standpoint feminism has been much discussed elsewhere (Harding, 1986, 1991; Smith, 1988; Cain, 1990). It has also been frequently criticized (Flax, 1987, 1990; Riley, 1988; Hekman, 1990). There seems little point in rehearsing the basic arguments over again, although we should recognize that standpointism is no longer as obviously naïve or essentialist as its critics were initially able to assert.

Harding (1991) in particular has done much to answer her critics by refining some of her basic concepts and rejecting charges of essentialism or a faith in the ultimately Truthful account. Other authors like Hill Collins (1990) who adopt a standpoint epistemology now argue against that early presumption that the more oppressed you are the more correct your analysis of the social organization of oppression. Moreover, Harding has argued that women's *experience* is not the fundamental element of standpointism. Rather she argues that standpoint epistemology must originate in the 'objective location of women's lives' and must proceed from there on the basis of democracy (1991: 123).

Standpoint epistemology therefore seems to accept multiple realities, contextualized and historicized accounts, and it has abandoned its hope of achieving a feminist Archimedean point (see Cain, 1990). On the other hand it retains a commitment to the idea that certain perspectives provide different and valuable ways of looking at the world and that these can amend or supersede the *more* partial accounts provided by elitist or orthodox masculine/white/heterosexual perspectives. Standpoint feminism can, it would seem, both have its cake and eat it.

It is with these recent developments, articulated by Harding and Cain, that I wish to take issue briefly. In her revised or more sophisticated version of standpoint epistemology, Harding appears to concede a great deal to her critics who adopt what is broadly referred to as a postmodern position. However, she stops short of abandoning standpointism because she desires to retain what she perceives as a means of distinguishing between more partial knowledge and less partial knowledge. Cain (1990) has referred to a similar desire but uses the term 'good quality knowledge' versus (presumably) poor quality knowledge. For Cain the key distinction between good quality knowledge and any old knowledge is the self-consciousness with which it is produced. Thus theory is made up of clearly articulated concepts in some logical relationship to one another. Because of the form it takes, theory can be easily communicated and is re-usable. This makes it, according to Cain, *objective*. Thus it is not the content of theory which contains the element of objectivity, it is the form or means of production of knowledge. This method does not promise to *uncover* the Truth, but it promises to be true to a set of procedural rules which can be clearly scrutinized. With such a system, feminism can monitor its own knowledge production and can be sure it does not simply produce *political* accounts. On the other hand feminism is provided with a tool or standard against which to judge other knowledge claims. We therefore have the legitimate grounds on which to find them wanting should they fail.

Harding makes a related argument but uses the term 'strong objectivity' to convey her approach to validating knowledge. Strong objectivity means bringing scientific observation to those background assumptions which are taken-for-granted as natural or unremarkable from the perspective of men's lives (1991: 150). This sounds similar to the strategy of revealing and challenging the doxa – those aspects of culture which are so normative as to be invisible. It also sounds perilously close to the practice of deconstruction which insists that one must never be satisfied with surface appearances but must *get behind* them to see how they are formed.

Both Cain and Harding agree that this newer, more sophisticated version of standpointism does not require the knower to be a woman. Indeed, both acknowledge the possibility of feminist men because they argue that what is required to produce feminist knowledge is the application of procedures not the attribution of *biological* or social gender. This move would seem to revoke all intimations of essentialism in standpoint epistemology and leave its critics breathless.

For both Cain and Harding standpointism remains the most attractive form of knowledge construction for one further reason. This reason is linked to the practice of feminist politics. While renouncing much of the epistemological basis of crude objectivism and realism, both insist that it is through the *reform* of these old concepts that the fundamental commitment to an emancipatory politics can be retained. Both construct postmodernism as apolitical or (worse) reactionary. Harding, for example, quotes Di Stefano (1988) approvingly when she states that the postmodernist project makes any kind of feminist politics impossible, even inconceivable.

Thus standpointism is defended on two apparently invincible grounds. First, it *gives* voice to knowledge arising from the lives of women and transforms this knowledge into knowledge with a scientific status. Second, it preserves the tradition of feminist politics started over a century ago, but refined in recent decades. Thus it can *prescribe* forms of knowledge deemed to be inadequate and evades the (supposed) pitfalls of relativism without positing a concept of alternative truth. It can *proscribe* in as much as its knowledge construction is intimately linked to a political venture and, if not exactly a programme, then lines of action appear to arise out of this knowledge. Finally there is a return to certainty. We have hovered on the brink of postmodernism (Lacey, 1992) and stepped back into the familiarity of traditional feminist politics. We do not have to doubt the existence of such categories as *Woman* because we talk to real women about the actualities of their lives. We can continue as before, revealing the exclusion of women and demanding that the state or the law respond to our scientifically verifiable knowledge of these lives.

Why then would one want to persist in a critique of standpointism? I want to suggest two reasons. The first is that although this new version answers its critics in its philosophical mode, when it is *applied* it seems to revert to the older more simplistic model. Second, I think standpointism is a means of preserving a method and politics more appropriate to modernity than it is to postmodernity. I shall explain these points in turn.

The philosophical mode versus applied mode
I enter into this section of my paper with some hesitation. At one level I know that it is all too easy to engage in an exercise which seems to be accusing a constituency of saying one thing, but in actuality doing another. Indeed, we should know that perfect consistency is a myth, or more worryingly, a stick to beat any critics who wish to change things but cannot produce the perfect blueprint for change.

So my purpose is not to berate standpoint feminists for failing to achieve complete consistency, but to suggest that the philosophical defence they mount is too nuanced for the practice of standpointism. Put simply, standpointism does not have the vocabulary to accommodate the complex meanings now attributed to it. It therefore celebrates difference but speaks of homogeneity, it denounces essentialism but takes for granted such things as *what men are like*. For example Harding states: 'Men love appropriating, directing, judging, and managing everything they can get their hands on – especially the white, Western, heterosexual, and economically overprivileged men' (1991: 280). Of course language and vocabulary are a problem for us all – but before I turn to this point I want to elaborate on the difficulties I see with this aspect of standpointism.

In her paper 'Realist philosophy and standpoint epistemologies or feminist criminology as a successor science', Cain (1990) mounts an extremely attractive case for standpointism. Her position is imbued with feminist politics and ethics and the promise of a powerful form of knowledge creation. In one section she goes on to address the possibility of whether it is possible to work from two standpoints at once. This would seem a *logical* possibility given her assurances that men can adopt the standpoint of feminism and so on. However, she hesitates about this possibility and states:

> If a person fully occupies two standpoints then it must be that she will be aware of the contradictions between them and try to theorize and make sense of these in order to achieve an improvement in the position of both groups, say women as a whole and black people or the working class or children too. (1990: 135)

What are we to make of this? Is Cain suggesting that there are several discrete standpoints such as the standpoint of women *and* of black people, or of women and of the working class, or of women and lesbians and so on? She does in fact say we must choose which standpoint we work from, and content ourselves with forming alliances with other groups. But what does this mean for black women, working class lesbians, Asian girls? Why should black feminists have to choose either 'women as a whole' or black people, or be forced to recognize the contradictions? Is this not exactly what black women in the US and UK have been complaining about (see, for example, Hull et al., 1982). Now clearly Cain is not saying that you have to be white to take a white standpoint, nor does she suggest that standpoints are fixed and unchanging. But she is providing us with the categories from which we can choose, namely women as a whole, blacks, the working class and children. It is precisely these traditional categorizations which are so problematic, and rather than accepting them and expecting those who do not fit into the categories to work with the contradictions, we may need to challenge the categories themselves.

Just in case my criticism is interpreted as a deep form of essentialism (see Cain, 1990: 134) I am not suggesting (any more than Cain is) that these identities are fixed and that, for example, black lesbians can only see the world as black lesbians and so forth. But I am saying we should take seriously the criticism that the category *Woman* hides other differences and we should not insist that women must choose *gender* over *ethnicity* or class, age, or sexual orientation or be required somehow to theorize their way out of a conceptual paradigm which is not of their making. Moreover, I am not sure that it is adequate for Cain to argue that the theoretician may be able to see the unity between these fractured identities which the actors themselves do not see (1990: 134). This seems to me to be a revived and disguised form of the discredited false consciousness argument. It suggests that those who analyse the world differently or according to different categories simply cannot see the whole picture which is only available to the theoretician who has followed the correct procedures of standpointism. At worst we may find ourselves in a position of positing a division between gender and ethnicity based on our orthodox sociological categories, but promising that we may be able to theorize a unity between the two, only to find that black women have not felt themselves to be fragmented in this way. (Indeed as many black feminists have argued, they are not women and black but are black women.) Or, if they have felt this specific form of fragmentation, we may need to recognize that it may in part have arisen from the dominant discourse of white feminism which has insisted that women are white and that blacks are men and has suggested that black women choose their location. It seems a shame that standpointism reproduces these categories as if they are unproblematic and as if these categorical divisions between *race* and *gender* are pre-given or natural.

In response to these points the standpoint feminist might argue that she would not insist on such broad categories as gender, ethnicity, class or age as the groupings on which a standpoint is based. Indeed, Harding and Cain both discuss other more *specialized* standpoints, for example women in prison. Harding argues:

> Are there not additional forms of situated knowledge and politics hiding in the logic of these analyses? One can begin to detect other identities for knowers, . . . secondary identities standing in the shadows behind the ones on which feminist and other liberatory thought has focused, identities that are also struggling to emerge as respected and legitimate producers of illuminating analyses. (1991: 273–4)

The question is what to do with the proliferation of accounts which emerge from increasingly *marginal* locations. Cain's answer, discussed above, is that the theoretician will be able to see the unity between such accounts even if the participants cannot. Harding proposes that these accounts need not compete, rather she suggests that the 'fundamental tendencies of each must permeate each of the others in order for each movement to succeed' (1991: 156). But it becomes clear that Harding suggests that feminist standpoints must be taken up by others (for example a standpoint from the position of disability) and vice versa. In other words she presumes that the problem of multiple accounts is *not* a problem of multiple *feminist* accounts. She presumes an ultimate consensus between the knowledge produced by people in *countercultures*. Even assuming this to be possible, it overlooks that within one *counterculture* like the Women's Movement there is no consensus. Issues of contention such as pornography and assisted reproduction surely make it plain that the problem facing the feminist knower is not simply one of bringing issues of ethnicity, sexuality, class, age and so on into an account, but how to deal with the various accounts that arise from the lives of even a relatively homogeneous group of women.

Harding's solution to this seems to be to 'apply rational standards to sorting less from more partial and distorted belief' (1991: 159). This, however, begs the question since it would seem that rational standards are hardly self-evident and indeed the very concept of *rationality* has been criticized by some feminists as a masculinist mode of thinking. Indeed it might almost seem that Harding is pressed to resort to a concept like rationality as if it is outside the debate, a final court of appeal or even Archimedean point which ultimately saves her version of standpointism from old fashioned or judgemental relativism.[1]

Once again, for the sake of clarity, let it not appear that I am saying that any account will do or that all accounts are equally valid; we do need some way of distinguishing between them. But I think we must acknowledge that a concept like rationality, or what we perceive to be rational, is also historically, politically and culturally located. Once we abandon ideas about a discoverable ultimate Truth or objective knowledge I would argue that we must recognize that the *rules* we set up to construct and validate knowledge are also far from being absolute. Yet it seems that what standpointism does is to try to compensate for the loss of this Archimedean point by positing impartial rules or guidelines. This then seems to lead to a tendency to construct a politically correct and ethically sensitive – yet invincible – feminist scientist who can be protected from criticism by the procedural rules of standpointism.

Yet, it seems a contradiction to suggest that an author like Cain constructs an invincible feminist scientist when she speaks so powerfully about accountability. Although on the one hand she argues that the academic 'can theoretically determine, and choose, for whom the knowledge she produces will be most useful' (1990: 136), Cain also argues that she 'will know to whom [she] is accountable for the quality of the knowledge' produced. So how can I argue that this emphasis on accountability presumes a certain invincibility? In my reading of Cain this element emerges from her clear presumption that if we follow the rules of standpointism we will produce knowledge that is unerring and reliable. She implies (albeit not consistently) that we will only 'get it wrong' if we do not follow the guidelines conscientiously enough. Thus she states, 'Just think of the suffering that has been caused to women by the mistheorizations of their atypical behaviours' (1990: 136). This suggests that had the theory been correct this suffering would have been avoided. This chance remark contains precisely what I find so problematic about standpointism.

I want to argue that there can never be this kind of certain relationship between understanding (formed at a precise moment in time/space/culture) and *future* events. Moreover, whether knowledge *works* or not is always contestable or open to reinterpretation. Thus the sort of accountability Cain talks of which is based on some future reckoning is either chimerical or ingenuous. Let me deal with this at an anecdotal level. If we consider the construction of knowledge from the standpoint of students we must concede that courses we teach should reflect some democratic process of modification according to the perspective revealed by this specific standpoint. Yet those of us who have followed these principles come to know quite quickly that if we change a course to meet the requirements of one cohort, the next cohort will find much of what has been changed to be deeply flawed and oppressive. We also know that the standpoint of the student may change during their period of study. We may also discover that not all students want the same programmes. Thus we can think of law schools in which there is a split between those who want black letter, doctrinal law courses and those who want more critical or theoretical courses. We might of course say that we (as radical teachers) will align ourselves with the latter, but what would this mean if the students who wanted the doctrinal training were the black students who most need a specific kind of degree in order to get what they perceive as decent jobs?

My point is simply that standpointism does not *tell* you what to do in policy terms. Nor can we rely on some future reckoning to judge whether we produced 'good quality knowledge'. If we accept that it does not *tell* us what to do in this simple way and that other factors must intervene in the development of policies and strategies, then the *failure* of such policies (as defined by specific groups for whom the knowledge was produced) cannot be reduced to a presumption that the foundations were rooted in poor quality knowledge. The knowledge may have been perfectly good as a retrospective but, as a basis for prediction, I would want to argue that *all* knowledge is *poor* quality.

As Bauman (1991) has pointed out, the presumed relationship between knowledge and some programme of action is based on a specific understanding not only of knowledge but also of the concept *society* or *structure on which* this knowledge *works*. Thus we presume a certain kind of system where we can change one or two variables and then monitor the effects. This is a very ordered universe, typically one in which the dominant agent is thought to be a (welfare) state which can direct resources in scientifically guided ways. His point is that this is no longer an adequate theorization of our conditions of existence. Our habitat is postmodern, so operating with a set of presumptions forged within modernism might perhaps now be seen as problematic.

This is a complex but vital discussion which brings me to my second point about the deployment of methods and politics which are linked to a social structure which may be rapidly vanishing.

Modern methods versus postmodern habitats
Much of the feminist critique of postmodernism has been targeted against a philosophy or mode of analysis. Postmodernism is felt to be a perspective which (maliciously?) directs us away from long-term concerns such as inequality, poverty, racism and sexism. What authors like Bauman (1991) and Smart (1991) argue, however, is not that power has vanished and we are all living the good life so that we do not need a politics of resistance, but that categories of class, race or gender are too cumbersome to accommodate fragmented sociality. Bauman for example argues that vocabularies or concepts such as *society* or *system* are now inappropriate to capture the 'processual modality of social reality, the dialectical play of randomness and pattern' (1991: 190) and the extent to which all found structures are emergent accomplishments.[2] He continues that sociology's focus should be on agency and the habitat in which agency operates. Linked to this is the notion that agents are themselves self-constituting. It is with these fluid concepts that he wishes to replace modernist theoretical concepts like class and community (he does not mention gender but then maybe this was never part of his vocabulary!).

Thus Bauman argues that we should no longer think in terms of a state which sets the agenda and against which we can campaign and organize. And we should recognize that rather than a single *goal-setting* agency there are numerous agencies with different goals, none of which is powerful enough to override the others. If we accept this model (or, for example, the model of law which argues that it is not a homogeneous unity) we cannot imagine that a given input like new knowledge will have a predictable or uniform effect. This does not have to be a reflection on the quality of the knowledge, at least not *unless* there really is a hidden presumption that standpointism can produce infallible knowledge.

So the problem that standpointism poses is not just epistemological, but that its success in producing purposeful and emancipatory good quality knowledge – and thus both its attractiveness to feminists and its *raison d'être* – is dependent on a particular Marxist inspired analysis of social relations. It is not clear to me that such a conceptual paradigm can any longer grasp the shifts, fragmentations and realignments that are occurring. It is not, I think, enough to acknowledge these fragments and to suggest that alliances resolve them, if what is retained is the idea that knowledge produced acts on *the* state and then manifests itself in policy directed by this univocal state.

The end of politics, ethics – or both?

So postmodernism opens up the possibility of thinking that we cannot be certain of the outcome of any knowledge intervention, even that good quality knowledge can produce unfortunate effects. It is this realization which seems to bring despair (although as Smart argues 'Little has actually been lost, beyond excessive faith, misplaced hope, and unrealistic expectations'; 1991: 219). Returning again to the level of anecdote, I once explained this to a North American feminist student who became appalled. She felt that if she could not believe that what she did would lead to a good outcome she should not bother to do anything at all. Why, she wondered, should she not just sit by the pool?

This, I think, is a brutally honest version of the feminist fear that postmodernism will rob us of our politics. The reasoning works on two levels. The first is that if we cannot tell *women in general* that feminist knowledge and subsequent policies will do them good then they will cease to join us or support us. The second is more of a personal despair born out of a real desire to right wrongs. It stresses the seemingly pointlessness of striving and making one's life difficult without any certainty that it will do good, or worse with the possibility of doing harm (as determined from some unforeseen point in the future).

Why would my student not be convinced that acting ethically and on the basis of the best knowledge available was enough? I think this is because she was so imbued with an instrumentalist version of knowledge propagated in the myopic, ahistorical – yet genuinely earnest – school of certainty in progress. To some extent there are echoes of a theological argument here. Thus the student might argue, 'Why should I be good (that is, ethical, honest etc.) if I cannot be sure that someone benefits?' When put like this I think this argument can be seen to be ethically bankrupt. Thus I also think that those who say that to rob feminism of its certainties and guarantees is to rob it of its purpose are equally ethically bankrupt.

Ironically the boot is usually regarded as being on the other foot. Thus my arguments in *Feminism and the Power of Law* (Smart, 1989) have been treated by some as a call for inaction and a celebration of theoretical *purity* (unsullied by the contradictions and compromises of action) (see Carlen, 1991; Lacey, 1992). How has this interpretation come about? Put briefly my argument was that we have misunderstood the power of law and that we should recognize that in using law to pursue certain goals we might be contributing to the legalization of everyday life, which currently seems to give greater legitimacy to a specific hierarchy of knowledge which subjugates alternative discourses, for example, feminism. However, I also argued that certain matters were already in the legal domain and thus could not be abandoned. I also argued that we might attempt some kind of calculus of harms, and decide that although deploying law was problematic that in certain circumstances it might be the best resource available. Finally I also argued that we might use the legal domain less for achieving law reforms than as a site on which to contest meanings about gender. But I offered no guarantees that any of this would *work*.

What I did not anticipate was that this would be interpreted as if it were a call for theoretical purity or inaction. I can only understand such responses if feminist scholars work with the presumption that when one argues that there are no certainties, one is implicitly saying (behind one's hand so to speak) that one should not bother to do anything.

To correct this assumption I think it has to be plainly stated that inaction is action, by which I mean it has consequences. So I have no concept of a theoretically *pure* position which remains somehow unsullied or *good* because it does nothing. But neither do I automatically assume that doing something is better than doing nothing. But this is not because I think that doing nothing is less risky than doing something, rather it is because I think both options (plus many others) should be considered. Thus I do not think that every time we identify a feminist *harm* we should demand a law against it. If this statement is then interpreted as a call to decriminalize rape, or as a form of purist indifference to something like sexual harassment then so be it.

The recognition that we live in postmodern times does not therefore mean that we have to abandon politics. But it does mean that we cannot make promises about what our politics will achieve. It may also mean that we should accept that there are different ways of *doing* politics, in particular that politics must entail a focus on issues of definitions and redefinitions rather than on programmes of action dedicated to a predetermined goal. This, of course, is not entirely novel for feminism because ideals of choice and autonomy (rather than blueprints) have been core demands for several decades. The question of how to be certain that women make the *right* choice when given this autonomy is of course another matter and is related to the question of morality and politics.

Morality and the morally competent subject

I have argued elsewhere that feminism is a strongly moral discourse (Smart, 1992b). I have no difficulty with this as long as the moral content and its contours are recognized. Thus I would want to argue that to suggest that one opts for theoretical purity over action is to make an implicitly moral statement rather than a descriptive statement. It attributes to the person who selects this theoretical purity (presuming such a state is possible) the ethics of a Pontius Pilot who washes his/her hands of affairs in some futile attempt to evade responsibility. So by chain of reasoning the person who says, 'maybe we should consider that we do not need a new law or right in relation to this harm', is seen as a moral reprobate who chooses to leave her sisters to the mercy of the Patriarchy – the more so if she cannot produce some equally tangible alternative programme of action.

My objection to this form of argument is not that it imports a dimension of moral evaluation, but that it does so implicitly. It marshals support on unexplicated grounds, namely the presumption that *real* or *good* feminists do certain kinds of things rather than others. The things that are good to do are laid down in a feminist history or tradition and are self-evident. My point is that this self-evidentness should now be challenged and brought into the open because:

1 We can no longer sustain the argument that feminism is a politics separated from a moral foundation.
2 Political organization based on social structures relevant to the past may no longer be relevant.

3 If we are to construct new feminist politics we should think in
   terms of politics based on clearly articulated ethics and good
   enough knowledge, not an ideal of good quality knowledge –
   judgement of which is necessarily deferred.

At a simplistic level what I am saying is that if we abandon the
idea of an ultimate Truth or correctness, then we have to allow
ethics back into the discussion. Ethics should not be the subtext on
which we rely to negate oppositional stances, they should be openly
addressed.

This is difficult for some forms of feminism. From one perspective
it might seem like a version of cultural feminism where the idea of
ethics is collapsed into *caring*. Thus we are seen to revert to caring
for and about others (that is, typical women's work) while the 'cut
and thrust' of politics is left to the boys. For others it might seem too
ephemeral, insufficiently concrete or programmatic. For yet others
ethics may seem just like patriarchal values writ large or discredited
because of being valued in the breach rather than the observance.

Yet in the field of feminist methodology the question of ethics has
been primary. More recently discussions of care and caring (Gilligan, 1982; Tronto, 1989) have made ethics a feminist issue. It is also
apparent that the Women's Peace Movement and Ecofeminism are
founded on ethical questions. Thus questions about whether we
should have weapons of mass destruction, for example, are not decided on the basis of scientific evaluations of whether deterrence
works or not, but on a repulsion against symbolic and actual violence and the cultural acceptance of violence as a mode of power.

Activities such as 'self-monitoring, self-reflection and self-
evaluation' (Bauman, 1991: 202) are not new to feminism and it is
these elements which go towards constituting the 'morally competent subject'. This morally competent subject may engage in
knowledge creation, or activist politics, but the basis of their action
is not a certainty, nor even a less partial objectivity, but an articulate
ethics.

This brings me back to feminist standpointism. As I have said earlier authors like Cain are very alert to the question of ethics and I
have not meant to imply that no consideration is given to this question. But Cain's version of ethics appears to me to collapse into accountability to others at the point at which one's knowledge
contribution can be judged to have *worked* or not. This seems like a
rather pragmatic ethics on the one hand and also a test that is too
easily avoided on the other (for example, the invincible feminist
scientist). Whereas ethics must of course be other-directed, I take
the view that the test is *self*-reflection not judgement by collective,

committee or cadre. This does not remove public accountability or peer review, but it does mean that ultimately responsibility lies with the moral agent, not some other grouping.

To a certain extent this concern within feminism over the production of knowledge and for establishing securely the grounds on which anything can be *said* seems a long way away from the practical exigencies of politics or law. Moreover, we can see a tendency among many feminist theorists towards becoming moral or social philosophers. It is as if (ironically) philosophy is exercising its old imperialism whereby we must all be grounded in a knowledge of all aspects of philosophy before we can participate in the debate. This can generate an irritability especially in an area like law which may be attractive precisely because of its practical application.

So is the move towards discussions of epistemology and social philosophy a kind of 'fiddling while Rome burns?' Is it to be regarded as a retreat in the face of newly recognized overwhelming odds? Or is it simply the pernicious effects of *ivory towerism* which activists warned about as soon as feminists started to enter the academe?

There may be some force to all of these points. However, there is another way to understand this development. This hinges on a reappraisal of the significance of knowledge as power. This is not to make the basic, but unremarkable, claim that information is empowering, but to reflect on the idea that the subject is constituted in knowledge or discourse. Knowledge is not something extra therefore, like the icing on a cake, but it is synonymous with power, politics and action.

There is a further point that should be considered, namely the extent to which feminists have now themselves produced a canon or body of knowledge. At the beginning of the second wave of feminism all we had to criticize was a dominant form of *masculine* knowledge or forms of knowing. Since then we have not only rediscovered a feminist heritage, but have produced a new one. We are now able to reflect on our own efforts. We even have the luxury of looking back at our early efforts and mounting our own critiques of ourselves. Feminist knowledge is thus no longer simply a critique of the *malestream*. I want to suggest that it is out of this critique of ourselves that the turning towards philosophical questions arises. We are now responsible for the production of knowledge and hence the production of the subject of knowledge. Such a responsibility should not be felt lightly.

The field of law

I want to suggest that in the field of law it appears particularly hard to abandon the language and perspectives of standpointism/modernism.

First, there is a purely pragmatic reason that feminist standpointism has produced the grounded and empirical knowledge that is able to gain entry both to the law schools and to the domain of legal policy making. The device of carrying out a study on (as in feminist empiricism) or for (as in standpoint feminism) women produces a form of knowledge which is acceptable (even if the conclusions are not). Such studies are accepted as revealing reality and are therefore deemed useful to the procedure of formulating policy (at least if we assume a model of political and liberal pluralism operates in the field of law).

The second reason is more conceptual. Basically we need to consider whether law is profoundly modern in the sense that it is wedded to social engineering and administering progress. If we conceptualize law in this way, it seems foolhardy to abandon the methodology of modernity when dealing with law. If however we abandon this supposition about law, we may see that we do not have to play out our politics of law on the terrain set by modernism.

We need therefore to ask certain questions concerning law. Is anything that seeks to legislate necessarily imbued with the values, practices and analyses of modernism? Is law inevitably part of the era of modernism because of its aim to regulate rationally, to create a deliberate order, and, for example, to apply *modern* concepts of punishment to those categorized as deviant or criminal. Certainly, as Bauman argues, the politics of *inequality* (and hence demands for equal rights, citizenship etc.) have been the dominant form of politics in the modern era. Moreover, he argues that as inequalities are unlikely to disappear in postmodern times, these modernist politics are likely to remain with us. So what are we to make of this? If modernist politics in the form of certain demands for rights from law are likely to remain, why should we not retain our modernist epistemology which provides the grounding for the claims for rights or different laws?

The problem, it seems to me, is that law is misconceptualized in this overconcise formulation. With this kind of formulation we merely seem to substitute the word *law* for the word *state*. If we no longer accept the idea of a univocal state, it seems perverse to substitute the concept of a univocal law or legal system. Equally, while the denial of rights which enable the individual to participate in social relationships should be resisted, it is not the case that law is simply about dealing with rights and inequality.

Thus rather than abandoning law to modernism, as if it were some atavistic domain or some unchanging set of rules and principles, we need to recognize the extent to which new ways of analysing law under postmodern conditions have emerged. In feminist work this can be identified in the shift towards analysing law as a 'technology of gender' (de Lauretis, 1987).[3] Such an approach understands law as a mechanism for *fixing* gender differences and constructing femininity and masculinity in oppositional modes. Thus law is no longer analysed as that which *acts upon* pre-given gendered subjects, rather law is part of the process of the continual reproduction of problematic gender differentiation (Smart, 1992b).

Once we understand law in this context we can see that standpointism is indeed a problem. This is because standpointism also *fixes* gender. Thus Cornell (1992) has provided a detailed critique of the work of Catharine MacKinnon precisely on the basis that the latter's realism or standpointism fixes the feminine. By this she means that for MacKinnon there is a feminine beyond the cultural and thus beyond change because it is *given*. This position arises out of MacKinnon's argument that the *feminine* as we know it under patriarchy is what male power lets women be. She does not therefore celebrate this feminine as perhaps Gilligan does but, in order to avoid the trap of being rendered completely silent (that is, MacKinnon's feminism is what male power allows it to be), she identifies sexual difference as the place which is beyond objectivity and subjectivity, beyond truth and falsehood, beyond male power. It is the thing which is knowable in an unmediated way, and is thus uncontaminated by the masculine system of knowing. Thus Cornell argues, 'Put very simply, MacKinnon's central error is to reduce feminine "reality" to the sexualized object we are for *them* by *identifying* the feminine totally with the "real world" as it is seen and constructed through the male gaze' (1992: 130, emphasis in original).

In order to get out of the trap her rhetoric lays, she then must reintroduce the idea of an *unmodified* (unmediated) objective reality somewhere beyond the pervasive reach of male culture on which to ground her account. Thus there is transcendental womanhood, the *real* feminine, knowable to those feminists who deploy consciousness raising. The aim of this sort of feminism is to fix gender in certain terms, in order that it becomes an extra-cultural standard against which to measure the wrongs of patriarchy and/or law.

This approach is quite antipathetical to one which sees gendering as a process without there being a place outside this sphere of cultural activity. The problem therefore is that it fixes Woman, or a specific group of women, into a pre-given gendered category which perpetuates the dualism of the gender divide. This in turn recreates the very problem that feminism wishes to resolve, namely that in asserting a fixed gender division it cannot transcend an oversimplistic dualism of male/female which in turn reaffirms the feminine on the subordinate side of this dualism.

Law, I want to suggest, is part of a process of fixing gender and is, even more than biological science, a discourse which insists on a rigid distinction between male and female, masculine and feminine. Thus law will not even acknowledge the idea of a continuum between maleness and femaleness (O'Donovan, 1985). In being more certain about biological anatomy than biological science is, law proceeds to insist that certain attributes follow this biological distinction. Moreover it takes its norm as the masculine against which to compare the feminine. The standpoint approach can do nothing to undermine this 'technology of gender' (de Lauretis, 1987) because it seeks to sustain this distinction at all costs. Law therefore continues to construct gender divisions (although obviously not law alone). Standpointism can only object to the content of this division. Moreover, it tends in practice to do this by asserting that it knows better than law the real interests of real women.

We have moved some way from the sophisticated standpointism of Cain and Harding but this should only affirm the point I have made above, namely that the nuances of revised standpointism collapse too readily into old problematic categories of women as a totality, or women's interests (see Phillips, 1991) when it enters into a legislative mode. At this stage it seems to me that there is only one way to avoid this trap. This is to cease to regard law in terms of policy and social engineering. Instead we should see it as a site on which to dispute meanings of gender. It is a very fruitful site for such activities. Thus we might see campaigns to extend the right to marry to lesbians and gay men as ways of disrupting gendered visions propounded in the law. Equally campaigns around rape or sexual harassment challenge the gendered vision of what men are and what women are – at least they do this as long as they do not posit some alternative fixed gender identity.

Such politics may seem less compelling than ones which appear to be based on the interests of a specific group and which appear to give rise to programmes of reform. And while such strategies will obviously not simply cease overnight (just as the transition from modernism to postmodernism is obviously not clear cut, self-evident and finished) it seems to me that feminism *ought* to give a more generous space to different ways of engaging with the problem of gender and through that the problem of law. It *ought* not to fall back on implicit moral arguments about how to be a real feminist (as opposed to a purist), nor *ought* it to wag a finger at those who find parallels between the thinking of feminists and postmodernists as if this is some form of *collaboration*. As the organization of social life shifts we need to allow our conceptual frameworks to shift also, this does not have to mean that we abandon the ethical goals of our previous mode but we may have to give up on proscription, prescription and certainty if we are really going to take diversity seriously.

Notes

This chapter was originally published in *Law, Politics and Society*, 1993, 13: 37–54.

1   Judgemental relativism is the sort of relativism which has been posed as the only alternative to *objectivism* and value neutrality. Thus in the simplified version of this timeless debate those who have claimed value neutrality, etc., have *disposed* of their opponent by suggesting that they are incapable of making any distinction between knowledge claims. Thus the claim that the earth is flat must be taken as being as valuable as the claim that it is spherical. Harding rejects these two preposterous oversimplifications and seeks to find an alternative way of disposing with the belief in ultimate Truth by constructing ideas of strong objectivism combined with the idea of historically and culturally located knowledge.

2   Some of the objections to this mode of analysis in the UK are based on the fact that these views can be seen to coincide with the views of the radical right. In the late 1980s Mrs Thatcher gave a speech in which she claimed that there is no such thing as society, only individuals. This was seen as a way of justifying the destruction of good social or community values and the celebration of selfishness. On a practical level it was also seen as the grounds for dismantling social organizations like the National Health Service, free Higher Education, and so on.

    Yet we can just as easily find feminist statements which coincide with the proclamations of right-wing women like Phyllis Schlafly in the US or Mary Whitehouse in the UK (see Smart, 1992b). We do not for this reason decry feminism as a whole. Nor would we feel that because Schlafly or Whitehouse opined that pornography was a *problem* that we as feminists think it is ideal. We must move beyond this kind of response to postmodernism also.

3   I am grateful to Barbara Yngvesson for bringing this work to my attention and for suggesting its value in conceptualizing law.

13

Postscript for the 1990s, or 'Still Angry After all These Years'

Looking back over these chapters which have been written over the last 10 years or more, it becomes apparent that the legal landscape I depict is peopled by certain distinct characters. Specific subjects appear and reappear. These are:

- The Criminal Woman
- The Prostitute
- The Raped Woman
- The Sexed Woman
- The Unruly Mother

These subjects do not appear by chance, nor are they simply there for discovery[1] and description. They are subjects constituted in and by legal and criminological discourses. When law addresses Woman it is almost inevitably in these forms. For example, even when law addresses Woman as worker, it is almost inevitably in terms of pregnancy (maternity rights) or some perceived disability (sex discrimination). My point is not merely that law differentiates on the grounds of gender, but that in so doing it takes Woman as sex or as body. An analogy might help convey my meaning here. Imagine a room full of men in a workplace or educational establishment. The door opens and a woman walks in. Her entrance marks the arrival of both sex and the body. A woman entering into such a room can hardly fail to recognize that she is disrupting an order which, prior to her entrance, was unperturbed by an awareness of difference or things corporal. The law is like this room full of men. When it notices women, it inevitably simultaneously sexes them and embodies them (us).

In suddenly noticing (again) these sexed and embodied subjects I realized that I was angry. This was not only the ongoing anger about the actualities of many women's lives, namely that they are (still) raped or are (still) poor and economically vulnerable, but an anger that such discursive constructions of Woman are so enduring and pervasive and that they underlie the actualities which render women rapable, vulnerable and victimizable. This discursive construction has women as mere bodies and, in turn, these bodies are deemed problematic and disruptive of the modern (masculine?) social order. In this construction women's bodies are atavistic, not rational or modern – in the sense that modern bodies are seen as mechanisms for the intellect to utilize but ultimately transcend. The 'reduction' of Woman to sex/bodies operates continuously to remind us of our tenuous positioning in a modern social world where bodies are regarded as primitive or disruptive.

It is this 'reduction' of Woman to sex/body which is such a source of anger. This is not because women want to be appreciated for their minds and/or to become disembodied (that is, to deny the significance of the body or even to accept the Cartesian divide between mind and body) but because of the meanings that are currently attributed to embodiment. Much early, popular feminist work was precisely about the celebration of women's bodies, so it is important to identify the difference between wanting to transcend a particular cultural mode of being embodied and the attempt to deny the significance or reality of the body as such. Put simply, feminism has wanted to bring the body back in to challenge the disembodied theories and perceptions which have dominated intellectual work for so long (see Turner, 1984). But in bringing the body back in, this body is not intended to be the equivalent of a centrefold of the masculinist pornographic gaze. Thus while wanting to place the body on the intellectual agenda, feminism has simultaneously wanted to challenge the perception of the female body as signifying only the sexual or the biologically reproductive.

The conflict of meanings about women's bodies is summed up for me in the debate over sexual harassment. According to one set of calibrations, sexual harassment is hardly as serious as rape. Rape may, after all, entail more physical damage, the penetration of the body is culturally regarded as worse than, say, inappropriate touching or words, and rape may be accompanied by a fear of death and mutilation. It is sometimes suggested therefore, that feminists should save their anger for real rapes and not risk losing sympathy by making waves over minor events, especially if these minor events are difficult to define and delineate. But this ranking of the seriousness of assaults is only one method of calibrating harm – albeit an important one – and it may be that on a different, more heuristic scale we can identify another kind of harm which does justify a similar degree of anger.

Again it may be useful to think in terms of an example. A woman is walking to the underground down a long passage which is quite busy with people. She is thinking of work, is carrying books and a briefcase and is hurrying along. She is preoccupied with her own concerns and is not looking at other people. In Riley's (1988) terms this is a moment when she does not feel herself to be specifically a woman. Then a passing man grabs her breast. It hurts, but fairly briefly, and the physical body is hardly harmed. It happens so quickly she only has time to turn to look at the man as he hurries off laughing. She has no time to retaliate, or shout, or do anything but stop. But then people crowd into her and look at her as though it is she who is troublesome or potentially so.

What does this incident mean? It is hardly a major incident, undoubtedly it happens many times a day on the London Underground. Given a choice, the woman would no doubt have rather this happened to her than she had been raped. But the incident is not to be dismissed so readily. She is not lucky; she is a woman who has been put in place. This place is a symbolic framework of meanings in which women are only their sexualized[2] bodies, and being such they are open to use and abuse. This act locates woman in her body; she had forgotten she had one, but the act makes her simply body. It is because this act invokes such a wealth of meanings that feminists like me remain so angry about sexual harassment. This form of abuse can be a 'look' or a comment, it need not even involve touch. But what it invokes, or calls upon, *is* the problem, not the actual physical harm. Both rape and sexual harassment do this and in this sense they are both demonstrations of the same problem of women being constituted as sexualized body.

The issue therefore becomes how to challenge this framework of meanings, how to resist this discursive construction of women as sex/bodies – while allowing that women are variously sexual and embodied and allowing that women should be able to enjoy being both sexual and embodied if they so desire. This focus accounts for why I have come increasingly to concentrate on law's discursive practices to try to encourage the emergence of, or more room for, other ways of 'thinking' about women and law's relationships with women.

Elements of the legal discursive construction of woman as body

The assertion that law constructs woman as body – and as unruly or disruptive body at that – needs some substantiation of course. So in this section I propose to explore these issues to draw together some of the evidence for such a claim. (In a later section I shall look at the process of sexing.) But first it is perhaps necessary to articulate what a discursive body is as opposed to a natural body: 'The body is a site of enormous symbolic work and symbolic production. . . . the body is both an environment we practise on and also practise with. We labour on, in and with bodies' (Turner, 1984: 190). From Turner's perspective, the body is not something that is simply given, it is a site of cultural production where there are no self-evident meanings or functions. Moreover, his insistence that we labour on, in and with bodies suggests that what meanings are constructed are not necessarily final or conclusive. It is true that our cultural repertoire of bodies may so far have been fairly restricted but the body has always been under constraint by aesthetic, religious and medical discourses. So while bodies are real, the way we experience our bodies, the meanings we give to them and the differences we perceive between them, are all historically and culturally located. They are therefore far from being natural. Given such an understanding we can turn to legal discourse to see what meanings have been given to women's bodies, and why such meanings may be problematic. I will not delve into the more speculative area of how this construction meshes with women's bodily subjectivity[3].

The discursively constructed disruptive body
In criminal law, women's bodies are constructed as a site for unlawful practices. Women are a problem because their bodies invite unlawful behaviour, or because their bodies escape the formal constraints that law attempts to impose on them. So, for example, in the rape trial, the entire focus of enquiry is on the woman's body and its emotions and responses. A woman's reason is invoked, but this reason is regarded as subordinate to her body (hormones, desire, primeval signals, etc.). And so, for example, it is understood that while a woman's reason may say 'no', her body (apparently) can be saying 'yes' and it is this discontinuity between reason and unreason that needs to be investigated. It is this body which is beyond reason which is seen as inviting the 'desire' which was enacted upon it.

Rape, incest and unlawful sexual intercourse – as legal notions – are all premised upon the idea of acts performed on the female body. The man's body (penis) is his instrument, the woman *is* her body. Ironically, it is the latter which is regarded as dangerous, unstable, vindictive. It is the latter which must be interrogated (physically and verbally). It is her body which is constructed as unruly, as outside the bounds of social and legal convention. It is true that the rape trial invokes the man's body as something which can slip beyond reasonable control as, for example, when a man's wife is pregnant and he turns to his daughter for sexual pleasure, or when he has become so inflamed that he cannot hold back. However, these behaviours are never the focus of interrogation and they are, in any case, seen as invited by the sexualized body of the woman. I am not suggesting here that the man's behaviour is never condemned but the rape trial does not challenge the fact of male sexual arousal, this is outside interrogation. In law, it is the nature of women's bodies to invite trouble. The trial considers whether or not this trouble was self-induced or not, but it does not subvert the idea that it is this body that is the problem. On the contrary, it continuously revisits this site to fix, ad nauseam, this meaning on the feminine body.

In family law we see a similar construction. Legal concepts of marriage, inheritance, legitimacy and illegitimacy all hinge on the female body and its constraints. A marriage is only lawful once it has been consummated; inheritance and the legal status of children all depend upon the lawfulness of the act of intercourse performed upon the woman's body. The status of her hymen has been crucial to her social status; laws of marriage, illegitimacy and inheritance have all been directed to one sole purpose – namely to ensure that a (good) woman's body is penetrated only under the correct legal and social conditions. Even now social policies are formulated with this in mind – even if there are few guarantees that they will work. For example, benefits to lone mothers are always discussed in the context of wishing to prevent conception outside marriage and deterring autonomous motherhood. The image of the unruly fecund female body haunts the legislature. It is feared that anything that helps the unsupported mother will simply mean that more women will opt out of marriage. It is even argued that the provision of minimal housing causes young women to get pregnant deliberately. This unruly fecund body must therefore be constrained and legislated against.

Men's bodies are simply not constructed as problematic in this way. They may be violent – but it is their actions that are problematic, not their bodies. Indeed the law has only rarely turned its attention to the reproductive capacities of men (as opposed to focusing on and punishing the results of this behaviour). The 1991 Child Support Act seeks, perhaps for the first time, to punish men for fathering too many children, or for doing so a little indiscriminately. Even so, this legislation constructs the father as inadequate 'economic man' rather than as an unrestrained reproductive body.

Regulating women's bodies

The law's strategy to deal with this supposedly disruptive body has predominantly been one of banning. For example, at common law the illegitimate child simply had no legal status or existence. The child was given no civil rights and the mother inadequate means to support it.[4] Matrimonial law before 1969 allowed a husband to divorce an adulterous wife, to keep most of the matrimonial assets and to deny her maintenance. In addition the legal definition and routine processing of rape cases has typically been so draconian for women that they have been deterred from seeking redress and literally had to let men get away with it (see Clark, 1987). Moreover the pregnant woman worker could be dismissed simply for becoming pregnant.

Although many of these legal wrongs have been modified, we still have modern versions of this banning or outlawing.[5] The old, established strategy returns in modified forms. For example, the Warnock Committee on Human Fertilisation and Embryology (1984) addressed the issue of how to regulate reproduction given the rise of new technologies and made a number of proposals concerning fertility treatment and surrogacy which have since entered into legislation. The resulting Human Fertilization and Embryology Act 1990 specified that a child of a married woman would only be born legitimate if her husband had given his consent to the infertility treatment – even if the infertility problem was his. Thus, in the 1990s we have a return to the powerful symbolic status of the husband's consent. Only his consent confers legitimacy and the woman is returned to her nineteenth-century status of being 'femme couvert de baron', namely under her husband's guardianship. Her pregnancy must occur only with patriarchal grace and she is to be kept in order by the patronage of the husband.

Another example of the return of this logic is the treatment of the frozen embryo. The posthumously implanted frozen embryo will be bastardized at birth even though he/she is created from the genetic material of a married couple. The 1990 Act treats this child in the same way that the old common law treated the child of an extramarital union. Section 27, subsection 6 (b) of the Act states that:

> Where the sperm of a man, or any embryo the creation of which was brought about with his sperm, was used after his death, he is not to be treated as the father of the child.

The Warnock Committee had found the idea that a woman might want to use her dead husband's sperm for AIH or might wish to implant a frozen embryo after his death, a complete anathema. This was seen as a form of unruly behaviour which required containment in a traditional way, namely by rendering the child illegitimate. This form of regulation is an indirect form of banning, but it is traditional in that the punishment is visited upon the child and therefore renders the mother both deviant and pathological. She is pathological because she would 'harm' her child by deliberately failing to provide for its legitimacy. This form of illegitimacy is, moreover, indelible –

unless another man adopts the child. And, for the first time, the law has created a category of illegitimacy which ignores both the biological links between the child and the father and the marital status of the parents.

The Surrogacy Arrangements Act 1985 was also brought into law soon after the Warnock Committee published its deliberations. This emergency legislation was brought in to stop women 'leasing' their wombs to infertile couples for financial reward. The mechanism deployed is the criminal law, and thus women who might seek to enter into such contracts in the role of so-called surrogate mothers are placed in a position highly analogous to that of the prostitute. In seeking to dissuade poor women from leasing their wombs the Act criminalized them in the same way as long-standing legislation on prostitution criminalizes poor women who seek to lease their sexual parts for payment. This strategy of banning is an old one, simply recycled to meet the needs of modern technologies. The status of the woman in the legislation remains that of the disruptive minor.

Women's fecund bodies have, therefore, been a focus of law and regulation for a long time, although the exact forms and specific concerns have changed. Women's bodies have given rise to a 'problem of order'. There are two elements to this. First, women's bodies are constituted as the archetypal site of irrationality. The female body, as constructed in legal discourse, is seen to have failed the test of subordinating desire to reason, and emotionality to rationality. The reproductive body is even more guilty in this respect; it threatens to disrupt the order which law seeks to impose on patriarchal family relations and on the production of children. The disorder that it threatens can only be accommodated if new forms of legal ordering are created (that is, through the restriction of infertility treatment to stable heterosexual couples). The second element concerns the response of law to those bodies which appear to be under 'rational' control. By rational here I am not applying a value judgement of my own but the dominant notion that economic rationality is the highest form of rationality. Hence the woman who could be so lacking in maternal emotion that she will lease her womb, as with surrogacy arrangements, becomes monstrous. The woman who is thought to get pregnant to avoid imprisonment is heinous. The woman who sells what should be given for free in the name of love (as with prostitution) merits punishment. So women's bodies are constructed as in need of constraint both when they appear irrational and (economically) rational. There is a powerful double bind here which we are still far from resolving but which constructs women's bodies as perpetually problematic.

Gendering and sexing the body

Thus far I have discussed ways in which law seeks to set boundaries around women's bodies and, in so doing constructs women as mere bodies. These bodies are, of course, both sexed and gendered. It is perhaps necessary to consider what is meant by this.

Gendering practices

To talk about gendering bodies probably presents few problems. Although feminist work has not always used precisely these terms, since the early 1970s we have been aware of the process of gendering. This process was originally conceptualized in terms of a process of socialization whereby girls were initiated into the feminine through child rearing practices and schooling. A similar process of gendering was also the focus of psychoanalytic feminism in which the Oedipal trauma became identified as the moment at which girls entered into the phallocentric universe and became heterosexualized and diminished women. This idea of becoming a woman has taken various forms but each form rests on the belief that gender is acquired.

We now talk of gendering practices. This new formulation suggests a variety of practices which do not necessarily constitute a single purpose, and which may at times be contradictory and various. It also frees us of the assumption that there is a perpetual patriarchal purpose or goal towards which all activity is directed. Moreover, it suggests a multitude of sources, without presuming that one has priority. Thus the idea that it is the mother–child relationship, or socialization within the family which fixes gender is now seen as problematic because of the more recent perception of gendering as a task which is never fully completed and is always open to modification.

In this formulation we can begin to see legal practices as gendering practices. We can move away from the idea that the family is primary, with education and the media in reserve to reinforce what the family has already achieved. In the latter model legal, medical, religious and other practices are always seen as supplementary layers which merely come along later as additional props. Whereas if we think instead of gendering practices, we need not create hierarchies, but rather analyse how different practices interweave in different circumstances. Thus, for example, if we are to look at early child rearing practice, we cannot ignore the way in which the family is always already encoded in a legal system which insists that men can only marry women, and vice versa. Such marriage laws are a gendering practice which already create the conditions for familial socialization processes.

I will not go on to identify every aspect of legal practice which is also a gendering practice because my aim is to convey a framework in which to understand law rather than to itemize it. Such an approach brings law back into a more central consideration rather than marginalizing it. I argued in the introduction to this book that there was a tendency for disciplinary boundaries to create false separations of knowledge and it is this problem I wish to overcome by treating law as one gendering practice among others.

Sexing practices

The idea that we may be sexed in ways that are similar to the processes of being gendered is a fairly recent innovation. This notion arises out of postmodern feminist work of the sort discussed in my introduction. Specifically, I see it as arising from the work of Judith Butler (1990) who was among the first to challenge the feminist orthodoxy of the distinction between sex and gender. The origins and purpose of this distinction are fully discussed in Chapter 7 and so I shall not repeat the discussion here. Suffice it to say that Butler turns the orthodoxy on its head and rejects the idea that sex is given in nature with gender as a cultural overlay to an inevitable, natural duality. Rather she argues that in the process of being gendered we are also sexed. That is to say that we comprehend sexual difference through the lens of gender, sex is therefore an artefact of gender not a separate a priori given to which we have to accommodate.

This is a difficult idea to incorporate because it is so counterintuitive. But once we acknowledge that intuition is culturally and historically constructed we have to give up our faith in it as an avenue to some inevitable Truth. This does not mean that Butler is 'right' of course. But it does suggest that we should not simply reject her ideas because they offend our idea of what is natural. I am more inclined to want to suspend my intuitive discomfort and to see how her ideas can be used. One way of using them is to think in terms of sexing practices which work alongside gendering practices. Thus, for example, we can interrogate law for practices which render women as perpetually feminine, but also which make women perpetual 'biological' women.

I suggest that my focus on the legal constitution of the female body achieves both of these enquiries at the same time. The body is the site of both sex and gender, and bodies do not exist which have not already been subject to both sexing and gendering. In focusing on the body we can, therefore, trace both of these practices rather than giving priority to the gendering process which has predominated in much feminist work. Thus, for example, we might wish to explore the extent to which women appear in legal discourse in terms of their reproductive function. We might ask why the law requires a biological difference to be established before couples can enter into the legal contract of marriage (it is not required for other legal contracts). We might ask why women's reproductive capacities are so closely guarded while men's are not (that is, no permission is required of a woman before a man donates sperm). Similarly we might ask why transvestite prostitutes are not treated as 'common prostitutes' for the purposes of criminal law and why only 'biological' women can be so constituted.

But . . . what is the use of these ideas?

Michèle Barrett (1992) has argued that feminist theory has become slanted towards cultural and literary theory as it has become more influenced by poststructuralist and postmodern thought. Where once sociology and political theory seemed to generate, or provide the basis of, a great deal of feminist thought, the impact of these new ideas seems to have virtually emptied these social sciences of useful insights. This, it seems to me, is a problem which we need to address. It is not simply that the 'old' disciplines must be kept alive at all costs, but that a discipline like sociology is ultimately about comprehending the social world, and representing social worlds to those who have no understanding save that derived from already embedded institutions and processes like schooling and the media. I am not suddenly trying to suggest that sociology floats above contamination by the social, or that it is a pure science which provides unassailable truths; but it does provide alternative accounts which are generated by an adherence to articulated methods. With sociological knowledge we can always see the packaging and the ingredients, it always provides the means for its own critique. Sociology always has the potential to construct subversive knowledge.

If we start to treat law as text/discourse and Woman as textual/ discursive construct (and all that this implies) we can see the operations of law in the field of gender in quite a new way. I hope I have shown this in the preceding chapters and I also hope I have shown that this direction does not imply the loss of politics. But are there other losses involved? Is it possible to follow a line of argument because it offers new insights, but then to find oneself in a different disciplinary framework which operates in ways quite dissimilar to one's starting point?

It is hard not to feel 'out on a limb' as one follows the various pathways that start to appear with the advent of postmodern thinking. This feeling is not about political values, which is to say that I do not think that the vertigo is about the loss of commitment. (In fact I have come to the conclusion that the whole argument about whether poststructuralisms or postmodernisms provide or renege on politics, conceals a rather different set of issues.) The problem is that the drift towards cultural and literary theories has taken feminist sociology into the terrain of theories about theories. We risk turning women into ideas or fictions which we then theorize about. We could, for example, create entire theories about women and law, without ever once addressing a woman, because we need only address the Woman of legal discourse.

I think we do need to address this Woman of legal discourse (or of medical discourse, or sociological discourse, etc.) because actual women are affected by being mistaken for her, or by failing to conform to her and so on.[6] So I am certainly not saying we should not do this kind of analysis. But this kind of analysis alone gives me cause for concern. I suggest in the introduction to this book that for me the main difference between poststructuralism and postmodern analyses is that the former provides analyses of 'things' (subjects, documents, accounts, discourses) while the latter is about critiques of philosophy and epistemology. I know this is a crude and not entirely accurate distinction but I, none the less, think the distinction is worth making because I retain such a strong commitment to the 'things'.

I would go so far as to argue that the idea of investigating the legal construction of, for example, the raped woman, is of little value unless we are also talking to women who have been raped. Indeed, we could not begin to conceptualize the legal construction as something quite so specific, if we did not already have other versions constructed from accounts provided by women. Putting this in more theoretical terms, we must never forget that women discursively construct themselves. It is not only legal, medical, sociological, etc., discourses that can do this. If we do forget this, we risk disempowering 'women' and overinflating the power of more organized discourses.

This argument brings me full circle it would seem. In Chapter 2, which is the earliest of my contributions included in this collection, I end with a suggestion that we need further research on women. I am saying something similar now when I say that for sociological feminism to survive we must resist the temptation to become solely concerned with metatheory and that we must keep talking to women (and men and children!). But do not be misled into thinking that the statements are identical. Unpacking the first statement reveals a fairly empiricist notion of doing research, as if it reveals something rather than constructing it. The women are biological givens and are presumed to be fairly – although not totally – homogeneous. By the time we get to the 1990s, empirical research is not given such a 'scientific' status and women are always 'women'. By this I mean that although we continue to speak of 'women' we also already know what a complex category (even non-category) this is.

So the usefulness of the ideas I have been discussing in this concluding chapter resides in our ability to integrate such forms of theorizing back into feminist sociology. This, in turn, may facilitate a new way of thinking about women and law. Barrett suggests that 'we shall have to reopen in new and imaginative ways the issue of humanism' (1992: 216) because an engaged feminist scholarship is probably not being served by either poststructuralist thought or its modernist predecessors. For her, as with many other feminists who seem to have reached this impasse, she is beginning to invoke ideas about values and principles which in turn invoke ideas of humanism and agency. However, as the 'old' kind will no longer suffice, she suggests we need a 'new' kind. This will hardly emerge overnight. Flax (1992) among others, has pointed out that postmodern thinking about difference was not parachuted into feminism by (male) theorists, but that it took root because it was a powerful argument within feminism itself arising from the voices of black women and lesbian women. The source of the issue does not make it a kind of new Truth of course, but the point is that it was a long-standing issue for feminism, not an esoteric point of debate from 'outside'. Notwithstanding this, I suggest that it has really taken us a decade to take difference seriously. The same slow process is probably occurring with the issue of values or ethics. That is to say, these are not 'external' ideas sent to distract us, but rather ideas that feminist scholars are developing to deal with conceptual and political questions identified within feminist theories and practices. There are no obvious 'solutions' to the problems generated by taking difference seriously which can be taken off a shelf and so we should recognize that the development of these ideas will continue to emerge slowly throughout the 1990s. We can anticipate ongoing conversations, but probably no certainties. We should also remain aware of our anger, since this anger is a manifestation of an ongoing commitment which may still need revision but is far from being redundant.

Notes

1   Marcus, for example, argues that 'Rape does not happen to pre-constituted victims; it momentarily makes victims' (1992: 391).
2   I refer in this chapter to the sexing of bodies and to sexualized bodies. The sexing of bodies means the giving of a biology (that is, male or female) to the body and this is explained later in the chapter. Sexualizing the body here means making it sexually desirable to the heterosexual, masculinist gaze.
3   This issue is arguably quite crucial, but it requires empirical work similar to that

carried out by Emily Martin (1989) on medical discourse and women's accounts of how they experience their bodies.

4   See Smart (1992a) for a fuller discussion of this point.

5   By 'outlawing' I mean the law's tendency to push these unruly women outside the domain of civil rights as with, for example, the common law's automatic refusal to allow a wife who had committed adultery to have any financial claim on her husband regardless of the circumstances.

6   This actual woman I am invoking is not an essence or a representative of all women, she does not have to be any of these things unless we elevate her to such statuses.

References

Adler, Z. (1987) *Rape on Trial*. London: Routledge.

Alcoff, L. (1988) 'Cultural feminism versus post-structuralism: the identity crisis in feminist theory', *Signs*, 13(3): 405–36.

Alexander, S. and Taylor, B. (1980) 'In defence of "patriarchy"', *New Statesman*, 1 February: 161.

Allen, H. (1987) *Justice Unbalanced*. Milton Keynes: Open University Press.

Allen, V. L. (1974) 'The common sense guide to industrial relations', *University of Leeds Review*, 17: 1.

Ardill, S. and O'Sullivan, S. (1986) 'Upsetting the applecart', *Feminist Review*, 23: 31–58.

Bankowski, Z. and Mungham, G. (1976) *Images of Law*. London: Routledge and Kegan Paul.

Bankowski, Z. and Mungham, G. (1981) 'Lay people and law people and the administration of the lower courts', *International Journal of the Sociology of Law*, 9(1): 85–100.

Bankowski, Z., Mungham, G. and Young, P. (1977) 'Radical criminology or radical criminologist?', *Contemporary Crisis*, 1(1): 217–38.

Barrett, M. (1980) *Women's Oppression Today*. London: Verso.

Barrett, M. (1992) 'Words and things: materialism and method in contemporary feminist analysis', in M. Barrett and A. Phillips (eds) *Destabilizing Theory*. Cambridge: Polity Press.

Barrett, M. and McIntosh, M. (1982) *The Anti-Social Family*. London: Verso Editions/NLB.

Barrett, M. and Phillips, A. (eds) (1992) *Destabilizing Theory*. Cambridge: Polity Press.

Bartky, S. L. (1972) 'Toward a phenomenology of feminist consciousness', in M. Vetterling-Braggin, F. A. Elliston and J. English (eds) *Feminism and Philosophy*. New Jersey: Littlefield, Adams & Co.

Bauman, Z. (1988) 'Is there a postmodern sociology?', *Theory, Culture and Society*, 5: 217–38.

Bauman, Z. (1991) *Intimations of Postmodernity*. London: Routledge.

Becker, H. (1963) *Outsiders: Studies in the Sociology of Deviance*. New York: Free Press.

Beechy, V. (1979) 'On patriarchy', *Feminist Review*, 3: 66–82.

Bell, V. (1993) *Interrogating Incest*. London: Routledge.

Bertrand, M. A. (1973) 'The insignificance of female criminality in the light of the hegemonic conceptions of sexual roles and the privatization of women', First Conference of the European Group for the Study of Deviance and Social Control, Florence.

Binney, V., Harknell, G. and Nixon, J. (1981) *Leaving Violent Men : A Study of Refuges and Housing for Battered Women*. London: Women's Aid Federation.

Blair, I. (1985) *Investigating Rape: A New Approach for the Police*. London: Croom Helm.

Bland, L. (1985) 'In the name of protection: the policing of women in the First World War', in J. Brophy and C. Smart (eds) *Women in Law*. London: Routledge and Kegan Paul.

Bland, L., Brundson, C., Hobson, D. and Winship, J. (1978) 'Women "inside and outside" the relations of production', in Women's Studies Group (ed.) *Women Take Issue*. London: Hutchinson.

Bodichon, B. (1869) *A Brief Summary in Plain Language of the Most Important Laws of England Concerning Women*. London: Trubner and Co.

Bourdieu, P. (1991) *Language and Symbolic Power*. Cambridge: Polity Press.

Braidotti, R. (1989) 'The politics of ontological difference', in T. Brennan (ed.) *Between Feminism and Psychoanalysis*. London: Routledge.

Brants, C. and Kok, E. (1986) 'Penal sanctions as a feminist strategy: a contradiction in terms?', *International Journal of the Sociology of Law*, 14: 269–86.

Bristow, E. (1977) *Vice and Vigilance*. Dublin: Gill and Macmillan.

Brownmiller, S. (1975) *Against Our Will: Men, Women and Rape*. London: Secker and Warburg.

Brunt, R. (1982) 'An immense verbosity': permissive sexual advice in the 1970s' in R. Brunt and C. Rowan (eds) *Feminism, Culture and Politics*. London: Lawrence and Wishart.

Butler, J. (1990) *Gender Trouble*. London: Routledge.

Butler, J. (1992) 'Contingent foundations: feminism and the question of "postmodernism"', in J. Butler and J. Scott (eds) *Feminists Theorize the Political*. London: Routledge.

Butler, J. and Scott, J. (eds) (1992) *Feminists Theorize the Political*. London: Routledge.

Cain, M. (1979) 'The general practice lawyer and the client: towards a radical conception', *International Journal of the Sociology of Law*, 7: 331–54.

Cain, M. (1990) 'Realist philosophy and standpoint epistemologies or feminist criminology as a successor science', in L. Gelsthorpe and A. Morris (eds) *Feminist Perspectives in Criminology*. Milton Keynes: Open University Press.

Campbell, B. (1980) 'A feminist sexual politics: now you see it, now you don't', *Feminist Review*, 5: 1–19.

Carlen, P. (1988) *Women, Crime and Poverty*. Milton Keynes: Open University Press.

Carlen, P. (1991) 'Women, crime, feminism and realism', *Social Justice*, 17(4): 106–23.

Chambers, G. and Millar, A. (1983) *Investigating Sexual Assault*. Edinburgh: Scottish Office, HMSO.

Chesney-Lind, M. (1973) 'Judicial enforcement of the female sex role: the family court and the female delinquent', *Issues in Criminology*, 8(2): 51–70.

Chodorow, N. (1978) *The Reproduction of Mothering*. London: University of Chicago Press.

Cixous, H. (1985) 'Sorties' in E. Marks and I. de Courtivron (eds) *New French Feminisms*. Brighton: Harvester Press.

Clark, A. (1987) *Women's Silence: Men's Violence*. London: Pandora.

Clark, L. and Lewis, D. (1977) *Rape: The Price of Coercive Sexuality*. Toronto: The Women's Press.

Clark, W. (1982) 'The dyke, the feminist and the devil', *Feminist Review*, 11: 30–9.

Cloward, R. and Ohlin, L. (1960) *Delinquency and Opportunity*. London: Routledge and Kegan Paul.

Cobbe, F. P. (1878) 'Wife torture in England', *Contemporary Review*, April: 55–87.

Code, L. (1988) 'Experience, knowledge and responsibility', in M. Griffiths and M. Whitford (eds) *Feminist Perspectives in Philosophy*. London: Macmillan.

Cohen, A. K. (1965) *Delinquent Boys*. New York: Free Press.

Connell, R. W. and Dowsett, C. W. (eds) (1992) *Rethinking Sex*. Melbourne: Melbourne University Press.

Coote, A. and Campbell, B. (1982) *Sweet Freedom*. London: Pan Books.

Cornell, D. (1992)*Beyond Accommodation*. London: Routledge.

Cousins, M. (1978) 'Material arguments and feminism', *m/f*, 2: 62–70.

Cousins, M. (1980) 'Men's Rea: a note on sexual difference, criminology and law', in P. Carlen and M. Collison (eds), *Critical Issues in Criminology*. Oxford: Martin Robertson.

Cowie, J., Cowie, V. and Slater, E. (1968) *Delinquency in Girls*. London: Heinemann.

Criminal Law Revision Committee (1982) *Working Paper on Offences Relating to Prostitution and Allied Offences*. London: HMSO.

Culler, J. (1981) *The Pursuit of Signs*. London: Routledge and Kegan Paul.

Dahl, T. S. (1984) 'Women's rights to money', *International Journal of the Sociology of Law*, 12: 137–52.

Dahl, T. S. (1987) *Women's Law: An Introduction to Feminist Jurisprudence*. Oxford: Oxford University Press.

Dally, A. (1982) *Inventing Motherhood*. London: Burnett Books.

Daly, K. (1989a) 'Criminal justice ideologies and practices in different voices: some feminist questions about justice', *International Journal of the Sociology of Law*, 17: 1–18.

Daly, K. (1989b) 'New feminist definitions of justice', Conference Proceedings, Institute for Women's Policy Research, Washington, DC.

Daly, M. (1979) *Gyn/Ecology*. London: The Women's Press.

Davidoff, L. and Hall, C. (1987) *Family Fortunes*. London: Hutchinson.

Davin, A. (1978) 'Imperialism and motherhood', *History Workshop Journal*, 5: 9–65.

Davis, A. (1971) *If they come in the morning . . . .*London: Orbach and Chambers.

Davis, K. (1966) 'Prostitution', reprinted in R. K. Merton and R. Nisbet (eds) *Contemporary Social Problems*. New York: Harcourt Brace.

DeCrow, K. (1975) *Sexist Justice*. New York: Vintage.

De Lauretis, T. (1987) *Technologies of Gender*. Bloomington, IN: Indiana University Press.

Delphy, C. (1977) *The Main Enemy*. London: WRRC.

Denning (Lord) (1980) *The Due Process of Law*. London: Butterworths.

Derrida, J. (1978) *Writing and Difference*. London: Routledge and Kegan Paul.

Diamond, I. and Quinby, L. (1988) *Feminism and Foucault*. Boston: Northeastern University Press.

Dinnerstein, D. (1978) *The Rocking of the Cradle*. London: Souvenir.

Di Stefano, C. (1988) 'Dilemma of difference: feminism, modernity and postmodernism', *Women and Politics*, 8 (3/4): 1–24.

Dixon, V. (1976) 'World views and research methodology', in L. M. King, V. Dixon and W. W. Nobles (eds) *African Philosophy: Assumptions and Paradigms for Research on Black Persons*. Los Angeles: Fanon Centre.

Donzelot, J. (1980) *The Policing of Families*. London: Hutchinson.

Douglas, J. (1967) *The Social Meaning of Suicide*. Princeton, NJ: Princeton University Press.

Duchen, C. (1986) *Feminism in France*. London: Routledge and Kegan Paul.

Duggan, L. (1988) 'Censorship in the name of feminism', in G. Chester and J. Dickey (eds) *Feminism and Censorship*. Bridport: Prism Press.

Duggan, L., Hunter, N. and Vance, C. (1988) 'False promises: feminist and anti-pornography legislation', in G. Chester and J. Dickey (eds) *Feminism and Censorship*. Bridport: Prism Press.

Eaton, M. (1986) *Justice for Women?* Milton Keynes: Open University Press.

Edwards, S. (1981) *Female Sexuality and the Law*. Oxford: Martin Robertson.

Eisenstein, Z. R.(1988) *The Female Body and the Law*. Berkeley: University of California Press.

Engels, F. (1972) *The Origin of the Family, Private Property and the State*. New York: Pathfinder Press.

Everywoman (1988) *Pornography and Sexual Violence: Evidence of the Links*. London: Everywoman Ltd.

Faragher, T. (1985) 'The police response to violence against women in the home', in J. Pahl (ed.) *Private Violence and Public Policy*. London: Routledge and Kegan Paul.

Farrington, D. and Morris, A. (1983) 'Sex, sentencing and reconviction', *British Journal of Criminology*, 23(3): 229–48.

Faulkner, D. (1971) 'The redevelopment of Holloway Prison', *Howard Journal of Criminal Justice*, 12(2): 122–32.

Fekete, J. (1988) *Life After Postmodernism: Essays on Value and Culture*. London: Macmillan.

Ferguson, K. (1993) *The Man Question*. Oxford: University of California Press.

Flax, J. (1987) 'Postmodernism and gender relations in feminist theory', *Signs*, 12(4): 621–43.

Flax, J. (1990) *Thinking Fragments*. Oxford: University of California Press.

Flax, J. (1992) 'The end of innocence' in J. Butler and J. Scott (eds) *Feminists Theorize the Political*. London: Routledge.

Foucault, M. (1973) *The Order of Things*. New York: Vintage Books.

Foucault, M. (1977) *Discipline and Punish*. London: Allen Lane.

Foucault, M. (1980) *Herculine Barbin*. New York: Pantheon.

Foucault, M. (1981) *The History of Sexuality, Vol. 1*. Harmondsworth: Pelican Books.

Fraser, N. and Nicholson, L. (1988) 'Social criticism without philosophy: an encounter between feminism and postmodernism', *Theory, Culture and Society*, 5 (2/3): 373–94.

Freeman, M. D. A. (1987) 'Feminism and Jurisprudence' in S. McLaughlin (ed.) *Women and the Law*. London: Faculty of Laws, University College London (working paper no. 5).

Fryer, B., Hunt, A., McBarnett, D. and Moorhouse, B. (eds) (1981) *Law, State and Society*. London: Croom Helm.

Fudge, J. (1989) 'The effect of entrenching a Bill of Rights upon political discourse; feminist demands and sexual violence in Canada', *International Journal of the Sociology of Law*, 17(4): 445–64.

Fuss, D. (1989) *Essentially Speaking*. London: Routledge.

Gandal, K. (1986) 'Michel Foucault: intellectual work and politics', *Telos*, 67: 121–34.

Gardiner, J. (1976) 'A case study in social change', in *Patterns of Inequality*, Open University, D302, Unit 32.

Garry, A. and Pearsall, M. (eds) (1989) *Women, Knowledge and Reality*. London: Unwin Hyman.

Gelsthorpe, L. (1986) 'Towards a sceptical look at sexism', *International Journal of the Sociology of Law*, 14(2): 125–52.

Gibson, P. C. and Gibson, R. (eds) (1993) *Dirty Looks: Women, Pornography, Power*. London: British Film Institute.

Gilligan, C. (1982) *In a Different Voice*. London: Harvard University Press.

Goodrich, P. (1986) *Reading the Law*. Oxford: Basil Blackwell.

Gordon, C. (ed.) (1980) *Michel Foucault: Power/Knowledge*. Brighton: Harvester.

Gouldner, A. (1973) *For Sociology*. London: Allen Lane.

Gregory, J. (1982) 'Equal pay and sex discrimination: why women are giving up the fight', *Feminist Review*, 10: 75–90.

Gregory, J. (1986) 'Sex, class and crime: towards a non-sexist criminology', in R. Matthews and J. Young (eds) *Confronting Crime*. London: Sage.

Griffin, S. (1971) 'Rape: the all-American crime', *Ramparts*, Sept: 26–35.

Griffith, J. A. C. (1977) *The Politics of the Judiciary*. London: Fontana.

Griffiths, M. (1988) 'Feminism, Feelings and Philosophy', in M. Griffiths and M. Whitford (eds) *Feminist Perspectives in Philosophy*. London: Macmillan.

Griffiths, M. and Whitford, M. (eds) (1988) *Feminist Perspectives in Philosophy*. London: Macmillan.

Hall, S. (1980) 'Reformism and the legislation of consent' in the National Deviancy Conference (ed.) *Permissiveness and Control*. London: Macmillan.

Hall, S., Chritcher, C., Jefferson, T., Clarke, J. and Roberts, B. (1978) *Policing the Crisis*. London; Macmillan.

Hanmer, J. and Saunders, S. (1984) *Well-Founded Fear*. London: Hutchinson.

Harding, S. (1986) *The Science Question in Feminism*. Milton Keynes: Open University Press.

Harding, S. (ed.) (1987) *Feminism and Methodology*. Milton Keynes: Open University Press.

Harding, S. (1991) *Whose Science? Whose Knowledge?* Ithaca: Cornell University Press.

Harrison, R. and Mort, F. (1980) 'Patriarchal aspects of nineteenth-century state formation: property relations, marriage and divorce, and sexuality', in P. Corrigan (ed.) *Capitalism, State Formation and Marxist Theory*. London: Quartet Books.

Hartsock, N. (1987) 'The feminist standpoint: developing the ground for a specifically feminist historical materialism', in S. Harding (ed.) *Feminism and Methodology*. Milton Keynes: Open University.

Hawkesworth, M. (1989) 'Knowers, knowing, known', *Signs*, 14(3): 533–57.

Heidensohn, F. (1985) *Women and Crime*. London: Macmillan.

Hekman, S. (1990) Gender and Knowledge: Elements of a Postmodern Feminism. Boston, MA: Northeastern University Press.

Hepple, B. (1984) *Equal Pay and the Industrial Tribunals*. London: Sweet and Maxwell.

Hill Collins, P. (1990) *Black Feminist Thought*. London: Harper Collins.

Hindess, B. (1973) *The Use of Official Statistics in Sociology*. London: Macmillan.

Hirst, P. (1975) 'Marx and Engels on law, crime and morality', in I. Taylor, P. Walton and J. Young (eds) *Critical Criminology*. London: Routledge and Kegan Paul.

Hirst, P. (1979) *On Law and Ideology*. London: Macmillan.

Hirst, P. (1980) 'Law, socialism and rights', in P. Carlen and M. Collinson (eds) *Radical Issues in Criminology*. Oxford: Martin Robertson.

Hirst, P. (1985) 'Socialism, pluralism and the law', *International Journal of the Sociology of Law*, 13: 173–90.

Holcombe, L. (1983) *Wives and Property*. Oxford: Martin Robertson.

Hollway, W. (1984) 'Gender difference and the production of subjectivity', in J. Henriques, W. Hollway, C. Urwin, C. Venn and V. Walkerdine (eds) *Changing the Subject*. London: Methuen.

Home Office (1974) *Working Party on Vagrancy and Street Offences Working Paper*. London: HMSO.

Hoskyns, C. (1985) 'Women's equality and the European Community', *Feminist Review*, 20: 71–90.

Howe, A. (1987) ' "Social injury" revisited: towards a feminist theory of social justice', *International Journal of the Sociology of Law*, 15(4) : 423–38.

Hull, G. T., Scott, P. B. and Smith, B. (1982) *But Some of Us Are Brave*. New York: The Feminist Press.

Jackson, M. (1987) ' "Facts of life" or the eroticization of women's oppression?', in P. Caplan (ed.) *The Cultural Construction of Sexuality*. London: Tavistock.

Jaget, C. (ed.) (1980) *Prostitutes: Our Life*. Bristol: Falling Wall Press.

Jaggar, A. (1989) 'Love and knowledge: emotion in feminist epistemology', in A. Garry and M. Pearsall (eds) *Women, Knowledge and Reality*. London: Unwin Hyman.

Jardine, A. (1985) *Gynesis*. London: Cornell University Press.

Jordonova, L. (1989) *Sexual Visions*. London: Harvester.

Kaluzynska, E. (1980) 'Wiping the floor with theory', *Feminist Review*, 6: 27–54.

Kellner, D. (1988) 'Postmodernism as social theory: some challenges and problems', *Theory, Culture and Society*, 5(2/3): 239–70.

Kenney, S. J. (1986) 'Reproductive hazards in the workplace: the law and sexual difference', *International Journal of the Sociology of Law*, 14 (2/3): 393–44.

Kingdom, E. (1991) *What's Wrong With Rights?* Edinburgh: Edinburgh University Press.

Kingdom, L. (1985a) 'The sexual politics of sterilisation', *Journal of Law and Society*, 12(1): 19–34.

Kingdom, L. (1985b) 'Legal recognition of a woman's rights to choose', in J. Brophy and C. Smart (eds) *Women in Law*. London: Routledge and Kegan Paul.

Kline, M. (1989) 'Race, racism and feminist legal theory', *Harvard Women's Law Journal*, 12: 115–50.

Koedt, A. (1970) 'The myth of the vaginal orgasm', in L. Tanner (ed.) *Voices from the Women's Liberation*. New York: Signet.

Konopka, G. (1966) *The Adolescent Girl in Conflict*. London: Prentice-Hall.

Lacey, N. (1992) 'Closure and critique in feminist jurisprudence: transcending the dichotomy or a foot in both camps?', paper delivered to Warwick Law School Seminar Series.

Lahey, K. (1985) '. . . until women themselves have told all they have to tell . . .' *Osgoode Hall Law Journal*, 23(3): 519–41.

Laing, R. D. (1968) *The Politics of Experience*. Harmondsworth: Penguin.

Land, H. (1976) 'Women: supporters or supported', in D. Leonard Barker and S. Allen (eds) *Sexual Divisions in Society*. London: Tavistock.

Laqueur, T. (1987) 'Orgasm, generation and the politics of reproductive biology', in C. Gallagher and T. Laqueur (eds) *The Making of the Modern Body*. London: University of California Press.

Laqueur, T. (1990) *Making Sex*. Boston, MA: Harvard University Press.

Lees, S. (1989) 'Trial by rape', *New Statesman and Society*, 24 November.

Lees, S. (1993) 'Judicial rape', *Women's Studies International Forum* 16(1): 11–36.

Linden, R. R., Pagano, D. E. H. and Star, L. S. (eds) (1982) *Against Sadomasochism*. Paolo Alto: Frogs in the Well.

Loach, L. (1992) 'Bad girls: women who use pornography', in L. Segal and M. McIntosh (eds) *Sex Exposed: Sexuality and the Pornography Debate*. London: Virago.

Lombroso, C. and Ferrero, W. (1895) *The Female Offender*. London: Fisher Unwin.

London Rape Crisis Centre (1984) *Sexual Violence: the Reality for Women*. London: The Women's Press.

Lord Lloyd of Hampstead and Freeman, M. D. A. (1985) *Lloyd's Introduction to Jurisprudence* (5th edn). London: Stevens and Son.

Lyotard, J. F. (1986) *The Postmodern Condition*. Manchester: Manchester University Press.

McCann, K. (1985) 'Battered women and the law: the limits of the legislation', in J. Brophy and C. Smart (eds) *Women in Law*. London: Routledge and Kegan Paul.

McClintock, A. (1993) 'Maid to order: commercial S/M and gender power', in P. C. Gibson and R. Gibson (1993) *Dirty Looks: Women, Pornography, Power*. London: British Film Institute.

McDonough, R. and Harrison, R. (1978) 'Patriarchy and relations of production', in A. Kuhn and A. M. Wolpe (eds) *Feminism and Materialism*. London: Routledge and Kegan Paul.

McGowan Tress, D. (1988) 'Comment on Flax's "Postmodern and gender relations in feminist theory"', *Signs*, 14(1): 196–203.

McIntosh, M. (1978) 'The state and the oppression of women', in A. Kuhn and A. M. Wolpe (eds) *Feminism and Materialism*. London: Routledge and Kegan Paul.

McIntosh, M. (1992) 'Liberalism and the contradictions of sexual politics', in L. Segal and M. McIntosh (eds) *Sex Exposed: Sexuality and the Pornography Debate*. London: Virago.

MacKinnon, C. (1982) 'Feminism, Marxism, method and the state: an agenda for theory', *Signs*, 7(3): 515–44.

MacKinnon, C. (1983) 'Feminism, Marxism, method and the state: toward feminist jurisprudence', *Signs*, 8(2): 635–58.

MacKinnon, C. (1987) *Feminism Unmodified: Discourses on Life and Law*. Boston, MA: Harvard University Press.

Mackintosh, M. (1979) 'Domestic labour and the household', in S. Burman (ed.) *Fit Work for Women*. London: Croom Helm.

McLeod, E. (1982) *Women Working: Prostitution Now*. London: Croom Helm.

Macmillan Report (1928) *Report of the Street Offences Committee*, Cmnd 3231. London: HMSO.

Marcus, S. (1992) 'Fighting bodies, fighting words: a theory and politics of rape prevention', in J. Butler and J. Scott (eds) *Feminists Theorize the Political*. London: Routledge.

Marsden, D. (1969) *Mothers Alone*. London: Allen Lane.

Martin, A. (1911) *Mothers in Mean Streets*. London: United Suffragists.

Martin, B. (1992) 'Sexual practice and changing lesbian identities' in M. Barrett and A. Phillips (eds) *Destabilizing Theory*. Cambridge: Polity Press.

Martin, E. (1989) *The Woman in the Body*. Boston, MA: Beacon Press.

Matthews, R. and Young, J. (eds) (1986) *Confronting Crime*. London: Sage.

Matsuda, M. (1987) 'Looking to the bottom: critical legal studies and reparations', *Harvard Civil Rights/Civil Liberties Law Review*, 22: 329–99.

Matza, D. (1969) *Becoming Deviant*. New York: Prentice Hall.

Merck, M. (1993) *Perversions*. London: Virago.

Mill, J. S. and Taylor, H. (1869) *The Subjugation of Women*. London: Everyman.

Millet, K. (1972) 'Prostitution: a quartet for female voices', in V. Gornick and B. K. Moran (eds) *Women in a Sexist Society*. New York: Basic Books.

Mitchell, J. (1971) *Woman's Estate*. Harmondsworth: Penguin.

Mitchell, J. (1975) *Psychoanalysis and Feminism*. Harmondsworth: Penguin.

Mitchell, J. (1987) 'Women and equality', in A. Phillips (ed.) *Feminism and Inequality*. Oxford: Blackwell.

Mitchell, J. and Oakley, A. (1976) *The Rights and Wrongs of Women*. Harmondsworth: Penguin.

Monture, P. (1986) 'Ka-Nin-Geh-Heh-Gah-E-Sa-Nonh-Yah-Gah', *Canadian Journal of Women and the Law*, 2(1): 159–70.

Morgan, T. (1993) 'Butch-femme and the politics of identity', in A. Stein (ed.) *Sisters, Sexperts, Queers*. Harmondsworth: Penguin (Plume).

Morris, R. (1965) 'Attitudes towards delinquency by delinquents, non-delinquents and their friends', *British Journal of Criminology*, 5(3): 249–65.

Mossman, M. J. (1986) 'Feminism and legal method: the difference it makes', *Australian Journal of Law and Society*, 3: 30–52.

Naffine, N. (1990) *Law and the Sexes*. Sydney: Allen and Unwin.

Nestle, J. (1981) 'Butch-fem relationships: sexual courage in the 1950s', *Heresies: The Sex Issues*, 12(3): 21–4.

Norton, C. (1982) *Caroline Norton's Defence*. Chicago: Academy Chicago.

Oakley, A. (1972) *Sex, Gender and Society*. London: Temple Smith.

O'Donovan, K. (1979) 'The male appendage – legal definitions of women', in S. Burman (ed.) *Fit Work for Women*. London: Croom Helm.

O'Donovan, K. (1985) *Sexual Divisions in Law*. London: Weidenfeld and Nicolson.

Pahl, J. (1980) 'Patterns of money management within marriage', *Journal of Social Policy*, 9(3): 313–35.

Pahl, J. (1982) 'The allocation of money and the structuring of inequality within marriage', unpublished paper, University of Kent at Canterbury.

Patullo, P. (1983) *Judging Women*. London: National Council for Civil Liberties.

Phillips, A. (1991) *Engendering Democracy*. Cambridge: Polity Press.

Picciotto, S. (1979) 'The theory of the state, class struggle and the rule of law', in B. Fine, R. Kinsey, J. Lear, S. Picciotto and J. Young (eds) *Capitalism and the Rule of Law*. London: Hutchinson.

Polan, D. (1982) 'Towards a theory of law and patriarchy', in D. Kairys (ed.) *The Politics of Law*. New York: Pantheon Books.

Pollak, O. (1950) *The Criminality of Women*. University of Pennsylvania Press.

Pringle, R. (1992) 'Absolute sex? Unpacking the sexuality/gender relationship', in R. W. Connell and C. W. Dowsett (eds) *Rethinking Sex*. Melbourne: Melbourne University Press.

Pringle, R. and Watson, S. (1992) 'Women's interests' and the post-structuralist state', in J. Butler and J. Scott (eds) *Feminists Theorize the Political*. London: Routledge.

Radclyffe Hall, M. (1950) *The Well of Loneliness*. New York: Pocket Books, Simon Schuster.

Randall, V. (1982) *Women and Politics*. London: Macmillan.

Rathbone, E. (1927) *The Disinherited Family*. London: George Allen and Unwin.

Reiss, E. (1934) *The Rights and Duties of English Women*. Manchester: Sherratt & Hughes.

Richardson, H. J. (1969) *Adolescent Girls in Approved Schools*. London: Routledge and Kegan Paul.

Rifkin, J. (1980) 'Toward a theory of law and patriarchy', *Harvard Women's Law Journal*, 3: 85–95.

Riley, D. (1988) *Am I That Name?* London: Macmillan.

Riley, D. (1992) 'A short history of some preoccupations', in J. Butler and J. Scott (eds) *Feminists Theorize the Political*. London: Routledge.

Roberts, H. (ed.) (1981) *Women, Health and Reproduction*. London: Routledge and Kegan Paul.

Roberts, N. (1986) *The Front Line*. London: Grafton Books.

Roberts, S. and Roberts, N. (1986) 'Stripping illusions', *New Statesman*, 17 January: 27–8.

Rorty, R. (1985) 'Habermas and Lyotard on Postmodernity', in R. Bernstein (ed.) *Habermas and Modernity*. Cambridge: Polity Press.

Rose, G. (1988) 'Architecture to philosophy – the postmodern complicity', *Theory, Culture and Society*, 5(2/3): 357–72.

Rowbotham, S. (1973) *Women's Consciousness, Man's World*. Harmondsworth: Penguin.

Rowbotham, S. (1979) 'The trouble with patriarchy', *New Statesman*, 21 December: 970–1.

Sachs, A. and Wilson, J. H. (1978) *Sexism and the Law*. Oxford: Martin Robertson.

Scales, A. C. (1986) 'The emergence of feminist jurisprudence: an essay', *Yale Law Journal*, 95: 1,373–403.

Scheff, T. (1974) 'The labelling theory of mental illness', *American Sociological Review*, 39: 444–52.

Schlafly, P. (1987) *Pornography's Victims*. Illinois: Crossway Books.

Schneider, L. (1984) 'In a different voice': reflections on a feminist view of rights', unpublished paper presented at the Feminism and Legal Theory Conference, University of Wisconsin, Madison, July 1985.

Schöttler, P. (1986) 'Friedrich Engels and Karl Kautsky as critics of "legal socialism"', *International Journal of the Sociology of Law*, 14: 1–32.

Segal, L. (1992) 'Sweet sorrows; painful pleasures', in L. Segal and M. McIntosh (eds) *Sex Exposed: Sexuality and the Pornography Debate*. London: Virago.

Segal, L. and McIntosh, M. (eds) (1992) *Sex Exposed: Sexuality and the Pornography Debate*. London: Virago.

Select Committee of the House of Lords on the Law Relating to the Protection of Young Girls (1881) *British Sessional Papers*. Volume 18. London: HMSO.

Select Committee on Violence of the Family (1975) *Report with Proceedings, Minutes of Evidence and Appendices*. Cmnd 53311. London: HMSO.

Sevenhuijsen, S. (1991) 'The morality of feminism', *Hypatia*, 6(2): 173–91.

Shoham, S. G. (1974) *Society and the Absurd*. Oxford: Basil Blackwell.

Smart, B. (1988) 'Modernism, postmodernism and the present', unpublished paper: University of Auckland.

Smart, B. (1991) *Modern Conditions, Postmodern Controversies*. London: Routledge.

Smart, C. (1976) *Women, Crime and Criminology: A Feminist Critique*. London: Routledge and Kegan Paul.

Smart, C. (1981) 'Law and the control of women's sexuality: the case of the 1950s', in B. Hutter and G. Williams (eds) *Controlling Women*. London: Croom Helm.

Smart, C. (1984) *The Ties That Bind*. London: Routledge and Kegan Paul.

Smart, C. (1986) 'Feminism and the law: some problems of analysis and strategy', *International Journal of the Sociology of Law*, 14(2): 109–23.

Smart, C. (1989) *Feminism and the Power of Law*. London: Routledge.

Smart, C. (1990a) 'Law's power, the sexed body and feminist discourse', *Journal of Law and Society*, 17: 194–210.

Smart, C. (1990b) 'Feminist approaches to criminology or postmodern woman meets atavistic man', in L. Gelsthorpe and A. Morris (eds) *Feminist Perspectives in Criminology*. Milton Keynes: Open University Press.

Smart, C. (1990c) 'Penetrating women's bodies: the problems of law and medical technology', in P. Abbott and C. Wallace (eds) *Gender, Sexuality and Power*. London: Macmillan.

Smart, C. (1992a) 'Disruptive bodies and unruly sex: the regulation of reproduction and sexuality in the nineteenth century', in C. Smart (ed.) *Regulating Womanhood*. London: Routledge.

Smart, C. (1992b) 'Unquestionably a moral issue: rhetorical devices and regulatory imperatives', in L. Segal and M. McIntosh (eds) *Sex Exposed: Sexuality and the Pornography Debate*. London: Virago.

Smith, D. (1974) 'Women's perspective as a radical critique of sociology', *Sociological Inquiry*, 44(1): 7–14.

Smith, D. (1988) *The Everyday World as Problematic*. Milton Keynes: Open University Press.

Snell, M., Glucklich, P. and Povall, M. (1981) *Equal Pay and Opportunities*. Department of Employment Research Paper 20. London: HMSO.

Spelman, E. (1988) *Inessential Woman*. Boston, MA: Beacon Press.

Spender, D. (1980) *Man Made Language*. London: Routledge and Kegan Paul.

Spender, D. (1983) *There's Always Been a Women's Movement*. London: Pandora.

Stanley, L. and Wise, S. (1983) *Breaking Out*. London: Routledge and Kegan Paul.

Stanton, D. C. (1992) *Discourses of Sexuality*. Ann Arbor: University of Michigan Press.

Storch, R. D. (1977) 'Police control of street prostitution in Victorian London', in D. H. Bayley (ed.) *Police and Society*. London: Sage.

Strachey, R. (1978) *The Cause*. London: Virago.

Sumner, C. (1979) *Reading Ideologies*. London: Academic.

Taylor, I. (1982) *Law and Order: Arguments for Socialism*. London: Macmillan.

Taylor, I., Walton, P. and Young, J. (1974) *The New Criminology*. London: Routledge and Kegan Paul.

Temkin, J. (1987) *Rape and the Legal Process*. London: Sweet & Maxwell.

Terry, R. M. (1970) 'Discrimination in the handling of juvenile offenders by social control agencies', in P. G. Garabedian (ed.) *Becoming Delinquent*. Chicago: Aldine Press.

Thomas, W. I. (1907) *Sex and Society*. New York: Little Brown and Co.

Thomas, W. I. (1923) *The Unadjusted Girl*. New York: Harper and Row.

Tronto, J. (1989) 'Women and caring: what can feminists learn about morality from caring?', in A. Jagger and S. Bordo (eds) *Gender/Body/Knowledge*. London: Rutgers University Press.

Turner, B. (1984) *The Body and Society*. Oxford: Basil Blackwell.

Valverde, M. (1985) *Sex, Power and Pleasure*. Toronto: The Women's Press.

Walker, N. (1973) *Crime and Punishment in Britain*. Edinburgh: University of Edinburgh Press.

Walkowitz, J. (1982) *Prostitution and Victorian Society*. Cambridge: Cambridge University Press.

Ward, D. (1968) 'Crimes of violence by women', A Report to the national US Commission on Crimes of Violence.

Warnock, M. (1984) *Report of the Committee of Inquiry into Human Fertilisation and Embryology*. London: Department of Health and Social Security. HMSO, Cmnd 9314.

Weedon, C. (1987) *Feminist Practice and Poststructuralist Theory*. Oxford: Blackwell.

Weeks, J. (1987) 'Questions of identity', in P. Caplan (ed.) *The Cultural Construction of Sexuality*. London: Tavistock.

Weeks, J. (1991) *Against Nature*. London: Rivers Oram Press.

West, D. (1969) *Present Conduct and Future Delinquency*. London: Heinemann.

West, R. (1988) 'Jurisprudence and gender', *University of Chicago Law Review*, 55: 1–72.

Whitbeck, C. (1989) 'A different reality: feminist ontology', in A. Garry and M. Pearsall (eds) *Women, Knowledge and Reality*. London: Unwin Hyman.

Whitehouse, M. (1977) *Whatever Happened to Sex?* London: Hodder and Stoughton.

Wiles, P. N. P. (1971) 'Criminal statistics and sociological explanations of crime', in P. Wiles and W. G. Carson (eds) *Crime and Delinquency in Britain*. London: Martin Robertson.

Wilson, E. (1977) *Women and the Welfare State*. London: Tavistock.

Wise, N. B. (1967) 'Juvenile delinquency among the middle class girls', in E. Vaz (ed.) *Middle Class Juvenile Delinquency*. New York: Harper Row.

Wishik, H. (1986) 'To question everything: the inquiries of feminist jurisprudence', *Berkeley Women's Law Journal*, 1: 64–77.

Wolfenden (1957) *Report of the Committee on Homosexual Offences and Prostitution*, Cmnd 247. London: HMSO.

Wollstonecraft, M. (1975) *Vindication of the Rights of Woman*. Harmondsworth: Penguin.

Woodhull, W. (1988) 'Sexuality, power and the question of rape,' in I. Diamond and L. Quinby (eds) *Feminism and Foucault*. Boston, MA: Northeastern University Press.

Young, I. M. (1990) *Justice and the Politics of Difference*. Princeton, NJ: Princeton University Press.

Young, J. (1986) 'The failure of criminology: the need for a radical realism', in R. Matthews and J. Young (eds) *Confronting Crime*. London: Sage.

Index

Index compiled by Meg Davies (Society of Indexers)